PAPERS IN LOGIC AND ETHICS

PAPERS IN LOGIC
AND ETHICS

A. N. Prior

Edited by P. T. Geach and A. J. P. Kenny

UNIVERSITY OF
MASSACHUSETTS PRESS
AMHERST

First published in 1976 by
Gerald Duckworth & Company Limited
The Old Piano Factory
43 Gloucester Crescent, London NW1

© 1976 The Estate of A. N. Prior

Published in the United States of America by the
University of Massachusetts Press

International Standard Book Number 0–87023–213–4
Library of Congress Catalog Card Number 76–9376

Printed in Great Britain by
Ebenezer Baylis and Son Limited
The Trinity Press, Worcester, and London

CONTENTS

PREFACE

In a paper found after his death Arthur Prior expressed a wish to publish a collection of his essays in addition to those which he had already published under the title of *Papers on Time and Tense*. We have collected from among his published and unpublished remains a score of papers which in our judgment he would have thought worth preserving. We have arranged the published papers in chronological order of publication and have inserted the unpublished papers into the chronological series as accurately as internal evidence permitted us to do so. We chose a chronological rather than a topical order with a view to showing the development of Prior's thought over the years.

We have left the text of published papers exactly as it stood with the exception of No. 4 'Definitions, Rules and Axioms'. This uncharacteristically contained many long footnotes, which have been taken up into the text. It also contained a mistake which was corrected in an erratum slip which Prior published in the same volume of the Aristotelian Society Proceedings; the substance of this erratum slip has now been incorporated in the text. Only very slight alterations have been made in the text of the unpublished papers, and these are practically confined to matters of style and punctuation. The original manuscripts of the unpublished papers may be inspected in the Bodleian Library, Oxford.

'The Ethical Copula' has appeared in the *Australasian Journal of Philosophy*, vol. 29 (1951), pp. 137–54; 'Entities' in the *Australasian Journal of Philosophy*, vol. 32 (1954), pp. 159–68; 'Berkeley in Logical Form' in *Theoria*, vol. 21 (1955), pp. 117–22; 'Definitions, Rules and Axioms' in *Proceedings of the Aristotelian Society*, n.s. vol. 56 (1955–6), pp. 199–216; 'Opposite Number' in *The Review of Metaphysics*, vol. 11 (1957), pp. 196–201; 'Epimenides the Cretan' in *The Journal of Symbolic Logic*, vol. 23 (1958), pp. 261–6; 'Thank Goodness That's Over' in *Philosophy*, vol. 34 (1959), pp. 12–17; 'The Runabout Inference-ticket' in *Analysis*, vol. 21 (1960), pp. 38–9, reprinted in *Philosophical Logic*, ed. P. F. Strawson, Oxford, 1967, pp. 129–31; 'The Autonomy of Ethics' in the *Australasian Journal of Philosophy*, vol. 38 (1960), pp. 199–206; 'Nonentities' in *Analytical Philosophy*, ed. R. J. Butler, Oxford,

1962, pp. 120–132; 'Some Problems of Self-reference in John Buridan' in *Proceedings of the British Academy*, vol. 48 (1962), pp. 281–96, reprinted in *Studies in Philosophy*, selected by J. N. Findlay, London, 1966, pp. 241–59; 'Oratio Obliqua' in *Proceedings of the Aristotelian Society, Supplementary volume* 37 (1963), pp. 115–26; 'Conjunction and contonktion revisited' in *Analysis*, vol. 24 (1964), pp. 191–5; 'The Cogito of Descartes and the Concept of Self-confirmation' in *The Foundation of Statements and Decisions*, ed. by K. Ajdukiewicz, Warsaw, 1965, pp. 47–53; 'Intentionality and Intensionality' in *Proceedings of the Aristotelian Society, Supplementary volume* 42 (1968), pp. 91–106; 'The Possibly True and the Possible' in *Mind*, n.s. vol. 78 (1969), pp. 481–92; 'Self-perception and Contingency' in *Analysis*, vol. 30 (1969), pp. 46–9. We are grateful to the Editors of the *Australasian Journal of Philosophy*, *The Proceedings of the Aristotelian Society*, *The Review of Metaphysics*, *Philosophy*, *Analysis*, *Proceedings of the British Academy* and *Mind* for permission to re-publish the papers originally published in them.

We are particularly grateful to Mrs Mary Prior who suggested that we should edit this collection and who assisted us in many ways in its preparation, in particular by preparing the index.

P.T.G.
A.J.P.K.

1. The Ethical Copula

Let me begin by referring to a sentence or two in a well-known passage from Hume's *Treatise*. We all know how he complains there that the typical moralist 'proceeds for some time in the common way of reasoning, and establishes the being of a God, or makes observations concerning human affairs; when of a sudden', Hume says, 'I am surprised to find, that instead of the usual copulations of propositions, *is* and *is not*, I meet with no proposition that is not connected with an *ought* or *ought not*'. One or two recent writers have raised the question why Hume speaks here of 'ought' and 'ought not' as new *copulae* replacing the ordinary 'is' and 'is not', and whether this way of speaking is justified. This point is raised, for example, in Professor Prichard's paper on 'Moral Obligation', and also in a critical notice by Mr Mackie in the *Australasian Journal of Philosophy* (1950)

Both Professor Prichard and Mr Mackie decide against special ethical copulae, and do so on at least partly the same ground. Both of them remind us that sentences containing 'ought' have an implicit 'is' in them. 'He ought to do X' means 'He *is* obliged to do X'. Now it can hardly be argued that Hume was ignorant of this fact. The dodge of 'putting propositions into logical form' was an ancient one by Hume's time, and Hume was not a logical tyro. The dodge is duly explained in the *Port Royal Logic*, which we know Hume knew; and also in Dr Isaac Watts's *Logick*, which was widely read in Hume's time and is quoted, for instance, by Reid. And one of Dr Watts's examples is structurally rather like Hume's. Watts doesn't deal with 'ought' at this point, though he does deal with it at another point, as we shall see; but he deals here with 'can' and observes that 'I can write' means 'I *am* able to write'.

We may take it, then, that it was not ignorance that led Hume to talk in this way. What, then, was it? Well, in the first place, the fact

9

that we have noted, that 'ought' is equivalent to a phrase with 'is' as a part of it, is only part of the truth about 'ought'. It is also true that in many sentences the whole phrase 'ought to be' may replace the word 'is', and still leave us with an intelligible sentence. For instance, we can substitute 'ought to be' for 'is' in 'He is going home', and thereby form the new proposition 'He ought to be going home'. And when Hume called 'ought' a copula, I doubt very much whether he had anything in mind beyond this obvious fact. But obvious as it is, it is a rather curious fact; and there are one or two curious facts connected with it. For instance, when we turn from 'ought' to 'ought not', we find that while 'He ought to do X' is equivalent to 'He is obliged to do X', 'He ought not to do X' is *not* equivalent to 'He is *not obliged* to do X', but rather to 'He is *obliged not* to do X'. Both these curiosities reflect the fact that 'ought' resembles 'is' in being what the grammarians call an auxiliary verb. Because of this, there is not just one verb, but two, in 'He ought to do X', though the second of them is only an infinitive. It is because of this that there are two places in the sentence where you can put 'not', giving a different meaning when you put it in different places. There are also two places at which you can split up a verb into the verb 'to be' together with something else. For 'He ought to do X' you can say either 'He *is* obliged to do X' or 'He ought to *be* a doer of X', or 'He *is* obliged to *be* a doer of X'.

I am not now merely drawing attention to the fact that the word 'ought' appears to signify a relation. I am wanting rather to emphasise what a very peculiar *sort* of relation it appears to signify. 'Ought' is not just a word like 'kills' or 'loves' which signifies a relation between one object and another. It signifies rather a relation between an object and something that that object can be thought of as doing. Its terms, in other words, are of different logical types. In this respect the obvious parallel is with 'can' and 'must' and the other modal words. This parallel between moral words and the modal words has recently been discussed at some length by Professor von Wright in his article on 'Deontic Logic' in *Mind* for January 1951, but of course Professor von Wright is not the first to have noticed that there *is* such a parallel, and it will be worth our while to glance at what was said on the subject by earlier writers, and in particular by writers who were either certainly or probably familiar to Hume.

We may begin with Dr Watts. In his section on the modalities of propositions, Watts begins by mentioning the ordinary four, the ones that Professor von Wright calls the 'alethic' modes—necessity, possibility and so on. Watts then goes on to say, 'Let it be noted that this quadruple Modality is only an enumeration of the *natural Modes* or Manners wherein the Predicate is connected with the Subject: We might also describe several *moral* and *civil Modes* of connecting two Ideas together (*viz.*) *Lawfulness* and *Unlawfulness*, *Conveniency* and *Inconveniency*, and etc., whence we may form such *modal Propositions* as these. *It is unlawful for any Person to kill an innocent Man*: *It is lawful for Christians to eat Flesh in Lent*: *To tell all that we think is inexpedient*: *For a Man to be affable to his Neighbour is very convenient*, etc.' And, like Professor von Wright, Watts does not stop at this, but says that beside the 'physical' and 'moral' modalities there are others; for, he says, 'there are several other *Modes* of speaking whereby a Predicate is connected with a Subject: Such as, *it is certain, it is doubtful, it is probable, it is improbable, it is agreed, it is granted, it is said by the Ancients, it is written*, and etc., all which will form other Kinds of *modal Propositions*.' These correspond broadly to the modes which Professor von Wright calls 'epistemic'.

These broadly 'epistemic' modes are also mentioned in the *Port Royal Logic*, and the way the Port Royalists introduce them is rather interesting. Their chapter on Modals comes immediately after their chapter on Complex Propositions, and they connect the two subjects in the following manner. By a 'complex proposition' they mean one with a complex subject or predicate or both. They then go on to say that 'beside the propositions of which the subject or the attribute is a complex term, there are others which are complex because they have incidental terms or propositions which regard only the *form* of the proposition, that is to say, the affirmation or negation which is expressed by the verb. When, for example, I say, *I maintain that the earth is round*, "I maintain" is only an incidental proposition, which must be a part of something in the principal proposition. Yet it is clear that it makes no part either of the subject or the attribute, for it makes no change in them at all; and they would be conceived in precisely the same way if I said *The earth is round*. And thus it can belong only to the *affirmation*, which is expressed in two ways, the one, which is the usual, by the verb *is*, and the other more expressly by the verb *I maintain*.' You see what the Port Royalists are saying here. In a statement like 'The earth that we live on is round', the clause 'that we live on' is part of the logical subject; it qualifies that subject and makes it a complex one; but in the statement 'I maintain that the earth is round' the introductory clause gives the proposition a complex copula—the simple 'is' has been replaced by 'is-maintained-by-me-to-be'. A more elaborate example given by the Port Royalists is the sentence *The reasons of astronomy convince us that the sun is much larger than the earth*. Here, you see, the subject is 'The sun', and the predicate is the phrase 'much larger than the earth', and the copula is, not just 'is', but 'is shown by the reasons of astronomy to be'. And then they go on to deal with ordinary modals under this head.

The treatment of modal words as affections of the copula is in fact the ordinary traditional way of treating them. Watts mentions this. He takes the example, 'It is necessary that a true Christian should be an honest Man'—an example, incidentally, which contains a curious blend of the logical and the moral—and he says of it, 'Logical Writers generally make the *Modality* of this proposition to belong to the *Copula*, because it shows the *Manner* of the Connexion between the Subject and the Predicate'. Watts himself, all the same, isn't quite in agreement with this. He says, 'If the Form of the Sentence as a *logical* Proposition be duly considered, the *Mode* itself is the very Predicate of the Proposition, and it must run thus: *That a true Christian should be an honest Man is a necessary Thing*, and then the whole *primary* Proposition is included in the Subject of the *modal* Proposition.' This way of analysing modals is traditional too; it is in the *De Interpretatione*, for instance, and it is clearly suggested by the common way of writing them, 'It is necessary that . . .', 'It is possible that . . .'. The traditional logic distinguishes here between the *dictum*, that is the proposition that is the implicit subject of a modal proposition, and the *mode* that is predicated of it; and it has been customary from Aristotle's time to point out that you get different results by denying the dictum and denying the mode. If we start with 'It is necessary that S should be P' and deny the dictum, we obtain 'It is necessary that S should not be P'; while if we deny the mode we obtain 'It is not necessary that S should be P', which is different. And if we deny both the dictum and the mode, we do not merely reconstitute the original proposition, but produce something different again. 'It is *not* necessary that S should *not* be P' does not mean 'It *is* necessary that S *should* be P', but only 'It is *possible* that S should be P'.

We may, then, find modal propositions expressed in two ways—either *cum dicto*, with a modal adjective predicated of an inner dictum or proposition, or *sine dicto*, with a modal adverb modifying the copula. Watts, as we have seen, regarded the second form of expression as somehow misleading; he possibly believed, as I understand that some in Sydney believe, that 'is' and 'is not' are intrinsically unmodifiable. But there are some cases in which the expression *sine dicto*, that is with a modified copula, seems essential to avoid confusion. Take the propositional forms 'Some S is necessarily P' and 'It is necessary that some S should be P'. I don't think these would naturally be interpreted as having the same meaning. Broad brings out the difference by this illustration: Suppose a man has some pennies in his pocket and takes them out one by one. Then it is necessary that there should be one penny that comes out first—it is necessary that some S should be P. But it doesn't follow that there is any one penny which is in itself fated to be the first—it doesn't follow that any S is necessarily P.

I shall not pursue this point further at present, but in the remainder of this paper I shall take it that the question 'Is "ought" a copula?' is one and the same with the question 'Is "ought" an expression of a modality?' Certainly the only sense in which 'ought' can be maintained with any show of reason to be a copula, is the sense, whatever it is, in which 'can' and 'cannot', 'must' and 'need not', may be said to be copulae. But is 'ought' a copula in this sense? The line I shall take is that 'ought' has some but not all of the characteristics which make words like 'can' and 'must' logically interesting; so that the description of it as a copula or sign of modality is illuminating in some ways and misleading in others, and we can really say what we like about it so long as we know how far the resemblances go, and where they end. Having made this clear, I shall go on to inquire whether the resemblances that undoubtedly exist between 'ought' and ordinary signs of modality throw any light on the stock issues of moral philosophy such as subjectivism versus objectivism.

Assertions of obligation resemble modal assertions, to begin with, in lending themselves to expression in a 'dictum and mode' form.

We can express 'I ought to do X' in the form 'It is obligatory that I should do X', and we can form different propositions from this by denying the dictum and denying the mode and denying both. For example, as we noted earlier, though we then considered a different form of expression, 'It is obligatory that I should not do X' does not mean the same as 'It is not obligatory that I should do X'. It should be added that the word 'ought' shares this feature not only with ordinary modal words but with a good many other words too. For instance, we can easily distinguish a 'dictum' and a 'mode' in the proposition 'A caused B to do C', and we can deny the dictum by saying 'A caused B not to do C', and deny the mode by saying 'A did not cause B to do C', and deny both by saying 'A did not cause B not to do C'. We can get more complicated cases of this sort too, like 'A's doing B caused C to do D', and here we might deny the first dictum by saying 'A's not doing B caused C to do D', or deny the second dictum by saying 'A's doing B caused C not to do D', or deny the mode by saying 'A's doing B did not cause C to do D'. Similar complications can be introduced into the moral modes too; for example, we might consider propositions of the form 'A's doing B obliged C to do D'. We shall confine ourselves here, however, to the simpler forms with which we have started.

Another resemblance between moral and modal assertions is that in both cases their expression *cum dicto* and their expression *sine dicto* may have different meanings. On the moral side of the comparison I have in mind those cases in which we determine our obligations by such methods as tossing up. We may say, for example, that it is obligatory that someone should wash up without saying that there is anyone with a definite and personal obligation to do so.

'Ought' also resembles modal words in the patterns of implication and opposition which its presence in sentences gives rise to. For example, although 'S is necessarily not P' is a different proposition from 'S is not necessarily P', the first implies the second (with certain minor qualifications that we need not go into here); and similarly, although 'A is obliged not to do B' is a different proposition from 'A is not obliged to do B', the first implies the second. This is by no means true of all the words or phrases that give rise to 'dictum-and-mode' propositions. For example, 'I have promised not to do B' does not imply 'I have not promised to do B'; and 'Aristotle has said that X is not Y' does not imply 'Aristotle has not said that X is Y'. For this reason alone, 'ought' has a stronger claim than the phrase 'Aristotle has said that' to be considered a logically interesting element in a proposition.

This last point is one at which there is not only a resemblance between moral words and ordinary modal words, but also a resemblance between both and signs of quantity. The difference and the connection between 'S is necessarily not P' and 'S is not necessarily P', or between 'A is obliged not to do X' and 'A is not obliged to do X', is very like the distinction between 'No X is Y' and 'Some X is not Y'. And in fact distinctions of quantity can be given exactly the same formal treatment as distinctions of modality. For example, we can put quantified propositions into a 'dictum-and-mode' form, and say that 'All S is P' means 'It is universally the case that what is S is P', and that 'No S is P' is derived from this by denying the dictum, and saying 'It is universally the case that what is S is not P', while 'Some S is not P' is derived from it by denying the mode and saying 'It is not universally the case that what is S is P', and 'Some S is P' by denying both, and saying 'It is not universally the case that what is S is not P'. This is in effect what the symbolists do when they express general propositions by prefixing a quantifier to what they call a 'statement-matrix' or 'propositional function'. Or we can express the quantity of propositions by an adverbial modification of the copula. Just as we can write 'S must be P' as 'S is-necessarily P', so we can write 'Every S is P' as 'S is-universally P', and 'No S is P' is 'S is-universally not-P', and so on. Again, just as you get curious ambiguities when you attach either moral or modal words to propositions which already contain a sign of quantity, so you get ambiguities when you attach a sign of quantity to a statement-matrix which already contains another sign of quantity. Consider, for example, Abraham Lincoln's statement, 'You can fool all of the people some of the time'. This might mean that there are some times at which you can fool the whole world at once—times, we might say, at which people are-universally foolable. Or it may mean merely that for everyone there is some time at which you can fool him, though maybe a different time for each person. When you express this kind of proposition symbolically, the two senses are distinguished by the order in which the quantifying symbols are placed; and in modern notations for modal logic the same device is used for distinguishing the two senses of such a statement as 'Some penny must come first'. This very exact analogy that exists between modality and quantity is no doubt what has led Professor von Wright to describe the distinctions of quantity as yet another set of 'modes', the 'existential' modes as he calls them.

There is one point, however, where the analogy between ordinary modality and quantity is kept up, but the analogy between 'moral modes' and both the others breaks down. In respect of their quantity, propositions do not just divide into universals and particulars, but into universals, particulars and singulars. Quite similarly, in respect of their modality, propositions do not just divide into apodictic and problematic, but into apodictic, problematic and assertoric. In between 'S must be P' and 'S may be P' stands the simple 'S is in fact P', just as 'This S is P' stands in between 'Every S is P' and 'Some S is P'. And just as 'This S is P' is implied by 'Every S is P' and implies 'Some S is P', so 'S is in fact P' is implied by 'S must be P' and implies 'S may be P'. But so far as I can see, there is nothing among the moral or 'deontic' modalities that corresponds to these intermediary 'existential' and 'alethic' modalities. We might be tempted to think that moral indifference provides the parallel here, but 'It is indifferent whether A does X or not' isn't really analogous to 'S is in fact P' or to 'This S is P'. It is analogous rather to 'S may but need not be P', or to 'Some S is P and some S is not'. 'It is indifferent whether A does X or not' doesn't really stand in between 'A is obliged to do X' and 'A is permitted to do X', being implied by the first and implying the second. On the contrary, 'It is indifferent whether A does X or not' is inconsistent with 'A is obliged to do X'. In point of fact it stands in between 'A is obliged to do X' and 'A is obliged not to do X' in the same way as 'S may but need not do X' stands in between 'S must be P' and 'S cannot be P', or in the same way as 'Some S is P and some is not' stands in between 'Every S is P' and 'No S is P', in the sense of being the proposition that is true when both the others are false. There is no moral word, then, which is related to 'ought' as 'is in fact' is related to the non-moral 'must be', or as 'This' is related to 'Every'.

Another important point at which the analogy between 'ought' and the ordinary modal words breaks down—another difference that makes us inclined not to admit that 'ought' is a copula or modification of the copula—is this: The ordinary modal adjectives may qualify propositions of any degree of abstraction or complexity, and with any subject-matter. We may attach them, for example, to quantified propositions, as when we say that it is necessary that some S should be P. Or we may attach them to propositions about obligation, as when we say that it is necessary that what is obligatory should be permissible. Or we may attach them to other ordinary modals, as when we say that it is impossible that it should be both necessary and impossible that a thing should be P; or to quantified ordinary modals, as when we say that it is impossible that anything should be necessarily P without its being necessary that something should be P. Signs of quantity may similarly be attached to propositions, or more accurately to propositional functions, of any sort and order of abstractness. But only acts can be obligatory: obligations themselves, for example, or necessities, cannot be obligatory—it cannot be obligatory that it should be obligatory that A should do X, nor can it be obligatory that it should be necessary that S should be P.

We may now consider the bearing of all this on the problems with which moralists customarily concern themselves. Does this quasi-modal functioning of the word 'ought' constitute so much evidence in favour of ethical naturalism, for example, or evidence against it? Or does it constitute evidence for or against ethical subjectivism? Or does it tip the balance in the issue between the deontological and teleological versions of ethics? So far as I can see, it does none of these things; all of these theories—naturalism and non-naturalism, subjectivism and objectivism, deontology and teleology—are consistent with the facts about 'ought' which we have been considering. They do, however, suggest a new way in which moral theories may be classified. For this quasi-modal behaviour of 'ought' may be differently explained and interpreted, and we may classify moral theories according to the different interpretations they put upon it.

In the first place we may hold that assertions of obligation resemble assertions of necessity because they *are* assertions of necessity of a relative or hypothetical kind. We do in fact quite often use the word 'ought' to express hypothetical necessity. For example, one burglar may say to another, 'If you want to open that safe, you ought to take a blow-lamp'. And this may just mean, 'To open that safe, it is necessary to take a blow-lamp', and there are theories that this kind of thing is all that the word 'ought' ever does mean—that when we use it, we are always really talking about what is necessary to the satisfaction of some desire or the achievement of some purpose, though this desire or purpose is not always expressed or even clearly before the speaker's own mind. Some such theory as this would be held, I take it, by Professor Anderson, and also by Mr Mackie. Their view of what the word 'good' means is, of course, of a different sort, but 'good' has no pretensions to being a copula, and we need not discuss it here.

If we reject this reduction of obligation to hypothetical necessity, what other alternatives are open to us? Principally two, I think. In order to see what they are, let us look for a moment at the ordinary copulae 'is' and 'is not', and ask what they signify. There are two different ways of approaching this question. In many of the traditional accounts of the function of the ordinary copula, what might be called a subjective approach is adopted. Here is what Watts, for example, says on the subject: 'A *Proposition* is a Sentence wherein two or more *Ideas* or *Terms* are joined or disjoined by one Affirmation or Negation . . . The *Subject* of a Proposition is that concerning which any thing is affirmed or denied. . . . The *Predicate* is that which is affirmed or denied of the Subject . . . *The Copula* . . . represents the Act of the Mind affirming or denying.' If what the copula does is to express the speaker's act of affirming or denying— and for my own part I am sure that this is at least one of the things that the copula does—then a modified copula, or a totally new copula, would be a word expressing some other act of the mind than affirmation or denial. And that is exactly what the words 'ought' and 'ought not' are said to do by many naturalistic moralists today. It is said to express not judgments, not affirmations and denials, but desires and aversions, or commands and prohibitions. Our English words 'mode' and 'mood' are both of them translations of the Latin *modus*: and when modern writers tell us that words like 'ought' signify that the sentences in which they occur are not really in the indicative but in the imperative mood, they might instead say that they are in the imperative 'mode', and treat this difference as in a broad sense a difference of modality.

But we may also approach the question as to what the ordinary copula means from what we may call the objective side. Propositions not only express judgments but attempt to represent facts, and we may ask what it is about facts that we attempt to represent by the copula. In such a proposition as 'John is kind', the copula seems to represent the inherence of the universal kindness in the particular John. In 'Richard is not kind', the negative copula seems to represent the absence of the same universal from the particular Richard. The word 'represent' must be taken here in a very broad sense, however; it is plain that the copula does not 'represent' the relation of inherence or absence in the same direct way as the name 'John' or 'Richard' represents the person, nor even in the somewhat less direct way in which the adjective 'kind' represents the universal kindness. Nor is the relation of inherence an element in the fact that John is kind in the sense in which John is, or even in the sense in which kindness is. We might express the matter as follows: The fact that John is kind contains the two elements John and kindness, but these elements enter into the fact in different ways, indicated in the proposition 'John is kind' by the fact that John is directly named but kindness is not—the proposition does not contain the word 'kindness' but only the word 'kind'. And the relation of inherence does not enter into the fact at all; it is rather, to use Professor Broad's expression, the 'form of unity' of this fact. Now consider the fact that kindness inheres or is present in John. The universal kindness seems to enter into this fact in the same way as John entered into the other; it is a fact about kindness, as the other is a fact about John; and the relation of inherence is an element of this fact, entering into it in substantially the same way as kindness entered into the other. There are differences due to the fact that inherence is a relation and kindness is a quality, but they are irrelevant in the present context, and as we proceed I shall adopt various dodges for avoiding the discussion of them; we may just note now that in the proposition 'Kindness is present in John', the relation of inherence is not named but is referred to by the adjective 'present' in just the same way as kindness is referred to by the adjective 'kind' in the proposition 'John is kind'. When we turn, finally, to the fact that inherence relates kindness and John, we have a fact that is about the relation of inherence; that is, a fact about the form of unity of the first of the three facts we have considered.

To turn now to 'ought' and 'ought not', it could be held that these words refer to modifications of these objective relations of inherence and absence which have just been mentioned, or that they refer to relations which may in some facts replace these modes of union. Let us consider the second form of this theory first—the form according to which there are facts in which the relation of obligation replaces the relation of inherence. Professor Prichard lays it down flatly that any such theory as this is quite inadmissible, because inherence and absence are the only possible relations that can ever subsist between a character or attribute and a particular or subject. He supports this astonishing dogma by an appeal to the Law of Excluded Middle. In his own words, 'the only relations in which a given subject of attributes can possibly stand to a given attribute are those of possessing and not possessing it, no third alternative being possible'. This seems to me just muddled. Take a parallel case. Every finite whole number is either odd or even—there is no third alternative. That is, every finite whole number is characterised by one or the other of these two determinates under this determinable, or respect in which numbers may differ; and there are no further determinates under that determinable. But this doesn't mean that finite whole numbers can have no other properties but this of oddness or evenness—they have, in fact, innumerable other properties. Returning to our subjects and attributes, the two relations of inherence and absence may be regarded as the two determinate forms of a single determinable relation for which we have no name—a single respect in which subject-attribute pairs differ. One of the determinate forms of this relation holds between any attribute and any subject whatsoever; and there are no other determinate forms of it but these two, inherence and absence. That is what the Law of Excluded Middle means. But of course this does not prevent subject-attribute pairs from being comparable in other respects as well. In particular, if we take an agent A and the character of acting in the manner X, either this character inheres in A or it is absent from A, and there is no possibility of its doing neither; but this does not prevent its standing in other relations to A as well as this relation of inherence or absence. Moreover, these other relations may, like inherence and absence, be possible 'forms of unity' of facts.

In connection with such a view as this, it is instructive to compare the following four facts (supposing that they are facts): (1) The fact that John is kind; (2) the fact that John ought to be kind; (3) the fact that kindness is present in John; and (4) the fact that kindness is obligatory upon John. On the view which we are now considering, the fact that John is kind and the fact that he ought to be kind are two first-order facts with the same elements but a different form of unity. The elements are John and kindness; and the forms of unity are those indicated by the words 'is' and 'ought to be'. On the other hand, the fact that kindness is present in John and the fact that kindness is obligatory upon John are two second-order facts with different elements but the same form of unity. The elements of the first are the character of kindness and the second-order character of inhering in John; the elements of the second are the character of kindness and the second-order character of being obligatory upon John; and the form of unity in both cases is the inherence-form indicated by the ordinary affirmative copula 'is'. On this theory, the peculiar logical importance that undoubtedly does attach to the copulae 'is' and 'is not', is due to the fact that no matter what may be the form of unity of the fact you start with, you can always find an equivalent fact of higher order in which the form of unity is inherence or absence.

An alternative to this theory is the following modification of it. We might hold that although there are other relations between attributes and subjects, obligatoriness being one of them, inherence and absence are the only relations between attributes and subjects which can constitute forms of unity of facts. On this view, the adjective 'obligatory upon A' may replace the adjective 'present in A' in second-order propositions about kinds of action; but 'ought to be' never really replaces 'is' as a copula in first-order propositions about agents. The grammatical form of the proposition 'John ought to be kind' is on this view misleading; the fact that it expresses is really the second-order fact that kindness is obligatory upon John. It is not, however, entirely misleading; the fact that we can use 'ought to be' *as if* it were a copula reminds us that obligatoriness does resemble inherence in being a relation between attributes and subjects.

We may now turn to the theory that the words 'ought' and 'ought not' signify modifications of the objective relations of inherence and absence signified by the ordinary copulae. What exactly can be meant by this? Suppose that John is not in fact kind. Then the character of kindness will not in fact inhere in John. Nor will the relational property of possessing kindness, that is, being inhered in by kindness, inhere in John. But that does not mean that there will be no such relational property as that of possessing kindness, nor does it mean that this relational property will stand in no relation to John at all. For one thing, this property of possessing kindness will be absent from John—it will at all events have *that* relation to him. And it may have others. The possession of kindness may, for example, be obligatory upon him. That is, John may stand to the character of kindness in the complex relation of being obliged to possess it, or being obliged to be inhered in by it; and we may call this complex relation, into which inherence enters as a part, a 'modification' of the relation of inherence.

Once again we may develop such a point of view in two ways. Taking the fact that John ought to be kind, we might say that the elements of this fact are John and the relational property of possessing kindness, and that its form of unity is the special form indicated by the word 'ought'. Or if we admit no such special form of unity, we could hold that the fact misleadingly expressed by the proposition 'John ought to be kind' is the fact that the possession of kindness is obligatory upon John, where the elements are the possession of kindness and the property of being obligatory upon John, and the form of unity is the ordinary inherence-form indicated by 'is'. Similarly, the proposition 'John ought not to be cruel' will express, on this view, the fact that to lack cruelty, that is, to have cruelty absent from him, is obligatory upon John, where the subject is the absence of cruelty, and the form of unity is the inherence-form, as before. The proposition 'John is not obliged to be cruel' will express the fact that the possession of cruelty is not obligatory upon John, where the subject is the inherence of cruelty, and the form of unity is the absence-form, indicated by 'is not'. The proposition 'John is permitted to be kind', or 'John is not obliged not to be kind', will express the fact that to lack kindness is not obligatory upon John, where the subject is the absence of kindness, and the form of unity is also the absence-form. It will be seen that this interpretation, though a little involved, has the advantage of enabling us to give to the word 'not' its ordinary meaning when we are dealing with the various 'dictum and mode' denials that arise with moral propositions. And it assimilates obligation more closely to modal relations than any other interpretation does; for modal relations do seem to be relations with abstract inherences and absences among their terms. 'S cannot be P', for example, seems to mean that the absence of P is necessary to S; or if we take possibility as our basic modal notion, 'S must be P' seems to mean that the absence of P is not possible to S.

I have done no more here than sketch an outline of what an objective theory of moral modalities might involve. Even on the points which I have discussed there are certainly other alternatives beside those which I have mentioned. One might, for example, put affirmations and denials on different logical levels, and say that while 'John ought not to be kind' is about the absence of kindness, 'John ought to be kind' is not about the presence of kindness, but just about kindness. I have also deliberately over-simplified matters at many points. One of these points is worth briefly mentioning. Mr Kneale has recently argued that singular modal statements are always elliptical, and contain a reference to some character in the subject beside that referred to by the predicate. For example, 'John cannot be kind' means 'John's known characteristics are incompatible with his being kind'. And assertions of obligation seem to be similarly elliptical. 'John is obliged to act in the manner M' is short for 'John is obliged by the character of the situation he is in, to act in the manner M'. A full development of this would lead to a consideration of the theory of fitnesses and unfitnesses of which the earlier eighteenth-century ethical rationalists were so fond. I suspect that when these writers used language which so often seems to us to confuse ethics with logic, they were trying to bring out the point that these relations of fitness and unfitness are of the same logical order as relations of necessitation, compatibility and so on. I think this is the point of the tortuous argument between John Balguy and his anonymous Hutchesonian opponent at the beginning of the Second Part of his *Foundations of Moral Goodness*. Balguy insists that moral appropriateness and inappropriateness are forms of 'agreement and disagreement' between ideas, although they are agreements and disagreements of a different kind from those studied in the non-moral abstract sciences. And this is the source of Hume's puzzlement in both the *Treatise* and the *Enquiry*, when he sees that the fundamental moral relation must be of the same order of abstractness as, for example, contrariety, but the only relations of this order that he himself can discover are a few logical and mathematical ones.

I should perhaps have one word in conclusion for those who will say that the moral of all this is just that an objective and non-reductionist interpretation of 'deontic' modalities involves us in a 'multiplication of entities' which makes any such theory utterly incredible. I cannot do better for such persons than quote a passage from Boswell's account of his last interview with Hume. They were discussing immortality, and Mr Hume argued 'that immortality, if it were at all, must be general; that a great proportion dies in infancy before being possessed of reason; that the trash of every age must be preserved, and that new Universes must be created to contain such infinite numbers. This appeared to me an unphilosophical objection, and I said "Mr Hume, you know Spirit does not take up space".'

2. Entities

I wish to maintain here that there are abstract entities. But as it is not easy to state the issue quite clearly in those terms, I shall concentrate on what I think it is fair to regard as a key question of a more specific sort. Virtue is undoubtedly abstract, and my left eye is undoubtedly an entity, and I shall adopt a technique of Professor Ryle's and say that virtue is an entity if we may take a statement in which the phrase 'my left eye' occurs and obtain another statement by replacing this phrase by the word 'virtue'. The statement I shall take is the statement that my left eye is not square. Replacing the phrase 'my left eye' in this by the word 'virtue', I obtain the statement 'Virtue is not square', and I shall contend not only that this *is* a statement but that it is a true statement. I shall even prove it, thereby proving, if this technique of Professor Ryle's is sound, that virtue is an entity in the sense in which my left eye is an entity; and since it is undoubtedly abstract, it will be an abstract entity, so that there are abstract entities. And I am strengthened in my view that these issues are connected, by the fact that people who deny that there are abstract entities will in general deny that the statement that virtue is not square is a genuine statement, let alone a true one.

My proof that virtue is not square is a simple syllogism—what is square has some shape, but virtue has no shape, therefore virtue is not square. That my left eye is not square would of course have to be proved a little differently; the point about my left eye is not that it has no shape but that it has *another* shape. But this difference in the character of the proofs that one would give for the two state-ments—and from a logical point of view the difference is not very great (it is only that between the mood Camestres and the mood Cesare)—this difference, whether great or small, is *only* a difference in the proofs one gives; it does not mean or entail that when I say that virtue is not square I am *saying* anything different about virtue

from what I am saying about my left eye when I say that my left
eye is not square. In neither case am I *saying* anything whatever
about what the object *is*, and in neither case am I saying *all* that it is
not. In saying that my left eye is not square, I am not saying that it
is of some other shape, and in saying that virtue is not square I am
not saying that it is not of any other shape either; in both cases I am
saying that the thing is not square, and that is *all* that I am saying.

This is very elementary stuff—I am almost tempted to apply to it
the mystic word 'tautological'—and I apologise for so solemnly
putting it forward in a learned journal. But I do not think it can be
denied that these things need to be said. For there are people who
do not agree with them, and moreover it is no new thing that there
are people who do not agree with them. At the turn of the present
century there were the idealists, people like Bosanquet and Bradley,
with their attacks on what they called *mere* negation or *bare* denial.
And then when it began to seem as if their position was vanishing
for good in face of the solid reasoning of people like Keynes and
Frege and Moore and Russell, there occurred that disaster from
which we have not yet recovered—Russell sold the pass. What
Russell did was no doubt done in all sincerity, and he gave in before
the *only* serious objection that the position I have outlined has ever
had to meet, but the fact remains that he did give in before it, and
as a result what we might call Bosanquetterie sprawls over the face
of Philosophy like a monstrous tumour, and on the whole the person
who maintains that virtue is not square must nowadays count himself among the heretics. The current dodge or 'gambit' is to say
that the question whether virtue is or is not square just doesn't
arise, and it is astonishing what a number of questions modern
philosophers have been able to dispose of by saying that they just
don't arise. Indeed it is hardly too much to say that the whole of
traditional philosophy has disappeared in this way, for among
questions that don't arise are those which, as it is said, nobody but a
philosopher would ask. And one only has to say that the question
whether these questions arise is itself one that doesn't arise (it is
certainly one that nobody but a philosopher would ask), for modern
philosophy to disappear as well, so that there is nothing for us to do
but shut up the shop and go home.

I have proved, then, that virtue is not square, and might well
leave it at that. But it would be only fair to indicate how I would

answer what I have admitted to be a serious objection (though the only one) to the sort of position I have been outlining—the objection that led Russell to sell the pass, as I have put it. And the study of this objection may serve the incidental purpose of making my general position clearer, if it requires any such further clarification. Russell was bothered by a paradox. One way of stating this paradox is as follows: If it makes sense, and is true, to say that virtue is not square, then presumably it also makes sense, and is true, to say that squareness is not square. The proof that it is true is, in fact, very much the same as in the other case. Squareness, though it *is* a shape, is not the sort of thing that *has* a shape; but whatever is square has a shape; therefore squareness is not square. One could show in a similar way that virtue is not virtuous, redness is not red, femininity is not feminine, and so forth. And this resemblance between squareness, virtue, redness and femininity may be summed up by saying that they do not inhere in themselves. It is natural to go on from this to saying that there is a property, in that broad sense of 'property' which covers negative properties, which squareness, virtue, redness and femininity all share, the property of non-self-inherence, just as virtue and my left eye share the property of non-squareness. But do they share this property of non-self-inherence with the property of non-self-inherence itself? In other words, is the property of non-self-inherence non-self-inherent? It is well known—there is no need to go over the proof—that if the property of non-self-inherence is non-self-inherent it isn't, and if it isn't it is. So that if there *were* such a thing as the property of non-self-inherence it would have contradictory properties. Therefore there is no such thing as the property of non-self-inherence. That is the paradox and its obvious outcome; and I am not going to deny that outcome—I too am compelled to admit that there is no such entity as the property of non-self-inherence. Indeed I admit it in a way in which Russell and those who have followed in his train *don't* admit it. For to my way of thinking the statement that there is no such entity as the property of non-self-inherence is a genuine statement, and is true, whereas a Russellian would call it the sort of thing that it is nonsense either to affirm or deny. And the question is, Why did Russell draw *this* moral, rather than the obvious one, from the paradox which he constructed?

The movement of Russell's thought, so far as I can see, was more or less like this. He felt that if it were really true that squareness, virtue, etc., are things that do not inhere in themselves, then there *must* be such a property as non-self-inherence; therefore it is not true that squareness, virtue, etc., do not inhere in themselves; therefore, again, it is not true that squareness is not square, that virtue is not virtuous, and so on. Yet it is obviously not true that squareness *is* square, that virtue *is* virtuous, and so on. So we must say that sentences like 'Squareness is square', 'Virtue is virtuous', and so on are neither true nor false but meaningless. But why are they meaningless? To answer this question, Russell sorted out subjects and predicates into what he called logical types, and argued that you only get genuine statements when subjects and predicates are matched in a certain way, according to their type. One of his principal rules might be stated thus: Suppose you have a sentence of the form 'X is Y' (e.g. 'Socrates is wise'). This is equivalent to 'X has the property of Y-ness', which has the appearance of stating a relation between the object X and the object Y-ness. Russell's rule is to the effect that 'X is Y' only makes sense if X and Y-ness are of different logical types, and in fact only if Y-ness is of a logical type one higher than X. (And of course in cases in which 'X is Y' does not make sense, 'X is not Y' does not make sense either.) Apply this to 'Squareness is square': if you turn this into 'Squareness has the property of squareness' the objects ostensibly related are not only of the same logical type but one and the same object, so we throw that one (along with its contradictory) into the limbo of The Meaningless without more ado.

This 'theory of types' has all kinds of internal difficulties on which I need not here dwell; let it suffice to point out that the attempt to meet them has driven its exponents into some very desperate straits. For example, a year or two ago Professor Smart was telling us that the reason why 'Squareness is square' and 'Squareness is not square' are not statements, is that they are the sort of thing that nobody would *want* to say. This, of course, is just plain false; to mention no others (though I could if I wanted to), *I* want to say that squareness is not square. Similarly I want to say, and do say, and consider it to be true to say, that the fourth figure of the syllogism does not like tripe, so that the fourth figure of the syllogism and I are a pair of non-tripe-likers; and that whereas my cat is not aware of its difference from the *consequentia mirabilis* because

I have no cat, and my grocer is not aware of his difference from the *consequentia mirabilis* because he is not given to philosophical reflection, the fourth figure of the syllogism is not aware of its difference from the *consequentia mirabilis* because it is not aware of anything.

However, from another formulation of Professor Smart's it would seem that he only meant that these are the sort of things that nobody but a cad would want to say. According to his amended version, they are the sort of thing which it is not 'natural' to say or to want to say. And this may very well be true—I just don't know, because I don't understand this use of 'natural'. When I myself say that something is 'natural', as I sometimes do (you will find the phrase being used, instead of being merely mentioned, three paragraphs back), I generally mean that it is a common and understandable human failing. For example, it is natural that the adolescents of New Zealand should behave as the newspapers tell us they do; and there are certain logical fallacies which it is natural that men should commit. Obviously to say that a thing is 'natural' in this sense is not to say that it is something we ought to do. But it is not at all surprising—it is even (in my sense) natural—that a Russellian should be driven to using the word 'natural' in a sense in which it does somehow follow from a thing's being 'natural' that we ought to do it. For this is the way the Thomists talk, and the theory of types, or the theory of categories as it is now often called, is essentially a Thomist theory. When we are told that there is a type-fallacy or category-mistake in saying that virtue and my left eye are both of them not square, we are irresistibly reminded of the way the Thomists tell us that we must not say that God and (for example) Mr Grave are both intelligent, because nothing that is predicable of God is predicable of Mr Grave in the same sense. It cannot even be said (according to this story) that God and Mr Grave both *are* in the same sense of 'are'; and just this, of course, is what your Bosanquettist or Russellian or whatever you like to call him would say of virtue and my left eye.

What is the way out of this Thomo-Bosanquo-Russellio-Rylean morass? Where, in other words, did Russell go wrong? He went wrong, I suggest, in assuming that from a statement of the form 'X is Y' it is *always* possible to infer the corresponding statement of the form 'X has the property of Y-ness'. It is indeed *almost* always the case that when X is Y it has the property of Y-ness, but this consequence fails in those odd cases in which there is just no property of Y-ness for X to have. For example, squareness is non-self-inhering, but it hasn't the property of non-self-inherence, because there is no such property. Note here that to say that there is no such property as Y-ness is not the same as saying that the property of Y-ness is not exemplified. The property of being a fire-breathing serpent, and the property of being at once ten feet tall and not ten feet tall, are neither of them exemplified, but I do not know of any reason for saying or believing that there are no such properties as these two. (That the second of them is self-contradictory is of course a reason for saying that it is unexemplified, but only its *having* self-contradictory properties—e.g. its being at once self-contradictory and not self-contradictory—would be a reason for believing that it didn't exist.) And note, secondly, that to say that there is no such property as Y-ness is not to say that statements which are ostensibly about the property of Y-ness are meaningless. There are a good half-dozen modern ways of exhibiting the sense of statements which are ostensibly about non-existent objects—Russell's theory of descriptions, for example—and we can adopt any of them that takes our fancy, or that we have some ground or other for preferring. The property of non-self-inherence, in other words, is in the same box as the present King of France, the integer between 3 and 4, and so on. As far as the point which worried Russell is concerned, it is not meaningless but simply false that the property of non-self-inherence is non-self-inherent, and also that it is self-inherent, just as it is false that the present King of France is non-bald and false that he is bald; and it is not meaningless but true that the property of non-self-inherence is not non-self-inherent, and also that it is not self-inherent, just as it is true that the present King of France is not non-bald and true that he is not bald. It is just as simple as that.

The reason why Russell did not see this way out was, I suspect, that he was half inclined to say that 'X is Y' and 'X has the property of Y-ness' cannot ever have different truth-values because they are just different ways of saying the same thing. This is a position which I propose to describe as 'pure nominalism'. On this view, a statement which is ostensibly about an abstract entity is a genuine statement if and only if it can be exhibited as a mere *façon de parler*, differing only in its verbal form from some statement which does not even appear to be about any entities but concrete ones. Thus 'Squareness does not inhere in my left eye' will pass if it is only a way of saying 'My left eye is not square', 'Political ability always accompanies noble birth' if it is only a way of saying 'Whoever is nobly born is politically able', and so on. This criterion certainly disposes of 'Squareness is not square' (for which no such translation seems possible), and so saves us from the paradox about non-self-inherence. And I should say that pure nominalism (as developed, e.g. by Nelson Goodman) is in its own way a consistent and respectable philosophical position. It has at all events the virtue of intelligibility. So often when we are told that such and such an expression is 'meaningless', the word 'meaningless' itself seems to be meaningless; but what a pure nominalist means by 'meaningless' is comparatively clear—when he says that an expression is meaningless, he means that there is no way of translating it into a certain sort of vocabulary, which he holds to be the only sort of vocabulary that he or anyone else can understand. And the position of Russell himself sometimes appears to be that of pure nominalism (the reason why only certain sorts of subjects can be intelligently attached to certain sorts of predicates sometimes seems to be just that the degree of artificiality—of façon-de-parletude, so to speak—of subject and predicate must be the same). On the whole, however, the evidence is against this interpretation of him; and I think we must say of Russell what I believe Quine has said of himself, that he would *like* to be a pure nominalist but cannot—the facts make it too hard for him. (Incidentally, any reader of Quine's *New Foundations for Mathematical Logic* will realise how much this present paper owes to that one, though I have not imitated Quine's odd fad of talking about 'classes' rather than about 'properties').

Why not be a pure nominalist? The counter-question 'Why be one?' is to me a sufficient answer; but I admit that there is a certain amount of temperament in this. I simply do not possess the sheer zeal for waving Ockham's razor about which seems to burn within so many of my contemporaries; my motto is rather *Entia non sunt subtrahenda praeter necessitatem*, and even the property of non-self-inherence I have given up with a sigh and only under extreme compulsion. Nor can I understand the *fear* of abstract entities by which so many nowadays are beset; it even seems to me a little comical. I have been told, for example, that one who starts by asserting the non-squareness of virtue will end by maintaining the existence of a 'State' distinct from and in addition to its individual citizens; and this may very well be the case, but what of it? Even if the State in this sense does exist, it has no particular claim upon our reverence; and indeed it would seem that if the State does exist I am in a much better position to thumb my nose at it than if it does not. But temperament apart, there is a *reason* for not being a pure nominalist, the simple reason that this theory throws out the baby with the bathwater. It may to some minds be very nice to have this short and easy way with 'Squareness is not square', but the same technique will also, so far as I can see, compel us to drop such unexceptionable statements as that squareness is a shape. And indeed these two statements, the 'good' one and the 'bad' one, are very closely connected, for it is just because squareness *is* a shape that it is not the sort of thing that *has* a shape, and so is not square. A connected point is that shapes can be *counted*—we can say that a certain six things are all of one shape, or only of two shapes, and so on. And although Russell and Quine do not seem to have been especially worried about shapes, they have been worried about numbers, and about the fact that there are some things we want to say about them that cannot be said in the vocabulary of pure nominalism.

Summing up, I would say that there are three principal positions which a man may incline to take up with regard to the two forms 'X is Y' and 'X has the property of Y-ness'. He may want to say that they have the same meaning, and so automatically have the same truth-value. That is the position I have called pure nominalism. Or he may want to say that the two forms have not the same meaning, and moreover have not always the same truth-value either. This might be called pure Platonism, though I am by no means sure whether, as a matter of history, Plato would have owned it. The third view is that although 'X is Y' and 'X has the property of Y-ness' have not the same meaning, they necessarily always have the same truth-value. And I would suggest that the real moral of the paradox about non-self-inherence is just that this third position cannot really maintain itself, the theory of types (with its unkempt and probably unexpected brood of philosophical children, some of them like poor horrible babes with old men's faces) being a desperate but incoherent attempt to preserve it.

3. *Berkeley in Logical Form*

In what follows I shall use the symbolism of Łukasiewicz[1] for the propositional and predicate calculi, enriched by a dyadic proposition-forming operator T and certain other operators defined in terms of it. The operator T has the peculiarity that it takes an individual name for one argument and a statement for the other. Operators of this sort are not at all uncommon in ordinary speech; we have, for example, '—says that—', '—thinks that—' '—wishes that—'; but they have in general been neglected by the constructors of symbolic systems. The form 'Txp', constructed by means of this operator, may be read 'x is imagining that p'; though nothing that will be here proved depends on how 'T' is interpreted. Our theorems will all hold if, for example, 'Txp' is read as 'x says that p' or as 'x wishes that p', with the derivative forms being analogously altered.

The operator 'T', it should be observed, does not strictly speaking express a relation, or to put the point syntactically, it is not a dyadic predicate. Where 'φ' is a genuine dyadic predicate a statement of the form 'φxy' is about the objects named by the two arguments of 'φ' (e.g. 'Plato admires Socrates' is about Plato and Socrates). A predicate may at this point be contrasted with a statement-connective like 'If'; a statement of the form 'Cpq' is not about the objects named by the two arguments of 'C', for these two arguments are not names at all but statements; rather, 'Cpq' is about whatever objects its two component statements are about (e.g. 'If Brutus does as he has promised, Caesar will die' is about Brutus and Caesar). The operator 'T' functions like a predicate in relation to one of its arguments but like a statement-connective in relation to the other. 'Plato is imagining that Socrates is talking to Theætetus' is indeed about Plato, the object named by the first argument of '—is imagining that—'; but it is not about the object named by its second

[1] As in his *Aristotle's Syllogistic* §§ 22–4 [cf p. 66 below].

2

argument, for this second argument (the statement 'Socrates is talking to Theætetus') is not a name at all; the whole statement is, rather, about the objects that the contained statement is about, i.e. Socrates and Theætetus. The statement does, indeed, assert that a relation holds between Plato and Socrates; and in general the form $Tx\varphi y$ asserts that a relation holds between x and y (for it asserts that x stands to y in the relation of imagining-that-it-φ's); but 'x' and 'y' are not here the arguments of the operator 'T', but rather of the complex operator '$T \ldots \varphi \ldots$', and it is this complex operator, not the operator 'T', which may be properly described as a dyadic predicate, and as expressing a relation (just as it is not the statement-connective 'If', but something more complicated into which it enters, which expresses the relation asserted to hold between Brutus and Caesar in the statement 'If Brutus does as he has promised, Caesar will die').

Turning now to our defined forms, the first two of them are '$T(t)xp$', which may be read as 'x is imagining truly that p', and '$T(f)xp$', which may be read as 'x is imagining falsely that p'. Their definitions are as follows:

Df. $(t): T(t)xp = KTxpp$
Df. $(f): T(f)xp = KTxpNp$

That is, we take 'x is imagining truly that p' to mean 'x is imagining that p; and p'; and we take 'x is imagining falsely that p' to mean 'x is imagining that p; and not p'. Given five laws of the propositional calculus, together with these definitions, I shall now prove in succession that imagining truly that p implies imagining that p (proposition 6 below), that imagining falsely that p implies not imagining truly that p (proposition 7), and from this we shall proceed to the more complicated theorem that if the mere fact of x's imagining that p implies his falsely imagining that p, then x does not imagine truly that p (proposition 11). The deduction is as follows:[1]

1. $CKpqp$
2. $CKpNqNKpq$
3. $CCpNpNp$

[1] In setting out proofs, Łukasiewicz's symbolism is slightly modified as in Bocheński, *Précis de Logique Mathématique*, § 8.

4. $CCpqCCqrCpr$
5. $CCqrCCpqCpr$
   1 $p/Txp, q/p \times \mathrm{Df}.\,(t) = 6$
6. $CT(t)xpTxp$
   2 $p/Txp, q/p \times \mathrm{Df}.\,(f) \times \mathrm{Df}.\,(t) = 7$
7. $CT(f)xpNT(t)xp$
   5 $p/Txp, q/T(f)xp, r/NT(t)xp = C\,7{-}8$
8. $CCTxpT(f)xpCTxpNT(t)xp$
   4 $p/T(t)xp, q/Txp, r/NT(t)xp = C\,6{-}9$
9. $CCTxpNT(t)xpCT(t)xpNT(t)xp$
   4 $p/CTxpT(f)xp, q/CTxpNT(t)xp,$
   $r/CT(t)xpNT(t)xp = C\,8{-}C\,9{-}10$
10. $CCTxpT(f)xpCT(t)xpNT(t)xp$
    4 $p/CTxpT(f)xp, q/CT(t)xpNT(t)xp, r/NT(t)xp$
    $= C\,10{-}C\,3\,p/T(t)xp{-}11$
11. $CCTxpT(f)xpNT(t)xp$

In a similar way we could prove that if x's saying that p implies his saying falsely that p, then x does not say truly that p; that if x's wishing that p implies his wishing unsuccessfully that p, then he does not wish successfully that p; and so on.

I shall now introduce a predicate 'τ', which may be read '—is being thought about (by someone)'. I shall take 'x is thinking about y' to mean 'For some φ, x is imagining that y φ's', i.e. $\varSigma\varphi Txp\varphi y$; and '$\tau y$' is the existential generalisation of this with respect to x. That is, we have the definition

$$\mathrm{Df.}\,\tau{:}\tau y = \varSigma x \varSigma \varphi Txp\varphi y$$

Using this definition, some further laws of the propositional calculus, and Łukasiewicz's rules $\varSigma 2$ and $\varSigma 1$ for introducing the existential quantifier, I shall prove in succession that if x is imagining that y φ's then y is being thought about (proposition 16); that if x is imagining that y is not being thought about then he is falsely imagining this (proposition 18); and so that nothing is ever truly imagined to be not-thought-about (proposition 22). The deduction is as follows (numbers below 12 referring to items in the previous deduction):

12. Cpp
13. $CpNNp$
14. $CCpqCpKpq$
15. $CNpCpq$

      12 $p/Tx\varphi y \times \Sigma 2\varphi \times \Sigma 2x \times \mathrm{Df.}\,\tau = 16.$

16. $CTx\varphi y\tau y$

      5 $p/TxN\tau y, q/\tau y, r/NN\tau y$
         $= C\,13\,p/\tau y - C\,16\,\varphi/N\tau - 17$

17. $CTxN\tau yNN\tau y$

      14 $p/TxN\tau y, q/NN\tau y \times \mathrm{Df.}\,(f) = C\,17 - 18$

18. $CTxN\tau yT(f)xN\tau y$

      11 $p/N\tau y = C\,18 - 19$

19. $NT(t)xN\tau y$

      15 $p/T(t)xN\tau y = C\,19 - 20$

20. $CT(t)xN\tau yq$

      20 $\times \Sigma 1y = 21$

21. $C\Sigma yT(t)xN\tau yq$

      3 $p/\Sigma yT(t)xN\tau y = C\,21\,q/N\Sigma yT(t)xN\tau y - 22$

22. $N\Sigma yT(t)xN\tau y$

The passage from 18 to 19, it may be noted, is a direct application of the theorem proved at the end of our first deduction; and the passage from 19 to 20 illustrates the following meta-theorem: 'If a formula of the general form $N\varphi y$ (y does not φ) expresses a logical law, i.e. yields a true proposition no matter what individual we take y to be, then the corresponding formula of the form $N\Sigma y\varphi y$ (Nothing φ's) also expresses a logical law.' For we may always deduce a law of the form $N\Sigma y\varphi y$ from the corresponding law $N\varphi y$ by the following steps (which are generalisations of the steps from 19 to 22 above):

3. $CCpNpNp$
15. $CNpCpq$

   I. $N\varphi y$

      15 $p/N\varphi y = C\,\mathrm{I} - \mathrm{II}$

  II. $C\varphi yq$

 III. $C\Sigma y\varphi yq$

      II $\times \Sigma 1y = \mathrm{III}$
      3 $p/\Sigma y\varphi y = C\,\mathrm{III}\,q/N\Sigma y\varphi y - \mathrm{IV}$

 IV. $N\Sigma y\varphi y$

(If the variable q happens to occur freely in I, we must replace it in 15 by one which does not, or we shall have trouble with the substitution for it in the last step.)

The philosophical interest of this deduction is that our final theorem 22, asserting that nothing is ever truly imagined to be not-thought-about, is that it is informally established by Berkeley in the following passage from his first dialogue:

> *Philonous:* If you can conceive it possible for . . . any sensible object whatever, to exist without the mind, then I will grant it actually to be so.
> *Hylas:* . . . What more easy than to conceive a tree or house existing by itself, independent of, and unperceived by, any mind whatsoever? I do at this present time conceive them existing after this manner . . .
> *Philonous:* Is it not . . . a contradiction to talk of *conceiving* a thing which is *unconceived*?

And it may very well be felt that our way of putting this reasoning of Berkeley's is not half as good as Berkeley's own. Nor would I wish to deny this. The logician probably has more to gain from the exercise we have gone through than the philosopher has—applying his technique to this type of material gives him practice in handling functions with odd structures. But there is, I think, something for the philosopher in it too.

Formally, Berkeley's argument so far is impeccable. Our formalisation of it would suffice to show that, if it were not obvious even without it. What, then, is wrong with the argument as a defence of the Berkeleyan philosophy? The trouble with it—and I think the formalisation really does help to show this—is that (a) it proves too much, and (b) it proves too little. When formalised, its premisses and rules of inference may be seen to be entirely logical, for the proof takes place from beginning to end within the propositional calculus and the theory of quantification. Its xs and ys, therefore, can be anything at all, and in particular the ys may be minds, so that whatever the argument proves about 'sensible objects' it proves about minds also. If, e.g., it proves that sensible objects cannot be truly thought of as unthought-of, it proves equally that minds cannot be truly thought of as unthought-of.

But (secondly) *does* it prove that even sensible objects cannot be thought of as unthought-of? A distinction which our symbolism makes it possible to express very neatly and clearly is that between the two propositional forms

(a) x is imagining truly that there is something which is not-thought-about; and

(b) There is something which x is imagining truly to be not-thought-about.

These work out respectively as

(a) $T(t)x\Sigma yN\tau y$: and
(b) $\Sigma yT(t)xN\tau y$.

The latter can never be true, since its negation expresses a logical law; but no reason at all has been given either by Berkeley or by anyone else for ascribing such impossibility to (a). It is (a), however, which Berkeley must show to be impossible if he is to establish his idealism; in thinking that he has done so, he has confused two possible orders of his operators. Aristotle would have described this as the 'fallacy of composition'; it is like confusing 'He is able-to-write when he is not writing' ($KM\varphi xN\varphi x$) with 'He is able to write-when-he-is-not-writing' ($MK\varphi xN\varphi x$).[1]

---

[1] Cf. *De Sophisticis Elenchis* 166a23–30.

4. *Definitions, Rules and Axioms*

Not so very long ago Professor Łukasiewicz gave to this Society, at its joint session with the Mind Association, a sketch of a small part of the logic of Leśniewski. I propose in this paper to develop more fully an aspect of Leśniewski's logic which Professor Łukasiewicz touched upon in passing, and which I think is of some philosophical interest, namely the Leśniewskian theory of *definition*.

It will perhaps be best to begin with a concrete example of a Leśniewskian definition, namely a definition of the word 'and' which was proposed some years ago in an important little paper by Sobociński.[1] What Sobociński proposed was that we should define the form '*p* and *q*' as something that could be roughly put into English as follows:

> I. Every truth-function of *q* and *p* has the same truth-value as that truth-function of *p* and the statement 'Every statement has the same truth-value as itself'.

I say that this is only 'roughly' what the definition amounts to because in the actual definition the statement in quotes is not mentioned but used, and the whole thing is as it were a one-level affair; but apart from that I have given the substance of it, and I will give it more accurately later. (The more accurate formulation will also remove the appearance of circularity.)

There is no doubt something a little fantastic about giving I as a definition of the form '*p* and *q*'—it seems to obscure rather than to clarify what is meant by 'and'—but try and forget about this in the meantime; we shall see shortly that Sobociński's procedure is not entirely pointless. And we can see almost immediately that I is at least true and false under the same conditions as the plain '*p* and *q*'.

[1] B. Sobociński, *An Investigation of Prototetic* (Brussels, 1949).

39

For, to begin with, the contained statement 'Every statement has the same truth-value as itself', is a *true* statement, so that so far as its truth-conditions are concerned, I amounts to this:

II. Every truth-function of q and p has the same truth-value as that function of p and a true proposition.

Now, (a) *if p and q are both true*, this amounts to

III. Every truth-function of a true proposition and a true proposition has the same truth-value as that function of a true proposition and a true proposition,

which is clearly true. And the simple 'p and q' is also true if p and q are both true.

But (b) *if p is true but q false*, II will amount to

IV. Every truth-function of a false proposition and a true one has the same truth-value as that function of a true proposition and a true one,

and (c) *if p is false but q true*, II will amount to

V. Every truth-function with a true first-argument and a false second-argument has the same truth-value as that function of a false first-argument and a true second-argument,

and (d) *if p and q are both false*, II will amount to

VI. Every truth-function of a false proposition and a false proposition has the same truth-value as that function of a false proposition and a true one.

IV, V and VI are all plainly false, and the form 'Both p and q' is similarly false when p is true and q false, when p is false and q true, and when q is false and p true.

This sort of thing can of course be set out more neatly with symbols. Using E for 'If and only if' and Πp for 'For all p', the contained statement 'Every statement has the same truth-value as itself' may be written as $\Pi p E p p$, 'For all p, if and only if p then p'. And before symbolising the rest, let me digress for a moment about this formula $\Pi p E p p$ and the verbal rendering I have just given to it. Our original version 'Every statement has the same truth-value as itself' is misleading in so far as it suggests that $\Pi p E p p$ is a statement *about* statements and their truth-values. The rendering 'For all p, if and only if p then p' removes this suggestion, but of course it is not English, but a kind of mixture of English and Mathematics which often occurs in logic-books and irritates their less reasonable readers. I call this irritation unreasonable because the logician has no alternative to talking in this way so long as the natural languages suffer—as all of them do suffer—from a paucity of quantifiers. But if I were given the task of improving standard English at this point, I think I should proceed as follows: In English we generally construct quantifiers out of question-words—'Whatever' out of 'What?', 'However' and 'Anyhow' and 'Somehow' out of 'How?', and so on. What we need at this point is a quantifier corresponding to the question *whether* it is the case that p; if we had such a quantifier we could read $\Pi p E p p$ as 'If and only if anywhether then thether'. The standard false proposition $\Pi p p$, 'For all p, p', which also occurs in Leśniewskian systems, could then be read, not roughly as 'Everything is true' but simply as 'Everywhether'.

We have, then, $\Pi p E p p$ for the contained statement in our definition of 'and'; and using δ as a variable which can stand for any operator forming a truth-function of a pair of statements, I as a whole can be written compendiously as

$$\Pi \delta E \delta q p \delta p \Pi p E p p,$$

'For all δ, if and only if $\delta q p$ then $\delta(p)(\Pi p E p p)$'.

The symbols also make it easy to see how this sort of definition can be generalised. The form 'For all δ, $\delta x y = \delta z t$', where δ forms truth-functions, will clearly be true when and only when x has the same truth-value as z and y the same as t. If x, y, z and t are so chosen that this happens when and only when p and q are both true, then 'For all δ, $\delta x y = \delta z t$' will have the same truth-conditions as 'Both p and q'. This is so when, as in the above definition, $x = q$, $y = p$, $z = p$ and $t = 1$ (i.e., something true), and Sobociński gives a number of other cases meeting this condition. Further, if x, y, z

and t are so chosen that x has the same value as z, and y the same as t, only when p and q are both false, then 'For all δ, $\delta xy = \delta zt$' will have the same truth-conditions as 'Neither p nor q', and can be offered as a definition of *this* form. Sobociński gives such definitions for 'Neither p nor q' and also similar ones for 'p and not q' and for 'q and not p'. And since this is being offered as a definition of 'and', we may express this fact as follows (using Kpq for 'Both p and q'):

$$Kpq = \Pi\delta E\delta qp\delta p\Pi pEpp.$$

It should be said at once, however, that this is *not* how Sobociński expresses his definition, and that the whole purpose of his procedure is to avoid having to express it in this way. You will remember that quite a fuss was made many years ago over the discovery that all truth-functions whatsoever can be defined in terms of alternative denial, that is, in terms of the form 'Not both p and q'. It was argued by Leśniewski, however, that this was a spurious economy, for the definitions given all involved a further undefined sign besides 'Not-both', namely the definition-sign itself ('=', or '= ... Df.', or whatever the symbolist might use). If, Leśniewski said, we could take for our one undefined form 'if and only if p then q', we could use this as the form for our definitions too. Hence the problem—to which the above of Sobociński's is one solution—of defining 'and' in terms of 'If and only if', K in terms of E. Remembering that this is the background, the definition should be written, not as above, but as

$$E(Kpq)(\Pi\delta E\delta qp\delta p\Pi pEpp)$$

But even this is not quite right. For Leśniewski stated all his logical laws, including definitions, not as mere schemata with free variables, but as actual statements, formed from the schemata by binding all otherwise free variables by a universal quantifier, thus:

$$\Pi pqEKpq\Pi\delta E\delta qp\delta p\Pi pEpp$$

('For all p and q, if and only if both p and q, then for all δ, etc.' The rules of inference are of course adjusted to this divergence from the usual type of symbolic calculus.) This last refinement is worth mentioning for two reasons. In the first place, it makes it clear that having to use Π as well as E in the definitions does not detract from the economy of the basic symbolism, since we must have Π in any case to express our theses as universal statements rather than as schemata. And secondly when the thing is thus written out in full we see that what is identified with the definition-symbol is not just the truth-operator 'if and only if', but this universalised; and that is a more plausible identification.

That is the essence of the theory of definition we have to consider. It is, in brief, the theory that definitions are universal equivalences which we lay down in the form of axioms whenever we wish to introduce a new expression. But before criticising it, there are one or two variations and extensions of it to be set out. In the first place, Leśniewski himself admitted that even if definitions are axiomatic equivalences, it does not strictly follow that our one undefined truth-function-forming operator must be the equivalence-operator E. For even if we start with 'Not-both', in the manner of Sheffer and Nicod, there are forms using this only which have the same truth-conditions as 'If and only if p then q', and we could use one of these forms for expressing our definitions. The simplest form of this sort appears to be one which we could arrive at as follows: 'If and only if p then q' amounts to 'p and q have the same truth-value', i.e. to 'p and q do not have different truth-values'. But 'p and q *do* have different truth-values' (i.e., are neither both true nor both false) amounts to

'(Both) not both p and q and not both not p and not q', so that the denial of this (i.e., what we want) amounts to

'Not both (not both p and q) and (not both not p and not q)', and since the plain 'Not p' is true and false under the same conditions as 'Not both p and p', this amounts to

'Not both (not both p and q) and (not both not-both-p-and-p and not-both-q-and-q)',

or in symbols (using D for 'Not-both')

$$DDpqDDppDqq.$$

So we can use this for definitions by replacing p by the *definiendum* and q by the *definiens* and universalising. For example, the definition of the form Epq itself as $DDpqDDppDqq$ could be expressed thus:

$$\Pi pqDD(Epq)(DDpqDDppDqq)$$
$$DD(Epq)(Epq)D(DDpqDDppDqq)(DDpqDDppDqq).$$

This is hardly a simplification of the procedure in which E is undefined, but it is, even from a Leśniewskian point of view, a permissible variation.

A further feature of Leśniewski's theory of definition is that he held that definitions may be 'creative'; that is, they may add to the deductive strength of a system, and that not merely in the trivial sense of enabling us to prove theorems containing the defined term, but in the significant sense of enabling us to prove additional theorems *not* containing the defined term. Neither of the definitions so far cited has this property; but we do have them in the logic of common nouns, which Leśniewski called 'ontology'. Here is an example which is of some historical importance: Consider the theorem

VII. 'For all a, b, c and d, if the c is an a and the b is a c and the d is a c, the b is a d',

or in symbols, using ab for 'The a is a b',

$$\Pi abcdCKK\varepsilon ca\,\varepsilon bc\,\varepsilon dc\,\varepsilon bd.$$

This theorem expresses the individualising force of the word 'The' —it is true because if *the c* is anything, say an a, then only one thing is a c, so that if the b is a c and the d is a c then the b and the d must be identical, and the b is a d because it is *the d*. This would not ordinarily be regarded as deducible from

VIII. 'For all a, b and c, if the c is an a and the b is a c, then the b is an a',

$(\Pi abcCK\varepsilon ca\,\varepsilon bc\,\varepsilon ba)$; for this only expresses the *transitiveness* of the operator 'The—is a—'; and many other operators, *e.g.*, 'Every—is a—', are also transitive without having the individualising force of ε. (Replace 'the' by 'every' in VIII and it will still be true, but replace 'the' by 'every' in VII and it will be false.) Yet all we need to prove VII from VIII, beyond the ordinary propositional calculus, is the following definition of the term-complex '*star-ab*':

IX. 'For all *a*, *b* and *c*, the *c* is a star-*ab* if and only if the *c* is an *a* and the *b* is a *c*'.
$(\Pi abcE\varepsilon c^*abK\varepsilon ca\varepsilon bc)$.

For the benefit of those who like to have chapter and verse for these things, the proof—simplified by dropping Leśniewski's initial quantifiers and using ordinary substitution and detachment—is as follows:

$$D^*:E\varepsilon c^*abK\varepsilon ca\varepsilon bc$$

1. $CK\varepsilon ca\varepsilon bc\varepsilon ba$
2. $CEpqCqp$
3. $CCpqCCKqrsCKprs$
4. $CEpKqrCpr$
5. $CCpqCCqrCpr$
   $2 \ p/\varepsilon c^*ab, q/K\varepsilon ca\varepsilon bc = C$ D*–6
6. $CK\varepsilon ca\varepsilon bc\varepsilon c^*ab$
   $3 \ p/K\varepsilon ca\varepsilon cb, q/\varepsilon c^*ab, r/\varepsilon dc, s/\varepsilon d^*ab$
   $= C \ 6 - C \ \text{I} \ a/^*ab, b/d - 7$
7. $CKK\varepsilon ca\varepsilon bc\varepsilon dc\varepsilon d^*ab$
   $4 \ p/\varepsilon d^*ab, q/\varepsilon da, r/\varepsilon bd = \text{CD*} \ c/d - 8$
8. $C\varepsilon d^*ab\varepsilon bd$
   $5 \ p/KK\varepsilon ca\varepsilon bc\varepsilon dc, q/\varepsilon d^*ab, r/\varepsilon bd$
   $= C7 - C9 - 10$
9. $CKK\varepsilon ca\varepsilon bc\varepsilon dc\varepsilon bd$

I owe this proof, as well as other details connected with the axiomatisation of Leśniewski's ontology, to Dr B. Sobociński.[1]

Neither VII nor VIII, it will be noted, contains the defined expression 'star-*ab*', but without the definition we cannot prove VII from VIII, while with it we can. And this proof has turned out to be

[1] But it can now be found, set out a little differently, on pp. 64–5 of J. Słupecki, 'St. Leśniewski's calculus of names', *Studia Logica* III (1955).

an important step in the simplification of the postulates for ontology. The original single ordinary axiom which Leśniewski used for this was a rather long one, namely

X. For all *a* and *b*, the *a* is a *b* if and only if
    (i) for all *c*, if the *c* is an *a* the *c* is a *b*,
    (ii) for some *c*, the *c* is an *a*, and
    (iii) for all *c* and *d*, if the *c* is an *a* and the *d* is an *a* then the *c* is a *d*

Note that on one side of this equivalence the term *a* is in the subject position while on the other side it occurs only in the predicate position. This enables us to meet an objection which might well be raised against definitions like IX, that they enable us to eliminate the defined term from the predicate position but not from the subject position and therefore not from all contexts in which they occur. For the term can always be shifted from the subject position to the predicate position by using X, and then we can deal with it by means of the definition.

X was replaced by successively shorter axioms, and finally by the quite short one

XI. For all *a* and *b*, the *a* is a *b* if and only if, for some *c*, the *a* is a *c* and the *c* is a *b*

This, like VIII, would still hold if 'the' were replaced by 'every'; but the original axiom X would not, but contains a part (the last part) which expresses the individualising force of 'the' (and another part, the second-to-last, which expresses its 'existential import'). It is therefore not surprising that the proof of VII from VIII should be an important part of the proof of X from XI, and without 'creative definitions' neither would be possible.

This is, I think, as far as we need go into the mysteries of Leśniewskian logic in order to have something concrete to discuss. To anyone brought up in a good Russellian home the whole thing is of course a piece of logical naughtiness (on a par with, say, substituting descriptive functions for variables which are only intended to stand for logical proper names). Beginning at the beginning, we may protest that the defining sign '=' or '= . . . Df.' is not something which requires to be eliminated in the interests of economy of primitive symbols; for definitions are not part of the system at all, but merely permissions to abbreviate the symbolism for ease of manipulation, and to expand it back to its proper form when we need to. And the Leśniewskian procedure not only multiplies axioms in this misguided attempt to introduce economy in un-defined symbols, but each of these new axioms is of a peculiarly objectionable kind, since it contains a symbol whose meaning has nowhere been explained in terms of the symbols whose meaning is assumed to be already known.

As to 'creative definitions', the Russellian will continue, they only serve to show what a slippery slide the Leśniewskian is on. 'You begin', he will say, 'by identifying definitions with axiomatic equivalences which do behave rather like them, but having once forgotten the gulf that lies between a definition and an axiom, you go on to obliterate even what remains of that distinction *within* the class of axioms; and the only end that all this can have is the treat-ment of all axioms alike as definitions'.

The use of IX to 'simplify' the one ordinary axiom of ontology is a particularly obnoxious procedure. As the deduction itself shows, this 'definition' does not merely introduce a new complex but conveys something quite substantial about the operator 'The—is a—', namely its individualising force; and we can show this inde-pendently of the deduction too. For suppose that in IX we replace 'the' by some word which has not this individualising force, say 'every'; we then obtain

XII. For all *a*, *b*, *c*, every *c* is a star-*ab* if and only if every *c* is an *a* and every *b* is a *c*.

And XII can be shown to be false *whatever* the term 'star-*ab*' is supposed to mean. For XII obviously entails:

XIII. For all *a* and *b*, there is some *d* such that, for all *c*, every *c* is a *d* if and only if both every *c* is an *a* and every *b* is a *c*.

This is the formal contradictory of:

XIV. For some *a* and *b*, there is no *d* such that, for all *c*, every *c* is a *d* if and only if both every *c* is an *a* and every *b* is a *c*.

Now XIV is clearly true. For let c be an empty term and b a non-empty term. Then, whatever d and a may be, 'Every c is a d' comes out true, but 'Every c is an a and every b is a c' comes out false, because its second conjunct is false. So if we take any term a and any non-empty term b, the equivalence:

Every c is a d if and only if both every c is an a and every b is a c

must fail for any empty term c; so there can be no d such that this equivalence holds for *all* terms c.

This proof of XIV, or disproof of XII, assumes the availability of non-empty terms. Dr C. Lejewski has pointed out to me that Ontology does not guarantee that any term is non-empty, so that XIV cannot be proved as a theorem of Ontology. In fact, in Ontology, as he has shown, XIV is *equivalent* to the assertion that there are non-empty terms. But XII is still clearly different from IX, because, unlike IX, XII is positively *inconsistent* with there being non-empty terms.

Thus the so-called definition IX breaks down when we substitute 'every' for 'the' for it so as to get XII; this shows that IX tells us something quite substantial about the operator 'The—is a—', and to slip this in as a 'definition' is just cheating.

I have put the Russellian case against the Leśniewskian procedure as forcibly as I can; but I think—and here I am registering a change of opinion—that it is not impossible to answer it. To begin with, we can stage a small counter-attack. If, as the Russellians allege, definitions are not axioms, then they can only be rules of inference, to the effect that if in any thesis of the system we replace an expression of the form Na, say, by the corresponding expression of the form Daa or *vice-versa*, the resulting formula will be a thesis also. Any economy in our axioms which is gained by taking definitions out of the class of axioms is therefore offset by a corresponding complication of the other part of our postulate-set, the rules. Certainly all of these new rules are of a single pattern, but that can be said of the corresponding Leśniewskian axioms too.

It may be said that the dichotomy of axioms and rules of inference is a naive one, and that definitions are a *tertium quid*; but that definitions, if they are not laid down as axioms, function effectively as rules, is shown by the notorious fact that they can be *inconsistent* with the other postulates, and can introduce *contradictions* into an otherwise innocent system if not laid down with due care. This can happen even without our wandering into type-fallacies, as the following example shows: Using the Łukasiewicz symbolism, and δ for any monadic statement-forming operator on statements, we might introduce a new statement-form Tp as follows:

$$DT:\delta Tp = N\delta p$$

This tells us simply that by any given function of Tp we simply mean the negation of that function of p. Now take the function 'p implies itself', which we might write as Vp. This can be laid down as a logical law, true whatever statement p may be. From this we can infer VTp, 'Tp implies itself'. But by the definition of T, this just means 'p does not imply itself'. So by means of DT we have inferred from a logical law the denial of that same law. Formally the proof could be set out thus:

1. Vp
     1 $p/Tp = 2$
2. VTp
     2 x $DT\delta/V = 3$
3. NVp.

In any properly-constructed calculus there will of course be rules for the introduction of definitions which will disqualify DT; but the very need for such rules is a testimony to the fact that definitions take their place among the rules and axioms of a system and interact with them at least *as if* they were rules or axioms themselves.[1] As a universalised equivalence, DT would be

XV. For all δ and p, δTp if and only if not δp

($\Pi\delta pE\delta TpN\delta p$), but this has not the form which Leśniewski prescribes for equivalences that we may lay down at any time to introduce a new symbol (where the new symbol is an operator

---

[1] The DT paradox is my own; but Leśniewski had an eagle eye for contradictions implicit in the methods of definition used by his contemporaries. *See* the fourth paragraph of Quine's review of his *Einleitende Bemerkungen*, etc., *Journal of Symbolic Logic*, vol. 25 (1940), p. 83.

on statements, one of his rules—broken by the above—is that the new symbol must be the *first* sign on its side of the equivalence); and by whatever *legitimate* process we might introduce the operator T, the above equivalence is false, for we can prove that its denial holds for *any* operator, *i.e.*, we can prove

XVI. For any γ, it is not the case that for all δ and p, $\delta\gamma p$ if and only if not δp

or in other words

XVII. For any γ, there is some δ and p such that $\delta\gamma p$ is not equivalent to $N\delta p$.

(The proof is simply a reversal of the paradox—let δp be 'p implies itself'; then 'γp implies itself' will not be equivalent to 'p does not imply itself', since the former will be true and the latter false.) If we do not express definitions (or what purport to be definitions) as equivalences, we will not dispose of DT in this way, but we shall need *some* way of disposing of it.

As to the alleged instability of the distinction between 'definitory' rules or axioms and other rules or axioms, the distinction can be made perfectly precise (and indeed must be, if our freedom to introduce definitions as we require them is not to lead to the introduction of things like DT); and at the same time it can be admitted that of the other rules and axioms, some resemble 'definitory' ones—again in perfectly precise ways—more clearly than others. For example, in a system of syllogistic logic using negative terms which was developed a few years ago by I. Thomas,[1] there is a rule to the effect that the terms *nna* ('not-not-*a*') and *a* may be interchanged in any formula; and while this is not exactly a definition (since it does not enable us to eliminate *n* from all contexts but only from ones in which it is iterated), it is quite like one—it is for example, quite correctly describable as a 'permission to abbreviate'. (It is therefore not very misleading, but only a little bit so, when Thomas writes down this rule as '*nna* = *a*', using the standard form for a definition.) The fashionable model of a 'spectrum' seems in place here—of rules and axioms which are not 'definitory', some are nevertheless

[1] I. Thomas, 'CS(n): an extension of CS', *Dominican Studies*, vol. 2 (1949).

closer to that end of the spectrum than others. Into this pattern the 'ontological definitions' or quasi-definitions of Leśniewski fit quite easily; and there is certainly no unfairness in using them to simplify the single ordinary axiom of ontology, since their use was allowed with the original long axiom too.

Finally, to the complaint that the equivalences which Leśniewski identifies with definitions contain symbols whose meaning is unexplained, it is extremely naive to identify any single routine procedure of formal logic with 'explaining what we mean' by an expression. Not only Russellian definitions, and not only Leśniewskian definitions and quasi-definitions, but even ordinary axioms, and for that matter ordinary theorems, may perform this function. At this point the notion of a definition *ought* to cover the whole syntactical spectrum. We might, for example, make clear what we mean by 'negation' by saying that it is an operator such that, if it is symbolised by N, certain formulae—*e.g.*, $ENNpp$—will express laws; and one might say that if these laws do not all hold for, say, intuitionist negation, then that is not what is here being symbolised. This type of definition is no doubt incomplete; one may not know *what* operators in fact conform to the given laws,[1] and there may be several which do so; but ordinary definition is incomplete also, though in another sense—it only takes us as far as the 'undefined' terms, so that whatever ambiguity attaches to these is transmitted to the defined terms too. And certainly if expressions which are alleged to be incapable of definition are to be made the subject of rigorous logical treatment, we cannot take a single step towards such treatment until some axioms or rules involving these expressions are laid down for us.[2] The expressions are then 'defined' in the sense that the logician knows as much about them as he needs to know for his particular purposes; and ordinary definitions 'define' in this sense too. This is still more obviously the case with the 'inferential definitions' of Popper.

I should like to record here my view that the real relevance of

[1] I have been told, for example (by Mr J. M. Shorter), that there are senses of 'has been', 'will be', etc., in which 'S is P' entails 'S has been going to be P' just as it entails 'S will have been P'; but I cannot for the life of me see what these senses are.

[2] Cf. J. Łukasiewicz in 'The principle of individuation', *Arist. Soc. Supp.* vol. 27 (1953), pp. 77–8; and C. Lejewski, in 'Logic and existence', *British Journal for the Philosophy of Science*, August 1954, p. 115 n.4.

Leśniewski's ontology to the problem of individuation is just this: It shows how we may define the singular statement-form 'The *a* is a *b*' without making any use of variables which stand for logical proper names. In Łukasiewicz's paper the form is 'defined' by means of an ordinary axiom, namely that numbered X in our text. In the variant of ontology developed by Lejewski, 'The *a* is a *b*' is in effect defined in terms of 'Every *a* is a *b*' (Lejewski gives a definition in terms of 'Every' of 'The *a* exists', and 'The *a* is a *b*' could then be equated with 'The *a* exists, and every *a* is a *b*').

To all this, the Russellian need not be entirely without an answer. He may admit that in a symbolic calculus considered purely syntactically, without reference to any interpretation, a permission to abbreviate is a permission to transform; and on the purely syntactical plane no rule of inference is anything more than that. But if we are using our formulae to express certain *truths*, and our rules of transformation to express means of deriving one such truth from another or others, we can distinguish between these things and the mere permission to express the same truths by different locutions.

There is no difficulty in dealing with the paradoxical definition *DT* on this basis. It won't do as a definition because it does not give an unambiguous indication of *what* alternative locution is being offered. *DT*, it will be recalled, reads thus: $\delta Tp = N\delta p$. This says to us in effect, 'Take the context (δ) of *Tp*, wrap it around *p* instead, and then negate the result'. But usually there is no such thing as *the* context of *Tp*—it usually has several. For example, in *NVTp* it has *V* for its more immediate and *NV* for its wider context. In fact the only circumstance in which *Tp* has one context only is when it occurs on its own; it then has what might be called the zero context, and is equivalent by the definition to *N*-(zero-context)-*p*, i.e., to the plain *Np*. So apart from any syntactical rules for definition-construction which *DT* may violate, it does not perform the *semantic* function of a definition, and it is no wonder that it lands us in trouble.

Since it has been admitted that syntactically a definition must appear either as an axiom or as a transformation-rule, we need not deny that other syntactical devices may be more or less close to definitions; but this 'spectrum' only acquires direction because we know at the outset what the definition-end of it must be like if the semantic function of definitions is to be effectively performed. We know, e.g., that what is meant merely to provide an alternative locution must enable us to fall back on the original locution whenever we wish to, and must not add to what we can prove when using the original locution only. Whether the precise syntactical device we employ is a replacement-rule or an axiomatic equivalence is generally of no great moment; but there are systems in which only the replacement-rule would give us both complete eliminability (of the defined symbol) and non-creativeness. In most systems an axiomatic equivalence will do the same because there is associated with the equivalence-operator E

(i) the rule that if $Ea\beta$ is a law, then a and β are interchangeable in any formula, and

(ii) the law of identity Epp.

Given (i) we may infer from the axiomatic equivalence $Ea\beta$ the rule permitting the replacement of a by β and *vice-versa* in formulae; and given (ii) we may infer the equivalence $Ea\beta$ from this permission to replace (by applying the permission to the result of substituting a or β for p in Epp); so that where we have both (i) and (ii) we can guarantee that these two devices will have the same deductive strength. But there are systems not containing Epp in which even such an equivalence as $EVpEpp$ will add to the theorems not containing V, though a mere permission to abbreviate Epp to Vp would not do so;[1] and there are systems not containing the rule (i) in which a definition will give us formulae which *do* contain the defined symbol which the corresponding equivalence would not give us.

When we remember the semantic function of definitions, the latter result will appear entirely in order. For example, a system in which it would not be reasonable to have the rule that logically equivalent expressions are interchangeable in all contexts, would be a system containing an operator B such that Bxp is interpretable as 'x believes that p'. Such a system might well contain the equivalence with which we began, asserting that 'Both p and q' (as ordinarily understood) is true if and only if every truth-function of q and p has the same true-value as that function of p and a true proposition.

[1] See my *Formal Logic*, pp. 98–9 for details.

But we would not want to pass, by a principle of interchangeability of logical equivalents, from 'x believes that both p and q' to 'x believes that $\Pi\delta E\delta pq$, etc.'; for x might be quite convinced that both p and q and yet require a great deal of persuading that $\Pi\delta E\delta pq$, etc. On the other hand it would be quite in order in such a system to introduce the form Kpq, not for 'Both p and q' as ordinarily understood, but as an abbreviation for '$\Pi\delta E\delta pq$, etc.', and there would then be nothing at all objectionable in passing from $BxKpq$ to $Bx\Pi\delta E\delta pq$, etc., since this would only be exchanging a short for a long way of saying the same thing. In such cases definitions are *syntactically* stronger than equivalences, that is they make possible more transformations, precisely because the transformations they effect are *semantically* more trivial, in fact without any content at all.[1] (This part of the debate is a little unhistorical, since Russellians have been almost, though not quite, as suspicious of 'non-extensional' systems as Leśniewskians. This is a pity, since the above seems to me quite the strongest point that can be made against the Leśniewskian procedure.)

An *axiom*, then, is a formula used to express a truth; a *rule of inference* a transformation rule used to express a means of deriving one truth from another; and a *definition*, a transformation-rule used to provide alternative ways of expressing the same truth. In this form, and at this level, the Russellian trichotomy can certainly be maintained. It must be insisted, however, that what we have now is just a proposal for the use of these three terms. (This is, we may say, a Russellian definition of 'definition' on two counts: it is a Russellian definition-of-'definition', i.e. it gives what Russellians mean by the term 'definition'; and it is a Russellian-definition of 'definition', i.e. it is itself a definition in the Russellian as opposed to the Lesniewskian sense.) As a description of actual logical procedure this way of making the distinction would be (and has been) extremely misleading. For just as what appears in a formal system as an axiom or set of axioms may function as an 'explanation of what we mean' by some expression, so conversely what appears in a formal system as an abbreviative definition may do much more than this.

Take, for example, the definition with which we began—

[1] On the general question on the relation of belief and meaning, see A. Church's excellent piece on 'Intensional isomorphism and identity of belief' in *Philosophical Studies*, October 1954.

$$Kpq = \Pi\delta E\delta qp\delta p\Pi pEpp$$

This is certainly not an explanation of what we ordinarily mean by 'and'; and while it could be represented as an introduction of a new and *non*-ordinary meaning of 'and', this would not be a very accurate account of what logicians are generally doing when they use symbol-sequences of this kind. If it is pure fantasy to say that $\Pi\delta E\delta qp\delta p\Pi pEpp$ is what we ordinarily mean by 'Both p and q', there is still a large element of fantasy in saying that when a logician does what he describes as 'defining K in terms of E and Π' he is simply introducing an arbitrary abbreviation for $\Pi\delta E\delta qp\delta p\Pi pEpp$. What is the point, we might ask, in having a special abbreviation for this particular formula, and why use K, the usual symbol for 'and'? To talk of arbitrariness here is in fact a pretence; we know very well that this formula is being 'abbreviated' to Kpq because we have shown by calculation that it is true and false under the same conditions as 'Both p and q', and the way we use the definition is as a kind of gearing device—it tells us that anything we may prove in the Π-E calculus (which is, of course, an extensional calculus) about the form $\Pi\delta E\delta qp\delta p\Pi pEpp$, we can safely take as having been proved about Kpq, and that in its ordinary sense. From the point of view of exhibiting what is actually going on, the use of axiomatic equivalences at this point is therefore if anything *more* accurate, (though also, I suspect more cumbersome) than the usual procedure; and the gearing of all other truth-operators to complexes formed solely from the gearing symbol itself is a genuine and striking technical achievement.

5. On Some Proofs of the Existence of God

Philosophers in the past have frequently put forward what they have claimed to be proofs of the existence of God, and other philosophers have subjected these proofs to criticism, sometimes leaving it at that, more often producing other proofs which they thought to be better, and sometimes producing what they claimed to be *dis*proofs of the existence of God. This sort of activity is nowadays, on the whole, in abeyance among philosophers, though there is a certain amount of interest in certain associated meta-theorems, as we might call them—alleged proofs that there cannot be *any* valid proofs of the existence of God, and sometimes that there cannot be any valid disproofs. More accurately, it is widely *taken as proven* that there cannot be any valid proofs of the existence of God. But I am not myself sure *how* this is supposed to have been proved, or how one would set about proving it. So it seems to me that particular proofs—and disproofs—of the existence of God must be examined on their merits; there is no 'short way' with them all. And I propose to examine one of them later.

There is *one* meta-theorem, though, that I should like to say something about to begin with—a theorem which concerns not only proofs of the existence of God, but proofs quite generally. For an argument to constitute a proof it must not only be formally valid; it is requisite also that those to whom it is addressed should be convinced of the truth of its premisses, at all events *more* convinced of the truth of its premisses than of the falsehood of its conclusion. Where this is not so, the argument—if those who are addressed know what they are about—will simply be contraposed, and the manifest falsehood of the conclusion made a ground for saying that at least one of the premisses must be false. This is something of a truism; but it has been explicitly applied to theological argumentation by Professor Smart, who seems to feel, I think quite rightly, that in that area it is something that needs to be pointed out.

In theological argumentation, and also in argumentation about the nature of logic, the notion that certain things are 'evident in themselves', and not merely evident *to* this person or that, has not yet died out. Thomists, for example, continue to make a distinction between what is evident in itself and what is evident to us. I must confess that this distinction, as propounded by Thomists, is totally unintelligible to me; but I don't think the Thomists are the only or even the chief sinners in this respect.

I said a moment ago that the notion of the 'evident in itself' continues to be appealed to not only in theological argumentation but also in argumentation about the nature of logic, and I think there is a connection. It is widely contended that what are sometimes called 'logically true propositions' are evident in themselves; that is, that if anyone does not know them to be true, it can in the nature of the case only be because he has not understood the words in which they are expressed—because, in other words, he has not the intended proposition before his mind. I cannot myself see that this is so; that is, I cannot see that a person may not mistakenly think that some proposition which is in fact logically true is false. Indeed it seems to me that mistakes of this sort are not at all infrequent, though they hardly ever occur with the *simplest* sorts of logically true propositions. Now if propositions are not evident in themselves but only evident to this or that person, then we must say that proofs are not proofs in themselves but only proofs to this or that person or class of persons; but if some propositions *are* evident in themselves then we may say that some proofs *are* proofs in themselves, namely those in which the conclusion is validly drawn from premises which are evident in themselves.

I think that those who have said that valid proofs of the existence of God are demonstrably impossible have usually meant that valid 'proofs in themselves' of the existence of God are demonstrably impossible. The demonstration they have had in mind is this: Only logically true propositions are evident in themselves, and it i? impossible to prove the existence of God or of anything else from a logically true proposition; therefore it is impossible to give something which would count as a 'proof in itself' of the existence of God.

The conclusion of this reasoning seems to me true but trivial, since I cannot imagine anything which would count as a 'proof in itself' of anything at all. And as to the premisses, the assertion that only logically true propositions are evident in themselves, seems to me true only if it means no more than that *no other* propositions are evident in themselves; if it means or implies that logically true propositions are evident in themselves, it seems to me false. The other premiss, that it is impossible to prove the existence of anything at all from logically true premisses, seems to me very sweeping and doubtful; I'm not at all sure where logically true propositions end and other sorts of propositions begin, but I imagine that the premisses of *Principia Mathematica* are logically true propositions, and yet there are innumerable existential propositions proved in that work—that there is a successor of the number 0, for example, and other things of this kind. However, if those who argue, on these or other grounds, that there cannot be a *demonstration* of God's existence, mean by a demonstration something which is a 'proof in itself' and not just a proof to someone prepared to admit the premisses, I do not deny their conclusion.

The fact that proofs of God's existence are inevitably thus limited in their appeal may be an awkward fact for those theists who have tried to claim something more for their proofs—who have tried, in fact, to claim for them more than can be justly claimed for *any* proof. But it also opens up the possibility of recognising the cogency, for the appropriate audience, of numerous proofs which have not been even considered by those who will not be content with anything less than a 'proof in itself'; that is, who will not be content with anything that *can* be had in this or any field.

I will only give one rather trivial example, which is however of some interest on the purely logical side. If a person is quite convinced that only if there is a God ought he to go to Church, *and* that he ought to go to Church, he is perfectly entitled to infer from these two premisses that God exists. It may be protested that it is inconceivable that anyone should be convinced of the premisses of this argument without being already convinced of the conclusion, and this may be so, but a state of mind not unlike this one seems to me perfectly conceivable and perhaps even not unusual. A man may be absolutely convinced that only if God exists would he be obliged to live in a certain way—for example, to respect certain freedoms in other people even when violation of these freedoms seems the only way to avoid some grave social disaster—and may also be absolutely convinced that he *is* obliged to live in this way; and a man in this state of mind would surely be not only rational in drawing the conclusion that God exists, but positively *ir*rational in not drawing it.

There is something a little bit peculiar about this argument all the same. The argument 'Only if God exists ought I to do X, and I ought to do X, therefore God exists', is unquestionably valid if assertions about obligations really are what they purport to be. But if we adopt the very prevalent view that what appear to be assertions about obligations are not really assertions at all but something else, let us say for simplicity's sake commands, the position is not quite so clear. In the logic of imperatives I think the weight of our inclination is to accept as valid the inference or quasi-inference

> If God exists, go to Church;
> and God does exist;
> So go to Church.

But what about the corresponding *modus tollens*, that is

> If God exists, go to Church;
> But don't go to Church;
> Therefore God doesn't exist?

And what about the analogous inference on the other side, that is

> If God doesn't exist, don't go to Church;
> But go to Church;
> Therefore God exists;

or in other words

> Only if God exists, go to Church;
> and go to Church;
> Therefore God exists?

I must confess that I am a little uneasy about these; though I must also confess that it is not at all clear to me why I should be uneasy about them. So I just put this up as a problem.

I want now to turn to one of the traditional proofs of the existence of God, to illustrate this policy which I have recommended, of examining all such proofs, and of course disproofs, on their logical merits. And the one on which I am going to concentrate is, I am afraid, that old chestnut the ontological proof. To anticipate my conclusion about this, I am going to say that the ontological proof contains a valid step and an invalid one, but the invalid step is not the one that is usually picked on by contemporary philosophers.

Leaving God right out of it for a moment, I suppose it would be agreed that the following argument is a perfectly valid one:

Sally is a trollop;
Therefore whoever has kissed all trollops has kissed Sally.
But some American has kissed all trollops.
Therefore someone who has kissed all trollops, namely this
American, has kissed Sally.

And of course not only this but any argument of the same form will be valid; that is, any argument of the form

X is a Y.
Therefore whatever is an R of every Y is an R of X.
But some Z is an R of every Y.
Therefore some R of every Y, namely this Z, is an R of X.

And in particular the following argument of this form is perfectly valid:

Real existence is a perfection.
Therefore whatever has all perfections has real existence.
But some object-in-the-mind has all perfections.
Therefore something which has all perfections, namely this
object-in-the-mind, has real existence.

And that is just the ontological argument, or as near to it as makes no difference.

Of course there *is* something wrong with arguments of this last *sort*, even if there's nothing wrong with arguments of that *form*. This is obvious because we can prove far too much by arguments of this sort. Some might say that the existence of God is itself far too much, but even apart from that, there are things like this:

> Real existence is one of the two properties, being-a-mermaid-in-the-Cherwell and real existence
> Therefore whatever has the two properties, being-a-mermaid-in-the-Cherwell and real existence, has real existence
> But some object-in-the-mind has these two properties
> Therefore some really existent mermaid in the Cherwell really exists.

And in case you protest that this is an empirical matter to be settled in empirical ways, I can prove similarly that there really exists a really existing mermaid in the Cherwell whom you will see with your own eyes next Tuesday.

This, of course, like Gaunilo's piece about the island, only shows there's *something* wrong with this sort of argument, and still leaves us to find out what it is. However, there is a chorus of voices to tell us what it is. In relation to the original argument, what the chorus says is that whatever is a perfection is a predicate, but existence isn't a predicate, therefore existence isn't a perfection; and the other first premisses are wrong for the same reason. Well, it may be so; but I doubt it. We take it for granted nowadays that we have Existence properly tied up and put in a bag, but I don't know. I don't see that it doesn't make sense to say 'This exists', though its sense is no doubt a kind of tautology; and I don't see that it doesn't make sense to say 'This doesn't exist', though *its* sense is no doubt a kind of contradiction. It certainly makes sense, as Moore pointed out some years ago, to say 'This might not have existed', and for all I know there may be, as the theological tradition affirms, objects of which this last is true and objects of which it is false.

But whether existence is a predicate or not, it seems to me that the *main* trouble with the ontological argument lies in the other premiss—'Some object-in-the-mind has all perfections'. Anselm's proof of this was simply that even atheists, in order to *be* atheists, must be able to *conceive* an all-perfect being. That is, we have here a subsidiary argument of the form

> *x* thinks that there is a *y* such that *y* is perfect
> Therefore there is a *y* such that *y* is in *x*'s mind and is perfect.

Now I don't think there's anything in *this* 'therefore' whatever, but it's worth trying to puzzle out why Anselm—and other people—should think that there is.

Consider this argument:

> *x* thinks that there is a *y* such that *y* is P
> Therefore there is a *y* such that *x* thinks that *y* is P

(e.g. 'I think someone is eating fish and chips, therefore there is someone whom I think is eating fish and chips'). This is clearly wrong, as I am sure even Anselm would have agreed. But it takes most people a second or two to see that it is wrong—there is something that makes this slip an easy one. And perhaps it is simply that the following similar argument is all right:

> It is true of *x* that there is a *y* which he loves
> Therefore there is a *y* such that it is true of *x* that he loves it.

'*x* thinks that there is a *y* such that *y* is P' looks as if it expresses a *relation* between *x* and some *y*, although in fact it doesn't. But we hanker after some way of pushing the quantifier to the beginning as we can with genuine relational propositions, and so, not being able to do it the straightforward way, we concoct queer ways of doing it—we say things like

> *x* thinks that there is a real *y* such that *y* is P
> Therefore there *is* an imagined-by-*x* *y* such that *y* is P.

And the logical importance of the ontological proof is that it shows that in the end this procedure is as fatal as the other one.

Aquinas, incidentally, thought that this modification of Anselm's argument would have been valid, though it wouldn't have yielded Anselm's conclusion:

> *x* thinks that there is a real *y* such that *y* is P
> Therefore there is an imagined-by-*x* *y* such that *y* is *thought by x to be P*.

But I can't see why this reduplication of the imagination-qualification should be necessary in the conclusion, and anyway we have to ask whether this imagined-by-*x* *y* *is* P or not, and Thomas provides no answer to this.

We could, indeed, introduce a new sort of quantifier by defining the form

There is-imagined-by-*x*-to-be a *y* such that *y* is P

as a verbal variant of

x imagines that there is a *y* such that *y* is P

but then there are no entailment-lines between this quantifier and the ordinary one, so that we cannot argue in this sort of way:

There is-imagined-by-*x*-to-be a *y* such that *y* is perfect and therefore really existent.
Therefore there is an imagined-by-*x* *y* such that *y* is perfect and really existent
Therefore there is a *y* such that *y* is perfect and really existent.

And it seems to me worth saying that this sort of argument is fallacious—an illegitimate jump from ordinary relational conversion —whether it leads to the existence of an Anselmic God or merely to, let us say, to the existence of an 'idea' as conceived by Locke or Berkeley.

6. *Opposite Number*

Suppose people reproduced like amoebæ, and suppose you and I are the two products of such a fission, each of us having a perfect memory of having been the one original person, though now the two of us are both being and doing quite different things, say me reading Plato and you not. This would put us in a situation not unlike that envisaged by John Wyndham in the story 'Opposite Number' in his *Seeds of Time*. Wyndham complicates the case a little by placing the two offshoots in different 'worlds', normally without any contact with one another, so that each regards the other as merely what he himself 'might have been'; but my more modest fantasy introduces the same awkward relativism into an area where experience as it is seems to provide us with absolutes. I can say, for example, 'I remember those sardines I ate before you were born', and you can say this to me too, both of us referring to the same occurrence and both referring to it equally correctly. And equally— just a little bit—incorrectly; for if both were quite correct I could say, for us both, 'I remember those sardines I ate before you were born, and you remember those sardines you ate before I was born'; but I cannot say this, for I cannot admit that I was not in existence when the sardines were eaten. Nor, for the same sort of reason, can you say it to me. For either of us this would be like (though not perhaps as like as Wyndham thinks) admitting to being a mere might-have-been.

I think—though this is not completely clear—that it would be accurate in the situation which I have envisaged, for me to say to you 'Once you were me', and for you to say this to me. For suppose we represent our joint life-history in the obvious way by a big Y. The left arm is not the right arm, and neither arm is the pedestal; but the word 'me' does not denote the present part of my life-history, represented by the left arm, nor any other part of my life-history (personal pronouns do not ordinarily denote life-histories), but rather denotes the *person whose* life-history is represented by the pedestal plus the left arm, and the word 'you' similarly denotes the *person whose* life-history is represented by the pedestal plus the right arm.[1] These two persons were *ex hypothesi* one and the same person before the fission, and given that pronouns have the reference just indicated, 'Once you were me' seems a correct way of describing this fact. 'Once I was you' would of course do as well; for it doesn't mean 'Once I was you and there was no me', which of course I cannot admit (and which indeed seems self-contradictory, at least unless we are prepared to add 'and no you either'), but just 'Once I was you', and that is fair enough. My memory of the sardine feast can then be expressed by 'I remember eating those sardines when I was you' (or 'before I had ceased to be you' or 'before you had ceased to be me').

Before going further with this, let us remember that while we perhaps *can* talk like this, we do not absolutely need to. We could slip past all purely logical dangers by either (a) saying that both your memory of the sardine-eating and mine of the same are illusory—the person who ate the sardines was someone other than either of us, and now non-existent; or by (b) saying that both our memories are veridical but they are of different events—there were really two of us all the time, and so two sardine-eaters, but before the fission no observer could distinguish these, and neither was aware of the other. I imagine, however, that in the circumstances envisaged, at all events if this sort of thing happened often, we would have to be very hard-pressed indeed to say either of these things. (If I may so put it, they smell too much of *finging hypotheses*.)

Just how hard-pressed, in fact, are we? Not very, it seems at first; and then it begins to seem rather more. Not very, because while 'You *are* me' entails 'Whatever is true of me is true of you', and this is *ex hypothesi* false in the matter of reading Plato, 'You *were* me' does not seem to have this consequence, but only 'Whatever *was* true of me was true of you,' and that is harmless. But is it? By the principle just admitted, if it was the case before the fission that I would now be reading Plato, then it was the case before the fission

---

[1] This difference between a person and his life-history is very properly and very fruitfully emphasised by N. L. Wilson in 'Space, time and individual', *Journal of Philosophy*, 52 (October 1955).

that you would now be reading Plato; but how can it have been the case that you would now be reading Plato if in fact, you are not now reading Plato?

This example suggests a method of proving quite generally that not only 'You are me' but even 'You were me' entails that whatever is true of me is true of you. In setting out this proof I shall use the Łukasiewicz notation[1] supplemented by Ixy for 'x is y', Pnp for 'It was the case n time-units ago that p' and Fnp for 'It will be the case n time-units hence that p'. Beside substitution and detachment I shall use the rule (RP) that if $C\alpha\beta$ is a theorem so is $PnC\alpha\beta$; the rule (RPF) that 'It was the case n time-units ago that it would be the case n time-units later that p' ($PnFnp$) is interchangeable with 'p now', i.e., the plain p; and the premiss (beside the principle of syllogism and the indiscernibility of identicals when identical) that if it was the case at any time that if p then q, then if it was then the case that p, it was then the case that q. Here is the proof:

1. $CCpqCCqrCpr$
2. $CIxyC\varphi y\varphi x$
3. $CPnCpqCPnpPnq$
   $2 \times RP = 4$
4. $PnCIxyC\varphi y\varphi x$
   $3 \ p/Ixy, \ q/C\varphi y\varphi x = C4{-}5$
5. $CPnIxyPnC\varphi y\varphi x$
   $1 \ p/PnIxy, \ q/PnC\varphi y\varphi x, \ r/CPn\varphi yPn\varphi x$
   $= C5{-}C3 \ p/\varphi y, \ q/\varphi x{-}6$
6. $CPnIxyCPn\varphi yPn\varphi x$
   $6 \ \varphi/Fn\varphi \times RPF = 7$
7. $CPnIxyC\varphi y\varphi x$.

This conclusion contradicts our original supposition (that you were me, but I am now reading Plato without you doing so), so it would seem that this supposition is allowable only if something from RP, RPF and 1–3 is discarded.

My own choice, for reasons I shall give later, is to drop RPF. But we should glance first at what looks like another way out. We might say that although 'Once you were me' is now true, at no time was this true: 'You are me'; so that the above rendering of 'You

---
[1] i.e. Cpq for 'If p then q', Kpq for 'p and q', Apq for 'p or q', Np for 'Not p'.

were me' as 'It was the case that you are me' (P*n*I*xy*) is not accurate. How one would express this solution formally I am not sure, but to begin with we might do it by distinguishing P*n*(I*xy*) from (P*n*I)*xy*, and denying that the latter entails the former; and if this is a bit clumsy we might introduce λxyP*n*I*xy* for the complex predicate P*n*I and re-write (P*n*I)*xy* as λxyP*n*I*xyxy* and keep P*n*I*xy* for P*n*(I*xy*). But whether elegant or not, this solution seems to me to confuse a denoting word with what is denoted. Whether or not the sentence 'You are me' could ever have been truly uttered, *your being me* was once the case; but when it was the case it was the same thing, entirely, as my being me (or your being you). It is only since the fission that my being me and your being you have been distinct facts and your being me not a fact at all.

The same goes, moreover, for all other facts about you and me. For example, before the fission there was no difference between my being a future (today at 4) reader of Plato and your being a future (today at 4) reader of Plato; nor between my being a future (today at 4) non-reader of Plato and your being a future (today at 4) non-reader of Plato. What, then, was actually the case before the fission about the future reading of Plato? Would I (you) have been right then in saying, '*n* time-units hence I shall be reading Plato', or ought I (you) to have said '*n* time-units hence I shall not be reading Plato'? My inclination here is to say 'Both'; it was true then that I was going to develop into a Plato-reading, etc., person, in fact into what I am now, and equally that I was going to develop into a non-Plato-reading, etc., person, in fact into what you are now. The one thing that was never true was that it was going to be the case after *n* time-units that I was both reading and not reading Plato; for neither you nor I nor anyone else can do that (read and not read at once), or ever be going to do that.

Taking this position means denying that F*np* and F*nq* together entail F*n*K*pq*, i.e., denying that CKF*np*F*nq*F*n*K*pq* is a law. And if identities fuse as well as divide we shall need to reject CKP*np*P*nq*P*n*K*pq* for a like reason; for if, e.g., you and I fuse after the Plato incident is over, I (you) will be able to say truly after the fusion both '*n* time-units ago I was reading Plato' and '*n* time-units ago I was not reading Plato'; but not '*n* time-units ago I was both reading and not reading Plato'. And since CKP*np*P*nq*P*n*K*pq* can be easily enough proved using RP and Prop. 3 in our earlier proof

(CP*n*C*pq*CP*np*P*nq*), we can only reject it if we reject one of these. We can leave that last hurdle, though, for somebody else; let us stick here to the case of fission. On the view propounded above, we have both P*n*F*n*φ*x*, 'It was then true that I was going to be reading Plato,' and P*n*F*n*φ*y*, 'It was then true that you were going to be reading Plato,' because *n* time-units ago there was no difference between your reading Plato and my doing so (between φ*x* and φ*y*) or between your being one who would do so and my being this (between F*n*φ*x* and F*n*φ*y*). But it does not follow that we now have both φ*x* and φ*y*, for since the fission these have been distinct, and indeed the former the case and the latter not the case. That is what I meant when I said my choice would be to deny RPF. And if that seems an odd thing to do, remember that (i) the two escape-hatches (saying that the fission only made manifest a two-ness that was there all the time, or that the pre-fission individual is now extinct) are always there for anyone that wants them; and that (ii) we are considering a very odd hypothesis anyhow, though not so odd that physicists as well as science-fiction writers will not play round at times with something very like it.

About alternative possibilities, which Wyndham in effect assimilates to this case, I want to say this: the comparison is between case A, in which *x* is going to divide into *y* which φ's and *z* which does not, and case B, in which there is no question of *x*'s dividing, but at the time being considered it is equally open to *x*, in the time ahead of it, to φ and not to φ. And these cases *are* alike, but also, even in their likeness, different. Just as I want to say in case A that in the time before the fission '*x* will φ' and '*x* will not φ' are equally true (but '*x* will φ-and-not-φ' not true at all), so I want to say in case B that at the time being considered '*x* will φ' and '*x* will not φ' are equally false, or at all events equally not true,[1] though '*x* will φ-or-not-φ' is as true then as ever—a course which clearly involves rejecting CKNF*np*NF*nq*NF*n*A*pq*. It also involves rejecting RPF, but whereas the fission case violates that by supplying examples of P*n*F*np* for which we have not *p* (it was the case, when you were me, that you would be now reading Plato, but you are not now reading Plato), case B violates it by supplying examples of *p* for which we have not P*n*F*np* (e.g., there is—let us say—a sea-battle going on, though it was not true this time yesterday that a sea-battle

[1] Cf. my *Time and Modality*, Lecture X.

would be going on a day later, as the future was not then closed in either this way or the other).

And I want to say this, not because there is nothing else I *could* say, but because the escape-hatch which is undoubtedly available— saying that even where there are still alternative possible futures, either it will be the case that p or it will be the case that not p, only nobody knows which and it may be that nobody *could* know which— is just too unattractive. This thing that is true now but not known till later is as elusive as (in case A) the other person who was eating sardines at the same time and apparently also in the same place as me; the supposition does no harm, certainly, and makes for a more streamlined past-future logic; but I cannot take the *existence* of this *ignotum* at all seriously—I am disposed to be a positivist about this *ignotum*—and it is anyhow worth seeing what sort of a past-future logic we get if we simply drop the hypothesis.

7. *Epimenides the Cretan*

What I am offering here is a reconsideration, and in the end a solution, of the ancient paradox of the Epimenides. What has provoked this new assault on so old a stronghold is L. Jonathan Cohen's article,[1] in which it is rightly pointed out that the Epimenidean as contrasted with the Eubulidean version of the Liar paradox is the one that threatens logicians who attempt to formalise the use of indirect rather than direct discourse. Among these he includes myself, referring to the system sketched on pp. 130–1 of my *Time and Modality*, and suggesting that I ought to have shown how a person interpreting this system in the obvious way can avoid semantic antinomies. Here too he is right, and my main purpose now is not to criticise his paper, but to fill in this lacuna in my own work to which he has drawn attention. I do want, however, to make one small criticism at the start, namely that Cohen fails to notice what it is that is really paradoxical about the Epimenides, and in consequence fails to perceive the same paradoxical character in a proposition which he is himself quite happy to accept as a 'logical truth'.

The point about the Epimenides, as was noted by Church,[2] is not that when we examine the truth value of a Cretan's assertion that nothing true is ever asserted by a Cretan we are led to contradictory conclusions, for we are not; the paradox is rather that such examination makes it seem possible to settle an empirical question on logical grounds. If we treat the Cretan's assertion as true, and so assume that nothing true *is* ever asserted by a Cretan, it follows immediately that the Cretan's assertion is false. If, however, we

[1] L. Jonathan Cohen, 'Can the logic of indirect discourse be formalized?' *Journal of Symbolic Logic*, vol. 22 (1957), pp. 225–32.

[2] Alonzo Church, review of A. Koyré's *The Liar* in *Journal of Symbolic Logic*, vol. 12 (1946), p. 131.

treat it as false, there is no way of deducing from this assumption that it is true. We can, therefore, consistently suppose it to be false, and this is all that we can consistently suppose. But to suppose it false (considering what the assertion actually is) is to suppose that something asserted by a Cretan is true; and this of course can only be some *other* assertion than the one mentioned. We thus reach the peculiar conclusion that if any Cretan does assert that nothing asserted by a Cretan is true, then this cannot possibly be the only assertion made by a Cretan—there must also be, beside this false Cretan assertion, some true one. Yet how can there be a *logical* impossibility in supposing that some Cretan asserts that no Cretan ever says anything true, and that this is the only assertion ever made by a Cretan?

Cohen establishes in a similar way the following more complicated proposition:

> If the policeman testifies that anything which the prisoner deposes is false, and the prisoner deposes that something which the policeman testifies is true, then something which the policeman testifies is false, and something which the prisoner deposes is true.

What he does not notice in his paper is that from the stated hypothesis it follows that *either* the policeman *or* the prisoner must have said something else beside the statements mentioned. For the prisoner's mentioned statement, that something that the policeman testifies is true, is either true or false. If it is true, then the policeman must have said two things, for the conclusion has already been drawn that something which the policeman says is false. If, on the other hand, the prisoner's mentioned statement is false, then *he* must have said two things, for the conclusion has already been drawn that he has said something true. So that if Cohen's proposition really is a 'logically true' one, something which is also logically true is this:

> If the policeman testifies that anything which the prisoner deposes is false, and the prisoner deposes that something which the policeman testifies is true, then either the policeman or the prisoner must have said something else as well.

That is, these *two* assertions cannot have even been made—not just cannot have been true—unless at least *three* statements have been made by these people. Yet it does not seem *logically* impossible that the policeman and the prisoner should make the assertions mentioned and no others (the court house being bombed immediately afterwards, say). The problem therefore cannot be (as Cohen's paper suggests that it is) that of constructing a system in which one can prove Cohen's proposition without proving paradoxes, for to prove Cohen's proposition *is* to prove a paradox, at least in the sense in which the Epimenides is a paradox. I am not saying that we cannot accept Cohen's proposition; on the contrary I think that in the end, despite all appearances, we *must* accept it, but we should know what we are doing when we do this.

Turning back, now, to the Epimenides: The references to Cretans, asserting, etc., are of course quite inessential; and for a verbal generalisation of the case we might offer the following: let us say that in the function δp the functor δ is 'satisfied by a fact' if δp is true and p also, i.e., if we have $K\delta pp$. Where our δ is of the form 'X believes that—' or 'X asserts that—', its satisfaction by a fact constitutes the 'truth' of X's belief or assertion (X's belief-that-p is true $\equiv$ X believes that p, and p); where it is of the form 'X wishes that—', its satisfaction by a fact constitutes the 'fulfilment' of X's wish; but the notion of satisfaction clearly applies in numerous cases in which we have no special word for it.[1] Now if it is a fact that no fact satisfies a given function, then obviously *this* fact (that no fact satisfies it) cannot satisfy it. If, for example, it is a fact that no fact disappoints us, then this fact that no fact disappoints us cannot disappoint us; if it is a fact that no fact amuses us, then this fact that no fact amuses us cannot amuse us; and if it is a fact that no fact is being asserted by me now (or is ever asserted by a Cretan), then *this* fact cannot be being asserted by me now (or ever by a Cretan). Hence, transposing, if a given function's not being satisfied by any fact is itself an argument that satisfies that function, then this argument cannot itself be a fact but must be a falsehood. If, for example, what amuses us is that no fact amuses us, then it cannot be a fact that no fact amuses us; and if what we are now asserting is that no fact is now being asserted by us, then it cannot be a fact that no fact is now being asserted by us. But if it is not a fact that the given

[1] For a group of simple theorems involving such 'satisfaction', see my 'Berkeley in logical form', *Theoria*, vol. 21 (1955) pp. 117–22.

function is satisfied by no fact, then the fact must be that the function is satisfied by *some* fact; and this fact that satisfies the function cannot be that the function is satisfied by no fact, since *ex hypothesi* that isn't a fact; so the function must have some *other* argument that satisfies it.

Doing it in pure symbolism, the paradox is easily derivable in the calculus of my own which Cohen mentions. Here we use the Łukasiewicz letters C, K, N, etc. for truth-functors; the ordinary propositional variable p, q, r, etc.; variables, δ, γ, etc. ranging over all monadic proposition-forming functors of propositions, whether extensional like 'It is not the case that—' or non-extensional like 'It is possible that—' or 'It is asserted by a Cretan that—'; and the quantifiers Π and Σ binding variables of both types. For postulates, we subjoin the Łukasiewicz rules for the quantifiers (designated hereafter as $\Pi 1$, $\Pi 2$, $\Sigma 1$, $\Sigma 2$) to any postulates sufficient for the ordinary propositional calculus without variable functors, but extending substitution to these functors and of course qualifying it in the presence of quantifiers. No other postulates are used and in particular no theses of extensionality such as $CCpqCCqpC\delta p\delta q$, which are obviously false when the functorial variables have the range indicated. We can now proceed with proofs as follows:

1. Cpp
2. $CCpCqrCqCpr$
3. $CCqrCCpqCpr$
4. $CCpNpNp$
5. $CNCpNqKpq$
6. $CCNpqCNqp$
7. $CI\!IpC\delta pNpC\delta pNp$ (1 $p/C\delta pNp$; $\Pi 1$)
8. $C\delta\Pi pC\delta pNpCI\!IpC\delta pNpN\Pi pC\delta pNp$ (7 $p/\Pi pC\delta pNp$; 2)
9. $C\delta\Pi pC\delta pNpN\Pi pC\delta pNp$ (8; 4; 3)
10. $CNC\delta pNp\Sigma pK\delta pp$ (5; $\Sigma 2$)
11. $CN\Sigma pK\delta ppC\delta pNp$ (10; 6)
12. $CN\Sigma pK\delta pp\Pi pC\delta pNp$ (11; $\Pi 2$)
13. $CN\Pi pC\delta pNp\Sigma pK\delta pp$ (12; 6)
14. $C\delta\Pi pC\delta pNp\Sigma pK\delta pp$ (13; 9; 3).

For example, if a man fears that whatever he fears isn't the case, then there is something which he fears that *is* the case. If we want to proceed from this to the thesis that there are at least two things that such a man fears, we can introduce Ipq, identifying not merely the truth values but the meanings of p and q, as an abbreviation for $\Pi\delta C\delta p\delta q$, and $\Sigma(2)p\delta p$, meaning that δ is satisfied by at least two arguments (e.g., 'X fears at least two things,' 'I am now asserting at least two things', etc.), as an abbreviation for $\Sigma pqKK\delta p\delta qNIpq$; and then prove

$$C\delta\Pi pC\delta pNp\Sigma(2)p\delta p;$$

but 14 takes us as far as we need go here.

It must be repeated that there is nothing actually contradictory about 14 (that is just not the trouble with this type of system); and this is sufficiently shown by the fact that, simply as a formula, 14 is obtainable in the ordinary forms of the extended propositional calculus in which the values of δ are confined by some law of extensionality to truth-functors. For the system we are using is, formally, simply a part of that one. In fact when the values of δ are confined to truth-functors 14 is not even surprising. For of the four monadic two-valued truth-functors the only one that satisfies the antecedent of 14 is the tautological functor V (such that $Vp = Cpp$) —we have $V\Pi pCVpNp$, but neither $F\Pi pCFpNp$ (where F is the contradictory functor) nor $N\Pi pCNpNp$ nor, letting $\delta p = p$, $\Pi pCpNp$. And with V for δ, the consequent $\Sigma pKVpp$ is demonstrably satisfied also (being an existential generalisation of $KVVpVp$). The surprising thing is not that this result is obtainable in the extended propositional calculus, but that so little of that calculus need be used in obtaining it—so little that there is nothing in the premisses to block our putting non-extensional functors for δ, despite the fact that if we can do that it seems possible to construct hypothetical empirical cases satisfying the antecedent of 14 but not its consequent.

I cannot avoid concluding that we are under some illusion here. Fearing that nothing we fear is the case, asserting that nothing we assert is the case and so on, must be more difficult performances than we at first take them to be. They may even prove to be categorically impossible, like thumb-catching. Of course a man can always *say the words* 'Nothing that I am now asserting is the case', or more formally 'For all p if I am now asserting that p then it is not the case that p'; but we take it too easily for granted that he is thereby *asserting that* nothing that he is then asserting is the case. For assertion is not a relation between a man and a sentence but one between a man and what the sentence is about; e.g., when Aristotle asserts that Plato is mistaken, this is a fact about Aristotle and Plato, not a fact about Aristotle and the sentence 'Plato is mistaken' (or any other sentence, Greek or English); and there may be many an unsuspected slip between the cup of uttering sentences and the lip of making assertions. This need not mean that there is something not well-formed about the sentence 'Nothing that I am now asserting is the case'; and in fact I can see nothing to prevent me from denying, doubting, fearing, wishing, believing, etc. that nothing that I am now asserting is the case, or from asserting that I am doing these things. It is just that I cannot use this sentence, or any sentence, to *assert that* nothing that I am asserting is the case. Or at any rate I cannot do this if there is not something else asserted by me at the time, and true. Thus what can be or not be the case, is not necessarily assertible by a given person, or a person in a given situation.

But when we turn to the Cretan who asserts, or thinks he asserts, that nothing asserted by a Cretan is the case, the paradox becomes more worrying. On the present hypothesis, this man really could be asserting that nothing asserted by a Cretan is the case, if only he were not himself a Cretan. And it could well be that he doesn't know he is a Cretan, and for that reason alone (rather than through any ignorance of the present sort of logic, in which we may suppose him well instructed) thinks that he is asserting this thing when in fact he is not asserting anything at all. Similarly he might (because he doesn't know he is a Cretan) *think that he thinks* that nothing thought by Cretans is the case, when in fact (because he really is a Cretan) he does not and cannot think anything of the kind. This, it is worth repeating, is still not self-contradictory, but it is a hard saying.

But this is drawing too sharply the line between the examples for which 14 seems plausible (simple supposed fears that nothing that we fear is the case, assertions that nothing we assert is the case, etc.) and ones for which it does not (introducing possibly unperceived complications like being a Cretan when one fears, asserts, etc.). There are intermediate cases which may help us in the end to see all the cases in the same way; e.g., the case of Cohen's poor policeman.

This man's evidence might well have been given before the prisoner's deposition, and before it was known what that deposition would contain; and at this stage of the proceedings it would certainly seem, to the policeman and most of the court, that the policeman had asserted something; and *what* he had asserted would also seem to be clear. But when the prisoner, his turn come, starts off with 'Something that the policeman has testified is true', and then pauses long enough for people to reflect upon what they have heard, the hearer's inclination is surely to say that 'no one has really said anything yet'. If, however, the prisoner then goes on to say something further, e.g., about what he is charged with, this opinion begins to be reversed—one begins to move towards the view that the policeman and the prisoner *were* saying something before too (though from our reasoning it would appear that we ought not to move right back to this unless and until either the prisoner or the policeman says something *true*). But even if we do conclude, at the trial's end, that the policeman really was asserting something, we ought surely to do it with a consciousness of where, but for the grace of God, he might have been—of where, in fact, he very nearly *was*—and with a realisation that asserting something is a performance in which a man could unexpectedly and for odd reasons fail. And could it not be like this also with the Cretan?

I would suggest, in fine, that if Epimenides the Cretan says 'Nothing asserted by a Cretan is the case', and no Cretan says anything else, then it is indeed the case that nothing asserted by a Cretan is the case, but Epimenides has not asserted this (and the reason why it is the case that nothing asserted by a Cretan is the case, is that no Cretan has asserted anything). If other things are said by Cretans which *are* assertions, but all false ones, then it is still the case that nothing asserted by a Cretan is the case, and still the case that in uttering the sentence mentioned Epimenides has not asserted anything. (It is still the case, in other words, that what we must reject is not *that which is supposed to be* asserted by Epimenides, but *the supposition that it is* asserted by him.) If, however, at least one true assertion is made by a Cretan, then it is *not* the case that nothing asserted by a Cretan is the case, and Epimenides *has* asserted, though of course falsely, that nothing asserted by a Cretan is the case. And all this regardless of whether or not Epimenides *knows* that he is a Cretan, or knows what other Cretans are saying.

To say such things as these is to suggest that the relations between direct speech and indirect are extremely tricky; we cannot just lay it down, for example, that whoever, speaking English, utters the sentence 'Nothing asserted by a Cretan is the case' will be making a true assertion if and only if nothing asserted by a Cretan is the case, for the circumstances in which this utterance is made can affect not only its truth-value but whether anything at all is being asserted by it. On the other hand, if we are prepared to say these things, the logic of indirect speech in itself can be kept extremely simple. To formalise that, the system sketched earlier on can stand, without any tinkering with its formation rules or transformation rules, and without any restrictions on the interpretation of δ (beyond the purely syntactical one that it must construct a proposition out of a proposition).

8. Thank Goodness That's Over

In a pair of very important papers, namely 'Space, Time and Individuals' (STI) in the *Journal of Philosophy* for October 1955 and 'The Indestructibility and Immutability of Substances' (IIS) in *Philosophical Studies* for April 1956, Professor N. L. Wilson began something which badly needed beginning, namely the construction of a logically rigorous 'substance-language' in which we talk about enduring and changing individuals as we do in common speech, as opposed to the 'space-time' language favoured by very many mathematical logicians, perhaps most notably by Quine. This enterprise of Wilson's is one with which I could hardly sympathise more heartily than I do; and one wishes for this logically rigorous 'substance-language' not only when one is reading Quine but also when one is reading many other people. How fantastic it is, for instance, that Kotarbiński[1] should call his metaphysics 'Reism' when the very last kind of entity it has room for is *things*—instead of them it just has the world-lines or life-histories of things; 'four-dimensional worms', as Wilson says. Wilson, moreover, has at least one point of superiority to another rebel against space-time talk, P. F. Strawson; namely he (Wilson) does seriously attempt to meet formalism with formalism—to show that logical rigour is not a monopoly of the other side. At another point, however, Strawson seems to me to see further than Wilson; he (Strawson) is aware that substance-talk cannot be carried on without tenses, whereas Wilson tries (vainly, as I hope to show) to do without them. Wilson, in short, has indeed brought us out of Egypt; but as yet has us still wandering about the Sinai Peninsula; the Promised Land is a little further on than he has taken us.

From this point on, then, I shall be quarrelling with Wilson, but

[1] T. Kotarbiński 'The fundamental ideas of pansomatism', *Mind*, October 1955, p. 488. Cf. also C. Lejewski, 'Proper names', *Arist. Soc. Supp.* vol. 31 (1957), pp. 253-4, and papers there cited.

from what has just been said I hope it will be clear that this is a dispute between allies—I want Wilson (with any Wilsonians there may be) to go further in a direction in which he has already started to go, for I do not think the place where he has left us is or can be a real resting-place. From such a place as that, we must either go forwards or go back.[1]

First let me sketch Wilson's position more fully, and mainly in his own words. Early (p. 592) in the paper STI, he says that when we pass from a space-time language to a substance-language, 'the time determinant is shifted across the copula of empirical sentences from subject to predicate'. Later (p. 594) he explains what he means by this. 'In our S-T language,' he says, 'we might record a simple matter of fact in a sentence like the following:' (here he gives the Russellian for 'The x such that x occupies u_1, u_1, u_1, t_1, is blue'). 'In substance-language we might say:

'a is blue at (time) t_1, where the copula "is" is used tenselessly'.

And again (p. 597) he says that 'the simplest kind of empirical statement in substance-language' is one of the form 'a has the quality Q_1 at time t_1'. 'It is so obvious, so necessary,' he goes on, 'that if Philip is drunk, Philip is drunk *at some time*, that if Scott wrote *Waverley*, he wrote it *during some period*—it is so obvious and necessary, that in ordinary language we generally drop the "at some time" and are left with the simple, the *too* simple, noun-copula-adjective form of sentence'. ('Perfidious ordinary language!' he adds in parenthesis at this point). Much of this is repeated in IIS. At the end of this (p. 48) Wilson says that although it may be true that a thing 'changes qualitatively and is numerically the same', e.g. 'If a leaf is green in August and red in September it is still *that* leaf', yet nevertheless 'a "complete" property of an individual is a compound, temporalized (or dated) property, like *being green in August* 1955 or *being born in* 1769, and there is no question of an individual changing in the sense of once having and later lacking one of these compound properties'.

---

[1] In thus asking for consistency above all else, I am consciously echoing J. J. C. Smart's note on 'Spatializing time' in *Mind* for April 1955. Smart's strictures upon those on his own side—the Quine-Kotarbiński side—who talk about 'consciousness crawling up world-lines' may be compared with what is said here.

This last conclusion should in itself have been enough to frighten him. From this leaf whose 'complete' properties never change, to the pure 'four-dimensional worm' of Quine, Kotarbiński, etc., is surely a very short step indeed. And this 'substance-language' goes wrong at the end because it goes wrong at the start. Wilson's basic sentence-form is '*S* is *P*', and his idea appears to be that you get from a space-time language to a substance-language by exchanging '*S*-at-*t* is *P*' for '*S* is *P*-at-*t*'; in this way the '*t*' 'crosses the copula', which is thought of as a sort of bridge between *S* and *P*. But if the 'is' in these two forms is tenseless, as Wilson explicitly says that it is, I cannot see what the difference between them amounts to. '*S*-at-*t* is *P*' presumably means that that part of the four-dimensional worm *S* which has the time co-ordinate *t*, is *P*; what else '*S* is *P*-at-*t*' could mean, i.e. what it means if it does not mean that *S* is *P* in the stretch of it specified by *t*, I cannot imagine. I can, indeed, see something different in the form '*S* *was* *P* at *t*', e.g. 'The leaf was green in August'; but here 'In August' is only intelligible as an answer to the question '*When was* the leaf green?', not as an answer to the question 'In what way is (was) it green?', 'What sort of green is (was) it?'. The thing then means, not 'The leaf was green-in-August' but 'The leaf was-in-August green'. The *t* in fact has not 'crossed the copula' but stopped *at* the copula; though it seems to me that this bridge theory of the copula is wrong anyway. Write 'The leaf is green' in the modern way as 'φx'; here '*x*' denotes the leaf, 'φ' means 'is-green', and there is no copula needed, but if we want one we can put '*S*' for 'It is the case that——' before the whole, i.e. in the place where we would put '*N*' or a tilde for 'It is not the case that——' if we wanted to construct a negative proposition. Then we can think of 'at *t*' as neither moving across the copula to the predicate nor staying with the copula on the way to the predicate, but as moving across the predicate to the copula, and changing 'It is the case that——' to 'It was the case in August that——'.

A parallel case will, I think, make the matter clear. A person, call him Owen, who is colour-blind, might see this leaf as green when it is in fact red. The leaf, we might then say, looks green to Owen; i.e. though it is not the case that, it does appear to Owen that, the leaf is green. And some philosophers would want to replace this by '*is* green-to-Owen', abolishing the explicit reference to looking or seeming in the same way as Wilson abolishes the explicit tense. But as in the other case, the supposed abolition is only a disguise. 'To Owen' is intelligible as an answer to the question 'To whom does it *look* green?'; as a description of the kind of green the leaf is, or of the kind of green leaf it is, 'green-to-Owen' is just nothing at all. Unless, indeed, we mean by calling it 'green-to-Owen' that the leaf is green where it is turned *towards* Owen—green on that side of it. And we might give 'green-in-August' a similar sense—we might mean that that part of the leaf which is in August (like 'that part of it which faces Owen') is green; but then it cannot be really a *leaf* that we are talking about, for it is not leaves but their world-lines that have parts of that sort. We are, in short, back in Pharaoh's House, with *S*-at-*t* being *P*.

I do not, however, want to make a difference where there is none; and in particular I do not wish to deny that there is such a property as that of *having been green in August* as well as the property of *being green*, i.e. being green now; nor even, for that matter, that there is such a property as *looking green to Owen* as well as that of *being green*, i.e. being green really. I only insist (*a*) that what is now in question with this leaf is not a property of *being* green in August which attaches to it tenselessly, but a property of *having been* green in August which attaches to it *now*; and (*b*) that having been green in August is not a way of being green now (I am not writing in August); (*c*) that neither is it a way of being green timelessly—there is in fact *no* way of being green timelessly (as Wilson very truly says, Philip cannot be drunk without being drunk at some time; and neither can a leaf be green without being green at some time); and (*d*) that the *internal* punctuation of 'having been green in August' is 'having in-August been green', not 'having been green-in-August'. Putting it yet another way: A leaf that was green in August is one sort of formerly-green leaf (because 'in August' is one sort of 'formerly'); but a formerly-green leaf is not one sort of green leaf. Indeed in common parlance being formerly-green and being green are often *inconsistent*—the 'formerly green' is precisely that which *is not* green but *was* green, just as a *soi-disant* philosopher is precisely someone who is *not* a philosopher but *says he is* one. And, of course, a leaf which is merely 'green-to-Owen' is precisely one which *is not* green but seems to that person to be so.[1]

[1] Cf. P. T. Geach on *alienans* adjectives in 'Good and evil', *Analysis*, December 1956, p. 33.

This is perhaps the most suitable point at which to consider a very strange argument put forward by Wilson in IIS, p. 47 on the subject of identity: 'When we say that the individual who wrote *Marmion* in 1807 is identical with the individual who wrote *Waverley* in 1814, we are not saying that the individuals are identical in 1807 or in 1814. They are identical outside of time, as it were. *Dates cannot be significantly associated with the identity sign.*' (Italics Wilson's.) In this passage perhaps more than any other we see the incompleteness of Wilson's emancipation from space-time language. Certainly to say in 1955 or 6 that X and Y (not 'were' but) 'are' identical in 1807, is to say something that grates upon the ear and the mind intolerably; but that is not what Wilson means, for it is clear from his conclusion that he would object equally to the result of repairing his syntax by due attention to tenses. If we do this, we will say that the individual who wrote *Marmion* in 1807 was not then identical with the individual who had written *Waverley* in 1814 because at that time (1807) nobody at all had written *Waverley*, or done either that or anything else in 1814. Was he identical, then, with the individual who *was going to* write *Waverley* in 1814? This, I admit, is a tricky one, but only because indeterminism makes me wonder whether there was yet any such individual; the question is not actually improper. Leaving that for the other date: the individual who had written *Marmion* in 1807 was certainly identical in 1814 with the individual who was then writing *Waverley*, and after that with the individual who had written *Waverley*. But Wilson does not want to say any of these things: he wants to say that the author of *Marmion* and the author of *Waverley* are 'identical outside of time', whatever that might be.

I cannot help thinking that Wilson is worried here about the relation between Scott-in-1807 and Scott-in-1814—there they are, separated for ever by seven years, and yet somehow the same person; but *when* can they be the same person?—clearly nowhen. But of course Scott-in-1807 and Scott-in-1814 aren't persons at all; they are year-thick slices of a four-dimensional worm (as Wilson says, '*S-at-t*' is a description from the space-time language, not from substance-language); and as they are distinct slices, there is no time whatever at which they are identical. Had he really left these 4-D worms behind—Scott-in-1807, Scott-in-1814, *and* Scott-from-his-birth-to-his-death (equally a no-person, a by-product of mispunctuating sentences like 'Scott, from his birth to his death, lived in the Northern Hemisphere')—and learnt again to talk simply about Scott, it is hard to see how this strange talk of identity-outside-time, in an enduring object, could have arisen.

Wilson also says on p. 47 of IIT that existence is not datable, but is 'a simple something or other which Napoleon simply has and Pegasus (for example) simply lacks'. This will surely not do; but before saying anything more about it let me interpose a *peccavi*. I have suggested elsewhere that just as there were no facts about me before I existed (not even this fact of there being no facts about me; though of course there is *now* the past-tense fact of there having been none then), so there will be no facts about me after my existence ends (if it does end). And my ground for saying this was the very weak one that if some facts about a thing imply that it still exists and some do not, nobody can state with any precision where to draw the line between these two classes of facts.[1]

This situation is not in fact anything like as hard for the logician as I made out. For he can use special variables, f, g, etc. for predicates entailing existence (call them E-predicates) without committing himself as to what these predicates are; and he can lay it down that E-predicates are predicates, substitutable for the usual predicate-variables φ, ψ, etc., and functions of E-predicates like Nf ('—does not f') and Pf ('—has fd in the past') are likewise predicates, substitutable for φ, ψ, etc., but these last (Nf, Pf, etc.) are not themselves E-predicates, substitutable for f, g, etc. Then we can say that there are facts about Napoleon still, e.g. the fact that no E-predicates apply to him now; and this not being itself an E-predicate, there is no contradiction in so speaking.[2]

So there is indeed a sort of 'being' that Napoleon has even after having ceased to 'exist'; he is at least a subject of predicates still, and cannot now ever cease to be that. But there is nothing timeless about this. For one thing, even this 'being' of Napoleon, i.e. there being facts about him, is something that had a beginning (when *he*

---

[1] A. N. Prior, *Time and Modality* (1957), p. 31. My present modification of the position there stated owes much to P. T. Geach's criticism in the *Cambridge Review*, May 4, 1957, p. 543.

[2] There is an instructive discussion of E-predicates and others in Walter Burleigh's *De Puritate Artis Logicae Tractatus Longior*, Franciscan Institute edition (1955), pp. 57–8.

had a beginning).[1] And for another thing, even now this fact that there are facts about Napoleon is not a timeless but a present (and abiding) one.

Turning now to a fundamental: I'm a symbol-man rather than an ordinary-speech man myself, but I can see what the ordinary-speech men are worried about when I find Wilson crying 'Perfidy!' at locutions which in fact constitute a more coherent and smoothed-out substance-language than his own. His chief quarrel with ordinary speech is, as he says, that it omits dates; but it is misleading to treat this as pretending to do without a time-reference. I do not know how it is with Wilson, but half the time I personally have forgotten what the date *is*, and have to look it up or ask somebody when I need it for writing cheques, etc.; yet even in this perpetual dateless haze one somehow communicates, one makes oneself understood, and with time-references too. One says, e.g. 'Thank goodness that's over!', and not only is this, when said, quite clear without any date appended, but it says something which it is impossible that any use of a tenseless copula with a date should convey. It certainly doesn't mean the same as, e.g. 'Thank goodness the date of the conclusion of that thing is Friday, June 15, 1954', even if it be said then. (Nor, for that matter, does it mean 'Thank goodness the conclusion of that thing is contemporaneous with this utterance'. Why should anyone thank goodness for that?)

Wilson seems to have the notion that a tensed copula is analysable into a tenseless one plus a date (which once obtained can be transferred to any other part of the proposition that we fancy); but the above example is sufficient to refute this assumption. The fact is that propositions with dates are just *not* 'the simplest empirical propositions', but are highly sophisticated propositions; well, medium sophisticated—an essential prelude, though only a prelude, to space-time talk. Just the bricks, in fact, for building half-way houses.

---

[1] I'm not taking that part back; nor the view that some statements have not always been statable. Nothing can be surer than that whereof we cannot speak thereof we must be silent; but this does not mean that whereof we could not have spoken yesterday thereof we must be silent today.

9. The Runabout Inference-ticket

It is sometimes alleged that there are inferences whose validity arises solely from the meanings of certain expressions occurring in them. The precise technicalities employed are not important, but let us say that such inferences, if any such there be, are analytically valid.

One sort of inference which is sometimes said to be in this sense analytically valid is the passage from a conjunction to either of its conjuncts, e.g. the inference 'Grass is green and the sky is blue, therefore grass is green'. The validity of this inference is said to arise solely from the meaning of the word 'and'. For if we are asked what is the meaning of the word 'and', at least in the purely conjunctive sense (as opposed to, e.g. its colloquial use to mean 'and then'), the answer is said to be *completely* given by saying that (i) from any pair of statements P and Q we can infer the statement formed by joining P to Q by 'and' (which statement we hereafter describe as 'the statement P-and-Q'), that (ii) from any conjunctive statement P-and-Q we can infer P, and (iii) from P-and-Q we can always infer Q. Anyone who has learnt to perform these inferences knows the meaning of 'and', for there is simply nothing more *to* knowing the meaning of 'and' than being able to perform these inferences.

A doubt might be raised as to whether it is really the case that, for any pair of statements P and Q, there is always a statement R such that given P and given Q we can infer R, and given R we can infer P and can also infer Q. But on the view we are considering such a doubt is quite misplaced, once we have introduced a word, say the word 'and', precisely in order to form a statement R with these properties from any pair of statements P and Q. The doubt reflects the old superstitious view that an expression must have some independently determined meaning before we can discover whether inferences involving it are valid or invalid. With analytically valid inferences this just isn't so.

I hope the conception of an analytically valid inference is now at least as clear to my readers as it is to myself. If not, further illumination is obtainable from Professor Popper's paper on 'Logic without assumptions' in *Proceedings of the Aristotelian Society* for 1946–7, and from Professor Kneale's contribution to *Contemporary British Philosophy*, Volume III. I have also been much helped in my understanding of the notion by some lectures of Mr Strawson's and some notes of Mr Hare's.

I want now to draw attention to a point not generally noticed, namely that in this sense of 'analytically valid' any statement whatever may be inferred, in an analytically valid way, from any other. '2 and 2 are 5', for instance, from '2 and 2 are 4'. It is done in two steps, thus:

2 and 2 are 4.
Therefore, 2 and 2 are 4 tonk 2 and 2 are 5.
Therefore, 2 and 2 are 5.

There may well be readers who have not previously encountered this conjunction 'tonk', it being a comparatively recent addition to the language; but it is the simplest matter in the world to explain what it means. Its meaning is completely given by the rules that (i) from any statement P we can infer any statement formed by joining P to any statement Q by 'tonk' (which compound statement we hereafter describe as 'the statement P-tonk-Q'), and that (ii) from any 'contonktive' statement P-tonk-Q we can infer the contained statement Q.

A doubt might be raised as to whether it is really the case that, for any pair of statements P and Q, there is always a statement R such that given P we can infer R, and given R we can infer Q. But this doubt is of course quite misplaced, now that we have introduced the word 'tonk' precisely in order to form a statement R with these properties from any pair of statements P and Q.

As a matter of simple history, there have been logicians of some eminence who have seriously doubted whether sentences of the form 'P and Q' express single propositions (and so, e.g., have negations). Aristotle himself, in *De Soph. Elench.* 176a1 ff., denies that 'Are Callias and Themistocles musical?' is a single question; and J. S. Mill says of 'Caesar is dead and Brutus is alive' that 'we might as well call a street a complex house, as these two propositions a complex proposition' (*System of Logic* I, iv. 3). So it is not to be wondered at if the form 'P tonk Q' is greeted at first with similar scepticism. But more enlightened views will surely prevail at last, especially when men consider the extreme *convenience* of the new form, which promises to banish *falsche Spitzfindigkeit* from Logic for ever.

10. *The Autonomy of Ethics*

It has often been said—in fact, I have said it quite emphatically myself—that it is impossible to deduce ethical conclusions from non-ethical premisses. This now seems to me a mistake, and my aim here will be first to show that it is a mistake, and then to try and find out what truth it is that has been confused with this falsehood by so many people, myself included. In the first bit at least—my *retractatio*—and perhaps in the other bit too, I shall not be particularly original; but I shall put the points in my own way.

Some of the recent writers who have denied this alleged non-deducibility of ethical conclusions from non-ethical premisses have concentrated on the word 'deduce', and have suggested that it ought not to be confined narrowly to logical entailment, and in the wider sense which they propose one could speak, e.g., of deducing the goodness of the welfare state from the fact that people are happier in the welfare state than in a strict *laissez-faire* economy. In favour of this suggestion it has been urged, for example by Toulmin in *The Uses of Argument*, that this wider sense of 'deduce' is much more like the sense it bears in ordinary speech. This does not seem to me a very important consideration; I have, all the same, some sympathy with the proposal to employ the term 'deduce' in such an extended sense, if only because I find it very difficult to draw a clear and non-arbitrary line between the logical and the non-logical.

It is not, however, *this* doubt about the common maxim to which I wish to give voice here. The point on which I want to concentrate now is rather one which has been emphasised by such writers as David Rynin,[1] namely that, even in quite a narrow sense of 'deduce', it is possible to deduce ethical conclusions from non-ethical premisses. In the illustrations that follow I shall not in fact use any principles of deduction beyond those of ordinary propositional calculus and quantification theory.

[1] D. Rynin, 'The autonomy of morals', *Mind*, July 1957.

Having thus disposed of 'deduce', I had better say something now about 'ethical' and 'non-ethical'. How shall we decide in a given case whether the conclusion we have deduced is an 'ethical' one? Well, in the first place, it must obviously contain at least one of the characteristically ethical expressions. I mean it must have in it some word or words like 'good', 'bad', 'right', 'wrong', 'ought', and so on, or some turn of speech in which these are implicit, like 'desirable' for what 'ought' to be desired (I shall in fact confine my examples to cases in which words like 'ought' occur directly and explicitly). But while this is a *necessary* condition for a statement's being an ethical one, I don't think anyone would accept it as a *sufficient* condition. It is also necessary, for example, that at least one of the ethical expressions which are present should occur 'essentially', i.e., should not be just replaceable by any expression whatsoever (of the appropriate grammatical type) without change of truth-value. For example, 'It either is or is not the case that I ought to fight for my country' is not an ethical statement, since the truth-value of the whole would be unaltered if the ethical phrase 'ought to' were replaced by 'frequently do' or 'am believed by my neighbours to', or if the whole clause 'I ought to fight for my country' were replaced by 'two and two are five' or 'bread is sixpence a loaf'.

I would go further than this too. (It will be appreciated that in piling on these conditions I am making my own job of deducing ethical conclusions a harder one.) I would not count as 'ethical' a statement in which *only* ethical and logical expressions occurred essentially. For example, I should not regard any of the following as ethical statements:

It is obligatory that what is obligatory be done.
If anything is obligatory it is permissible.
It is forbidden to do anything that is incompatible with what is obligatory.

I would say that statements of this sort belong to the *logic* of ethics, or 'deontic logic' as it is sometimes called, but not to ethics itself. In genuinely ethical statements like 'Tea-drinking is wrong' there must be a non-vacuous mention of something, like tea-drinking in this example, which is *brought into relation* to ethical concepts.

Even these conditions are not quite stringent enough; for they would let through, for example, 'Tea-drinking is common in England, and if anything is obligatory that thing is permissible'. Here the expressions 'tea-drinking', 'obligatory' and 'permissible' all occur essentially, but the statement as a whole is not an ethical one but a mere conjunction of an empirical statement with one from deontic logic. I would in fact accept the principle that no truth-function with non-ethical arguments only can be counted as being ethical as a whole.

Finally, in case my conditions are not stringent enough, I shall with all my examples proceed as follows: Wherever I claim that a certain statement is an ethical conclusion, and give a deduction of it from purely non-ethical premisses, I shall also give a deduction of the same conclusion from premisses which are *not* all non-ethical, and the deduction will be of a sort generally recognised as leading to an ethical conclusion. That is, to anyone tempted to query the 'ethical' status of my conclusion, I shall say 'Look, you can also get it *this* way; and if that was where you had first met with it, you wouldn't have dreamed of denying its "ethical" character'.

Any doubts as to where 'ethical' statements end will of course *ipso facto* be doubts as to where non-ethical ones begin, but it is at least clear that if any one of the above conditions for a statement's belonging to Ethics is not met, then that statement must be non-ethical, and all but the last of the examples of 'non-ethical premisses' which I propose to use will not meet even the first condition of being counted ethical, i.e., they will not explicitly or implicitly contain any of the distinctively ethical expressions 'good', 'ought', etc. (The one exception at the end is an inference which will have a premiss from deontic logic.) I shall also exclude *self-contradictory* premisses and sets of premisses, from which one could deduce not only ethical conclusions but any conclusions whatever, trivially. (This amounts to re-stating the common maxim as 'Ethical conclusions never follow from *consistent* premisses all of which are non-ethical', but I don't imagine anyone will object to this.)

The way is now sufficiently prepared for my first demonstration of an ethical conclusion from a non-ethical premiss, namely this: 'Tea-drinking is common in England; therefore either tea-drinking is common in England or all New Zealanders ought to be shot'. There is nothing peculiar about this deduction as a deduction; it has the form 'P; therefore either P or Q'. The premiss is certainly non-ethical, and the conclusion ethical. If you are tempted to wonder whether this *is* an ethical conclusion, see how it looks when deduced in the following manner:

> Anyone who does what is not common in England ought to be shot;
> All New Zealanders drink tea;
> Therefore either tea-drinking is common in England or all New Zealanders ought to be shot.

No doubt what the conclusion expresses is not a simple duty but a duty with a proviso, but much ethical information has this form.

With regard to disjunctions of ethical and non-ethical statements, the 'autonomists' are in fact in the following dilemma: Either such statements are as a whole ethical or they are not. If they are, we may deduce ethical from non-ethical propositions as above. And if they are not, we may deduce ethical from non-ethical propositions by using the form 'Either P or Q, but not P, therefore Q': e.g. either grass is blue or smoking is wrong (now counted as non-ethical), but grass is not blue, therefore smoking is wrong.

Here is another case; and this time I'll put the unimpeachable deduction (from partly ethical premises) first: 'There is no one who is allowed to sit in a chair which will not bear his weight, and no ordinary chair will bear the weight of a man over 20 feet high; therefore there is no man over 20 feet high who is allowed to sit in an ordinary chair.' Certainly some ethical information, about what is allowed and what not, is conveyed by the conclusion of this inference; and why shouldn't it be, considering how we got it? But we could equally have got it thus: 'There is no man over 20 feet high; therefore there is no man over 20 feet high who is allowed to sit in an ordinary chair.' And here the sole premiss is non-ethical.

These inferences are of course non-syllogistic, and Dr T. H. Mott, who first pointed out to me[1] the possibility of using 'P, therefore P or Q' to disprove the common maxim, observed at the same time that it does hold where syllogistic inferences are concerned. It must obviously do so if the premisses are 'non-ethical' in the sense of not containing ethical expressions, for the conclusion of

[1] In a letter of February 9, 1954.

a syllogism cannot contain any expression (beyond purely logical constants in the narrowest sense) that does not occur in at least one of its premisses. It is worth adding, though, that the converse maxim, that non-ethical conclusions cannot be deduced from premisses all of which are ethical, does not hold even for syllogistic inferences. Consider, for example, 'One should always wear a coat on a rainy day, but there's no need to wear a coat today, therefore it's not raining today', i.e., 'All rainy days are days on which one ought to wear a coat, today is not a day on which, etc., therefore today is not a rainy day'.[1]

Further, although one cannot syllogistically deduce an ethical conclusion from a non-ethical premiss, one can do so by forms of inference which are very close to syllogisms. For example, since the two premisses 'All Church officers ought to be reverent' and 'Undertakers are Church officers' jointly imply that undertakers ought to be reverent, the single ethical premiss 'All Church officers ought to be reverent' implies that *if* undertakers are Church officers they ought to be reverent, and the single *non*-ethical premiss 'Undertakers are Church officers' implies that *if* all Church officers ought to be reverent undertakers ought to be. In fact this non-ethical premiss 'Undertakers are Church officers' implies that *whatever* all Church officers ought to do, undertakers ought to do. This conclusion is comparatively complex, but its complexity is not of such a kind as to deprive it of all ethical content, as should be plain when we see it deduced not as above but as follows: All who have to do with the dead, whether they are themselves Church officers or not, ought to do whatever all Church officers ought to do; undertakers have to do with the dead; therefore undertakers ought to do whatever all Church officers ought to do (e.g. if all Church officers ought to be reverent, undertakers ought to be reverent).

In view of such examples as these, it is hard to see how anyone can any longer maintain that ethical conclusions are never formally deducible from premisses all of which are non-ethical. It must be admitted, however, that there is *something* peculiar about each of the examples I have given, though it is not easy to pick out a single oddity that attaches to them all, and when picked out not easy to see it as having any very profound significance.

[1] Cf. P. T. Geach, 'Imperative and deontic logic', *Analysis*, January 1958, and C. D. Broad, *The Mind and its Place in Nature*, pp. 487–91.

In the first two cases one obvious peculiarity is that the premisses suffice to prove not only that a certain thing *ought* to be done but also that that very thing *is* done, so that the duty established is not one that we need ever be practically anxious about. Thus from the non-existence of men over 20 feet high we inferred in effect that no men over 20 feet high ought to sit on ordinary chairs; but it equally follows from this premiss that no men over 20 feet high *do* sit on ordinary chairs. Similarly, from the fact that tea-drinking is common in England it follows not only that either tea-drinking is common in England or New Zealanders ought to be shot, i.e., that New Zealanders ought to be shot-if-tea-drinking-is-not-common-in-England, but also that either tea-drinking is common in England or New Zealanders *are* shot, i.e., that New Zealanders *are* shot-if-tea-drinking-is-not-common-in-England (in view of the premiss, this is of course a very harmless sort of shooting). And this peculiarity is absent from the parallel cases in which the same conclusion is drawn from mixed premisses; i.e., in the parallel cases the obligation established is one which *could*, consistently with the given premisses, fail to be discharged. Thus, given that whoever does what is not common in England ought to be shot, and that New Zealanders drink tea, while it does follow that New Zealanders ought to be shot if tea-drinking is not common in England, it does *not* follow that they *are* shot if tea-drinking is not common in England. Similarly with the man-over-20-feet-high example.

Moreover, it is clear that in the first two examples the moral expressions which occur in the conclusions have what we might call a *contingent vacuousness*. If a conclusion containing an expression E is validly inferred from a certain premiss or set of premisses, and the inference would remain valid if E were replaced by any expression whatever of the same grammatical type, then I say that in that inference the expression E is contingently vacuous. The expression 'ought to' is in this sense contingently vacuous in the inferences 'Tea-drinking is common in England, therefore either tea-drinking is common in England or all New Zealanders ought to be shot' and 'No men are over 20 feet high, therefore no men over 20 feet high ought to sit in an ordinary chair', since the validity of neither of them would be affected if we replaced 'ought to' by 'think they are going to', for example. And it is very tempting to say that any 'ought' that is deduced by ordinary modes of inference from a pure 'is' *must* be contingently vacuous in this sense. For since there is no 'ought' in the premisses, it would seem that no 'ought' can possibly get into the conclusion except by processes which would bring anything at all into the conclusion in the same position.

My third example shows, however, that this last conjecture, for all its plausibility, is mistaken. For if we consider the inference

Undertakers are Church officers,
Therefore undertakers ought to do-whatever-all-Church-officers-ought-to-do,

the first and principal 'ought to', i.e. the one which expresses the duty of undertakers, is *not* contingently vacuous in the above sense. It will not do, for example, simply to omit it, for it does not follow from the given premiss that undertakers *do* whatever all Church officers ought to do, but only that they do whatever all Church officers *do*; similarly it does not follow that they *think they* do whatever all Church officers ought to do, but only that they think they do whatever all Church officers think they do. (That is, this last follows in the sense 'For all F, if all Church officers think they F, then undertakers think they F', though of course it does not follow in the sense 'Undertakers think that for all F, if all Church officers think they F, they themselves F', for the premiss only states that undertakers are in fact Church officers, not that they know they are.)

In the above example, it is evident, the principal 'ought' is only prevented from being contingently vacuous by the presence of a second 'ought' in a subordinate clause; and it is also evident that the only duties that are not contingently vacuous and that may nevertheless be inferred from purely non-ethical premisses are ones whose statement does thus require the use of at least two 'oughts' (or other distinctively ethical expressions). They are all, one would say, *parasitic* duties, presupposing other duties. They are in this way rather like many propositions of deontic logic, e.g., 'We ought not to do anything incompatible with what we ought to do'. They are not, however, propositions of deontic logic, since other expressions occur non-vacuously in them beside ethical and formal ones (in our example, the expressions 'undertaker' and 'Church officer'), and we must resist any suggestion that duties of this parasitic sort are not, as far as they go, perfectly genuine and significant duties, or that they are duties only in some special and abnormal sense. No one could seriously say this, for example, of the duties expressed in such precepts as that one *ought* not to promise to do what one *ought* not to do, or that one *ought* to be punished for doing what one *ought* not to do, or that one *ought* to spend some time, though not too much time, in finding out what one *ought* to do.[1] Nor is it odd or unusual for the duties of one class of people to be parasitic upon the duties of another class of people, which may or may not include the former class as a sub-class. For example, it could be the duty of, say, magistrates to impose unpleasant experiences upon all those (including, it may be, magistrates) who have done what they ought not to do.

It is, indeed, difficult to see how any of the duties just mentioned, e.g., that of not promising to do what one ought not to do, could be deduced from purely non-ethical premisses; so perhaps those parasitic duties which are so deducible all fall into some subclass of parasitic duties which do have something peculiar or empty about them. I have not, however, been able to identify any such subclass. Moreover, if one includes propositions of deontic logic among non-ethical propositions, the impression that such principles as the above could not possibly follow from purely non-ethical premisses is erroneous. For example, the following valid deduction has for its sole premisses a proposition of deontic logic and a proposition with no ethical terms in it at all, while its conclusion expresses a duty of the kind we are considering:

No one ought to do what is invariably accompanied by the doing of something wrong;
X.Y. invariably acts as he says he will act;
Therefore X.Y. ought never to say that he will do anything that he ought not to do.

(I am not saying that the deontic-logic premiss is *true*, only that it and the other premiss do formally imply the conclusion.)

It is true that in our example about undertakers a *sort* of contingent vacuousness attaches to the two 'oughts' in the conclusion taken together, in that the inference ('Undertakers are Church

[1] Cf. T. Reid, *Essays on the Active Powers*, II.iii.

officers, therefore undertakers ought to do whatever all Church
officers ought to do') will remain valid if *both* 'oughts' are replaced
at once, and by the same replacement; and it is evident that at least
this sort of contingent vacuousness will be present in *any* inference
of an ethical conclusion from non-ethical premisses. This, however,
seems to me a very trivial sort of contingent vacuousness, since it
does not even imply that the duties inferred are automatically discharged. Thus in the given case, as we noted earlier, it cannot be
inferred from the premiss that undertakers in fact *do* whatever all
Church officers ought to do; so the duty that one *can* infer is by no
means something that they have no real choice about.

I am driven to admit, therefore, that one simply *can* derive
conclusions which are 'ethical' in a quite serious sense from
premisses none of which have this character. The undertaker, for
example, who learns that he is a Church officer, can learn as a logical
consequence of this something about his duty that he did not know
before. This something will indeed require supplementation by
other things—I mean other things of an *ethical* sort—before the
undertaker is in possession of a precise recipe for action or absten-
tion from action at place P and time T; but in this it resembles much
else that nevertheless constitutes, as far as it goes, significant
information about what one ought to do.

11. *It Was To Be*

One feature of the ordinary unreflective view of free will is that it presupposes an enormous difference between the future and the past. Over what has already happened, the ordinary view would be, we have no further control; but we do have some control over what is going to happen. Whatever is past, we might say, is now *unpreventable*; we cannot now stop its having happened; but what is still as it were on the way to happening, we *can* sometimes stop happening, and whether it actually happens or not may depend on what we decide and do.

Some philosophers, however, have argued against this view as follows: Whatever is *logically equivalent* to something unpreventable must itself be unpreventable; but every fact about the future can be shown to have corresponding to it a logically equivalent fact about the past, so whatever unpreventableness is admitted to attach to the past must attach to the future also. The proof that to every fact about the future there corresponds a logically equivalent fact about the past, is roughly as follows: We need only concern ourselves, for the purposes of this argument, with what we might call elementary facts about the future, i.e. facts to the effect that something or other will take place at some definite future time, say *n* time-units hence. Now corresponding to any fact-about-the-future to the effect that X *will* take place *n* time-units *hence* there is always a logically equivalent fact-about-the-past, in fact a whole infinite *range* of logically equivalent facts-about-the-past, to the effect that *m* time-units *ago* the statement 'X will take place *m + n* time-units hence' *was* true. To take a simple example: if and only if it is a fact-about-the-future that I *shall* have a smoke *tomorrow* then it is a fact-about-the-past that *yesterday* the statement 'Prior will have a smoke the day after tomorrow' *was* true, and for that matter the statement 'Prior will have a smoke a million years and a day hereafter' *was*

4

true a million years ago. But these, being facts about the past, are about what's over and done with now; they're things, therefore, that it's now too late for us to stop; *ergo* it's equally too late now for us to stop myself smoking tomorrow, since I could only do this by undoing the million-year-old truth that I've mentioned, which is absurd.

There are, of course, a variety of ways of breaking this chain, if one doesn't like what one finds oneself with at the end. One way of sliding out, on which I don't think it's necessary to waste much time, is to make nonsense of most of the argument by denying that you can attach a time to a truth-value. But in fact we all use phrases like 'was true yesterday' perfectly happily when we are not philo-sophising, and we even *have to* use them if we are talking about the truth-values of statements with words like 'was' and 'will' in them. Not that I think we can settle all philosophical questions by con-sidering what we do when we are not philosophising; but the con-sideration is relevant in the present case. For the argument that I stated professes to demonstrate an incoherence in our ordinary unreflective notions; it puts together a few premisses that men are ordinarily disposed to assent to, and draws from these a conclusion which they are ordinarily disposed to deny; and it won't do as a defence of the ordinary unreflective point of view to deny that there is an intelligible use of phrases like 'true yesterday', for this is simply *abandoning* the ordinary unreflective point of view at another point. In any case, the whole argument can pretty obviously be re-phrased without using the words 'true' and 'false' at all; for example we can say that if and only if I *am* going to have a smoke tomorrow then yesterday I *was* going to have a smoke the day after the follow-ing day.

For my own part, I would say that the argument I stated not only claims to show but *does* show that our ordinary unreflective view of these matters is a little bit incoherent, and how we ought to straighten it out is partly a matter of what is true and partly a matter of how it's most convenient to talk. Whether or not we ought to accept the conclusion that we have no control over what will be, seems to me a matter of what is true; but assuming that in fact we *have* some control over what will be, which premisses of the argument we reject or how we modify them seems to me to be a linguistic matter, and this is what I want now to talk about in some detail.

The argument has two principal premisses—the unpreventableness of the past, and the logical equivalence of every statement whose principal verb is in the future tense to a set of statements with the principal verb in the past tense. So ways of avoiding the conclusion will divide into ones which deny the logical equivalence just mentioned, and ones which deny the unpreventableness of the past. Denials of the logical equivalence just mentioned—denials for example, of the equivalence between 'There will be a sea-battle tomorrow' and 'It was true yesterday that there would be a sea-battle the day after the following day'—are often associated with denials of the law of excluded middle. That is, it may be said that statements to the effect that X *will* take place at a certain time are only true if it is already settled and determined that they will take place, and are false only if it is already settled and determined that they will *not* take place, and are some third thing, say neuter or undecided, if it is still an open question whether X will take place or not. If, let us say, a sea-battle tomorrow is now past stopping but might have been stopped yesterday, then on this three-valued view we would say that the statement 'There will be a sea-battle tomorrow' is now true while yesterday the statement 'There will be a sea-battle the day after tomorrow' was not true but neuter; and this of course suffices to destroy the logical equivalence between future-tense and past-tense statements on which the argument we are considering depends.

But we can also destroy this equivalence, as I tried to show in the tenth chapter of my *Time and Modality*, *without* denying the law of excluded middle. For we might say that if a sea-battle tomorrow is now past stopping but wasn't past stopping yesterday, then the statement 'There will be a sea-battle tomorrow' is true today, but yesterday the statement 'There will be a sea-battle the day after tomorrow' was not merely neuter but *false*. This sounds almost like a contradiction, but I don't think it is one—we escape contradiction by distinguishing two senses of the phrase 'will not', these senses being what I think Miss Anscombe would call the external and the internal negation of the plain 'will'. We may write down these two senses of 'There will not be a sea-battle the day after tomorrow' as follows:

Ext.: It is not the case that
        it will be the case two days hence that
           there is a sea-battle going on.

Int.: It will be the case two days hence that
        it is not the case that
           there is a sea-battle going on.

On the view I'm trying to sketch, as on the three-valued view, the simple statement that it will be the case two days hence that a sea-battle is going on is not *true now, true already*, that is to say *in positive accordance with the present facts*, unless the sea-battle is already in a manner present—present in its causes, to use an old locution—and indeed in such a way that we cannot now prevent it happening. If it is *not* so present, whether because it has already been prevented or merely because it is still preventable, the positive 'will' statement is false, and the direct external negation, asserting that it is *not* the case, i.e. not now the case, not yet the case, that there will be a sea-battle in two days' time, is true. On the other hand the *internal* negation of the simple future, which doesn't merely deny the future being but asserts the future non-being of the sea-battle, is only true if the sea-battle is not merely still preventable but has already been prevented; only then is it true now, true already, that it *is going to* not-happen. This way of talking gives us the distinction that we want to make between necessary, contingent and impossible futures without introducing a third truth-value.

Nevertheless, the way of talking that I have just sketched shares with the three-valued way of talking one big disadvantage, namely that it is grossly at variance with the ways in which even non-determinists ordinarily appraise or assign truth-values to predictions, bets and guesses. Suppose at the beginning of a race I bet you that Phar Lap will win, and then he does win, and I come to claim my bet. You might then ask me, 'Why, do you think this victory was unpreventable when you made your bet?' I admit that I don't, so you say 'Well I'm not paying up then—when you said Phar Lap would win, what you said wasn't true—on the three-valued view, it was merely neuter: on this other view of yours, it was even false. So I'm sticking to the money.' And I must admit that if anyone treated a bet of mine like that I would feel aggrieved; that just isn't the way this game is played.

What one would like to see is a systematisation of ordinary betting talk that is quite unfatalistic. And this I think can be provided; but only, I would suggest, if one is prepared to deny or qualify the other premiss of the original argument I gave, namely the unpreventability of the past. And to bring this out in detail I shall try to pass on a way of talking that was originally put to me by my New Zealand colleague Mr Michael Shorter as a kind of gloss on the second chapter of Professor Ryle's *Dilemmas*, from which of course I have pinched the title of this present paper. Basically what must be abandoned, if we are to use betting language correctly and yet indeterministically, is the assumption that the present truth of an assertion must consist in its accordance with something in the non-linguistic world around one at the time the assertion is made. For the whole peculiarity of future tense assertions is precisely that with them this assumption fails. There may be just nothing in the world around us that verifies a statement like 'Phar Lap will be the winner in two minutes' time' at the time when it is made; that is to say there may be *no grounds* for making any pronouncement as to its truth-value at that time; there only come to be such grounds two minutes later, and then we can look back and say 'That statement *was* true' or 'That statement *was* false', as the case may be. But does this mean that when it was made the statement was neither true nor false? Not at all. At all times, including the time when they are made, the two statements

A1. Phar Lap *will* win in two minutes

A2. 'Phar Lap will win in two minutes' *is* true

are exactly equivalent and on exactly the same footing; and if A1 is what you might describe as a wait-and-seeish sort of statement, meaning by that that when it is made there are no grounds for judging it true or false, but if you wait and see there will be grounds for saying that it was true or was false—well, if A1 is a wait-and-seeish statement in this sense, so is A2, despite the fact that its main verb is present; and the same also goes for

A3. 'Phar Lap will win in three minutes' *was* true a minute ago,

despite the fact that the main verb of *this* one is past. It's about what was the case—the truth-value of a certain statement—a minute ago; nevertheless we have no way of assigning a truth-value to it until two more minutes have gone.

This is a procedure which, Mr Shorter has pointed out, could be applied to other types of sentences which are sometimes said to be either permanently or temporarily without a truth-value. Imperatives, for example. We are tempted to say that ' "Shut the door" is true' must be false or senseless because by the ordinary conventions about the word 'true' it ought to be equivalent to the plain 'Shut the door', but it can't be because the plain 'Shut the door' is an imperative whereas ' "Shut the door" is true' is an indicative. But why should we not use the sentence ' "Shut the door" is true' as a way of *endorsing* the imperative 'Shut the door', and so as another imperative? We *don't*, of course, as our language now is, use the sentence ' "Shut the door' is true' in that or any other way, but it is at least arguable that we do use sentences like 'He is quite right to tell him to shut the door' in precisely that way, despite their indicative grammatical form. And as with imperativeness, so it could be with futurity or wait-and-seeishness.

Wait-and-seeishness, we might say, is not in this language acquired by statements from their main verb only; let even a subordinate clause, or something in quotes, be of the wait-and-seeish kind, and the wait-and-seeishness *may* be transmitted to the whole. And along with this wait-and-seeishness goes preventableness. An example that Mr Shorter sometimes used was giving up smoking. 'I have given up smoking' is past in form but does it really describe something which I cannot now undo? On any analysis, it contains a compound to the effect that I used to smoke, and that is certainly something that I cannot now undo. But what about the rest of it? Well, there are two possible analyses of this remainder, namely

B1. For some time I haven't smoked, and I shall not smoke any more.

B2. It has been the case for some time that I shall not smoke any more.

On the view I sketched earlier, these could be different in force. On that earlier-sketched view, both B1 and B2 are only true if I have now effectively prevented myself from ever smoking again; but B2

is only true if this effective prevention took place some time ago—
B1 would be true, but B2 false, if for some time I haven't smoked
but still could have done, though now I can't any more. But on what
one might call the Shorterian or perhaps Rylo-Shorterian view B1
and B2 are equivalent forms and in any case they both express
something that could still be preventable. If I do prevent my never
smoking again by having another smoke, then of course I shall say,
looking back, that B1 and B2 were false when said, and that at that
time I *hadn't* in fact given up smoking; but on the other hand this
may never happen, in which case B1 and B2, and along with them
B3. B1 and B2 are true will be retrospectively verified.

Now I want to suggest that the difference between this way of
talking and that sketched earlier is *just* a difference in ways of
talking and not in what is said. And what shows this is that within
either of these languages you can give the basic rules of the other
language. Suppose I use capital letters for the tense-forms of the
language in which it is important to distinguish the internal from
the external negation of the plain future; and small letters for the
tense-forms of the betting language. Now I can easily *mention* the
small-letter 'will' in the big-letter language, but it's a tricky matter
to explain how it works when you can only *use* the big-letter 'Will'.
It obviously won't do to say, e.g.

C1. 'Phar Lap will win' is true if and only if Phar Lap WILL
win.

Nor will it do to say

C2. It WILL be right to say ' "Phar Lap will win" was true' if
and only if Phar Lap WILL win.

This is true but unhelpful—it only tells us that the future rightness
of the thing in quotes is now unpreventable if and only if Phar
Lap's winning is now unpreventable, but it's the use of the small-
letter 'will' and 'was' when Phar Lap's win isn't unpreventable that
we want to explain. And the way to do it is like this.

C3. If anyone says 'Phar Lap will win 2 minutes hence'
then it WILL be the case 2 minutes hence that
'what he said was true' is true if and only if Phar Lap is
the winner.

The big WILL in the main consequent of this is justified because although nothing compels Phar Lap to win and nothing compels the man to say he will, once the man *has* said that Phar Lap will win he has in a manner put his hand in the fire and *one* thing cannot now be stopped, namely that when the time comes what he has said will stand or fall under the conditions stated. But note that the big WILL governs the whole 'if and only if' statement—we get things that we don't want at all if we try to put the big WILL into one or both of the *parts* of the biconditional—we go all wrong if we try to replace 'It WILL be that if and only if . . .' by 'If and only if it WILL be that . . .' Of course C1 is only the first of a whole series of statements needed to explain the small-letter usages, but it will do for a start.

Conversely, the way to introduce the big-letter language into the other is by supplementing the pure tense apparatus of the betting language with a modal operator 'It is inevitable that . . .' 'It WILL be the case that . . .' can then be explained as 'It is inevitable that it will be the case that . . .' The difference between the internal and external negation of 'WILL' then becomes simply that between 'It is inevitable that it will not be the case that' and 'It is not inevitable that it will be the case that'. This makes the rules for 'will' in themselves very simple; there's no need, for example, to distinguish different senses of 'will-not'—'It *is not* the case that it *will* be' is just the same as, I mean logically equivalent, to 'It will be that it is not the case that'. And similarly with disjunctive forms—'It either will be that p or it will be that q' is just the same as 'It will be that either p or q'. There's nothing as simple as that with 'WILL'; e.g. it WILL be that either p or not-p even in cases where it neither WILL be that p nor WILL be that not-p. But in the betting or Shorterian language the complications come in with the relation of 'WAS' to the 'It is inevitable that' and 'was'. Let us begin consideration of this by noting that the internal and external negations of 'WAS' statements are the same, the big-letter language being designed precisely to give direct expression to the idea that whereas for every p it either WAS the case that p or WAS the case that not-p, at any given time ago, there are ps such that it neither WILL be that p nor WILL be that not p—the clear expression of this felt difference between past and future is the special merit of that system. But if you define 'WAS' simply as 'It is inevitable that it was', it would seem that you'd only get the required simple bifurcation of the past if you could assume that all 'wases' are now inevitable; and that, as we have seen, isn't the case. This is a bit tricky, so let's put up an example. In big-letter language this is a law:

> D1. Either it WAS the case yesterday that p or it WAS the case yesterday that not p.

But the following

> D2. Either it is inevitable that it was the case that p or it is inevitable that it was the case that not p.

is *not* a law in little-letter language, for if p is a sufficiently future-tense statement it may be still open to us to prevent or not to prevent its having been the case that p; e.g. it is still open to me to prevent or not to prevent its having been the case yesterday that I would have a smoke two days from then.

I think the position is more or less as follows: Little-letter statements aren't universally translatable into big-letter ones, e.g. simple 'will' statements have no exact equivalents in the big-letter language—they're not statements in the big-letter sense. But simple 'will' statements preceded by 'It is inevitable that' *are* translatable as the corresponding 'WILL' ones. *Simple* 'was' statements even when not preceded by 'It is inevitable that' translate directly as the corresponding 'WAS' ones, likewise 'was' statements that have no subordinate 'wills' except ones preceded by 'It is inevitable that'. But 'was' statements containing unqualified 'wills' are no more translatable into big-letter language than the simple 'will' ones are. All you can do for these in big-letter language is to explain their syntax in the way I've outlined; so that you *can teach* a big-letter speaker how to talk little-letter, but cannot always supply big-letter translations. And the law D1 only applies where the ps stand for statements in the big-letter sense.

We might say briefly that 'It WAS the case that p', where p is a genuine big-letter sentence, *is* always translatable into little-letter language as 'It is now inevitable that it was the case that p', but the converse translation with p a genuine *little*-letter sentence is not always possible. And with regard to the limitations of translating little-letter language into big-letter language, the following general-isation may be made: The only expressions which count as indica-tive sentences in big-letter language are ones which state what already is or already is not the case, i.e. which state what is now either beyond prevention or—if the sentence is false—already prevented. We can, of course, state in big-letter language that it neither WILL be the case that p nor WILL be the case that not-p, i.e. we can state in big-letter language *that p is now a future con-tingency*; but this thing that we state is not itself a future contingency, i.e. it is not now a future contingency *that p* is now a future con-tingency; on the contrary this present contingency of p is itself either a fact which it is now too late to prevent or a falsehood which it is now too late to make true. The big-letter language, in other words, can only set forth truly or falsely that which has already come to be the case, in such a sense as to be now beyond prevention, including now unpreventable futures. The future, one might say, is only describable in the big-letter language to the extent to which it is assimilable to the present and the past. There are no wait-and-seeish statements in big-letter language, so no wait-and-seeish statements are translatable into it.

We *can* all the same explain in big-letter language how the wait-and-seeish statements of little-letter language are used. That is, we *can* explain in big-letter language how our ordinary appraisals of bets and guesses work. Bets and guesses don't have present truth-values in the sense in which big-letter statements of all tenses have present truth-values. And this entails that they haven't big-letter past or future truth-values either; for X big-WAS true if and only if X's truth big-WAS present. We can, however, introduce into big-letter language, firstly, *names* for bets and guesses, i.e. bets and guesses in quotes, and secondly, a special unanalysable semantic predicate '(little)-was-true' which attaches to bets and guesses according to rules that can be stated in a pure big-letter way. The paradigm is like this:

(a) It is, always WAS and always WILL be the case that
(b) *if* a man says 'Phar Lap will win in two minutes', then
(c) it WILL be the case in two minutes that
(d) if and only if Phar Lap is winning, what the man said was-true.

Here the big WILL in (a) is justified because the totality of what follows exemplifies a *law* of the logic of guesses and bets and so is not only now but at all times unpreventable. The big WILL in (c) is justified because once a man has committed himself to the bet or guess recorded in (b), nothing can prevent his bet or guess being appraised, when the time comes, in the manner described in (d). He has, as it were, once he has betted, put his hand in the fire, and *must* now take the consequence of standing or falling, when the time comes, in the manner (d). But note that to convey what we want to do, the big WILL must be placed *before* the whole biconditional (d), and not within it. For if we say instead of (c)-(d), the following:

(e) If and only if it WILL be the case in two minutes that Phar Lap wins, it WILL be the case that what the man said was-true,

this will be true enough as far as it goes, but only tells us that the future appraisal was true is now beyond stopping if and only if Phar Lap's win is now beyond stopping, and what we want is a rule for the use of this appraisal that can be applied even when we *aren't* thus betting on a certainty.

I'd like to repeat that this semantic term 'was-true' that I have introduced in the above manner is *not* a compound of the ordinary big-'WAS' and the ordinary 'true', as that term applies in big-letter semantics to big-letter statements. And I don't mind at all if you put this point, as I think Ryle puts it, by saying that 'true' is not *quite* the right word to apply to bets and guesses, and that bets and guesses aren't in the ordinary sense statements. But I would add that you *can* use a language in which bets and guesses and statements are all put in a single box, similar semantic appraisals used for all of them, and the same expression used for the 'was' of 'was-true' and for the ordinary past tense. My little-letter language is in fact just that: in the little-letter language, one might say, you can't distinguish between a formal *assertion* and a mere bet or guess; while in the big-letter language you can't distinguish between what will be so and what will inevitably be so. But in both of them you can express consistently the hypothesis of freedom—in little-letter language by saying that what will be, and in some cases even what has been, is not always beyond stopping, and in big-letter language by saying that there are some things of which it is not yet true either that they WILL be so or that they WILL be not-so.

Neither big-letter language nor little-letter language, so far as I can see, supplies us with a means of reconciling free power over the future with foreknowledge. For, to take big-letter talk first, it is obvious that if you define foreknowing that *p* as knowing that it big-WILL be the case that *p*, and adopt the usual view that what is known is true, then nothing can be foreknown in this sense but what big-WILL be the case, that is, what is unpreventable. With little-letter talk the question is a bit more tricky, but if you define fore-knowing that *p* as knowing that it little-will be the case that *p*, I cannot see how any such thing can take place if what is said to be known is of a *strictly* wait-and-seeish sort. If one *has to*, in *principle*, 'wait and see' whether it will be the case that *p*—if there is *nothing* presently round about one which decides the matter one way or the other—I cannot see that one can talk of *knowing* that *p*. And this doesn't seem to me an avoidable defect of either of these languages, for I must confess I can't see that foreknowledge *is* compatible with preventability. And I am *not* now doing anything so silly as to treat foreknowledge as any sort of *cause* of what is foreknown. What is known must be so in order to be known rather than vice versa, so that the knowing is much more like an effect of what is known than a cause of it. But that only makes what is foreknown less preventable than ever; for what has already got so far as to have *effects*, and effects which nothing but that thing *could* have, is surely beyond stopping. Uniformly correct *prediction* compatible with prevent-ability, yes; but foreknowledge is surely more than that.

12. Nonentities

1. There is a philosophical dilemma which, reduced to its simplest terms, is just this: We are half disposed to say that some things exist and some do not, for Socrates exists but Pegasus does not; and half disposed to say that everything whatever exists, for 'everything' is just 'all there is'. And what could be more natural than to resolve this dilemma by distinguishing between a large sense of 'exists', in which it would be self-contradictory to say of anything at all that it does not exist, and a narrow sense, in which we can say of some things that they exist and of others that they do not? This simple and obvious solution was once favoured by Russell, but he later abandoned it at the promptings of what he was pleased to call a 'robust sense of reality'. To this point of dispute between Bertrand drunk and Bertrand sober I shall return later (defending Bertrand drunk); but before that I want to raise the question as to whether 'exists' can be defined, particularly in the sense in which some things (e.g., Socrates) exist and some (e.g., Pegasus) do not.

2. What, then, is this 'existence' or 'reality' which Socrates possesses but Pegasus does not? An equivalence which has often commended itself to philosophers is that between 'being' *simpliciter* and 'being something' (using 'be' in the copulative sense). Whatever is something (e.g. is red) surely is; and whatever simply is, must be something (if not red, then something else). But is 'being something' really what distinguishes Socrates from Pegasus? Pegasus, it might be argued, is a winged horse; *ergo* there is something that Pegasus is; *ergo* Pegasus exists, in this sense of 'exists'. This argument could, however, be reversed: Pegasus, we could say, does not exist, therefore he is not a winged horse, but is at most said to be one. All right then; but does not this still leave us with something that Pegasus is? He is not a-winged-horse; but he is still said-to-have-been-a-winged-horse, and being at least that, he is something,

i.e. he exists. Again, whether Pegasus be a winged horse or not a winged horse, he is a-winged-horse-if-he-is-a-winged-horse, and a not-a-winged-horse-if-he-is-not-a-winged-horse; so once again, there is something that he is (a-winged-horse-if-a-winged-horse, and also not-a-winged-horse-if-not-a-winged-horse).

3. It is not difficult to turn this last argument for the existence of Pegasus into a formal proof, in a symbolic system, of the existence of anything whatever, say x. For by our definition, 'x exists' means 'For some φ, x φs', $\Sigma\varphi\varphi x$. Now let Vp be short for Cpp, 'If p then p'. $V\varphi x$ will then be short for $C\varphi x\varphi x$, 'If x φs then x φs', i.e. $V\varphi$-ing is φ-ing-if-one-φs. This is something which anything whatever, say x, is bound to do, i.e. the formula $V\varphi x$ ('x $V\varphi$s', or '$x\varphi$s-if-it-φs') expresses a logical law. But the formula $C\varphi x\Sigma\varphi\varphi x$, 'If x φs then there is something that x does', also expresses a logical law. Hence, substituting for the free φ in this, $CV\varphi x\Sigma\varphi\varphi x$, 'If x $V\varphi$s, there is something that x does', expresses a logical law, and since its antecedent $V\varphi x$ expresses a logical law, so does its consequent $\Sigma\varphi\varphi x$, or 'x exists'. Or setting the thing out formally

Df. V. $Vp = Cpp$
1. Cpp
2. $C\varphi x\Sigma\varphi\varphi x$
    1 $p/\varphi x \times$ Df. $V = 3$
3. $V\varphi x$
    2 $\varphi/V\varphi = $ C 3–4
4. $\Sigma\varphi\varphi x$

4 is not, as it happens, a theorem of *Principia Mathematica*, but it quite easily could be, and *Principia Mathematica* does contain one theorem. *62.22, which amounts to the same thing. What *62.22 asserts is that the domain of the relation of class membership is the universe, i.e. everything whatever is a member of some class. Since being a member of a class is equivalent, in the Russellian system, to possessing the class's defining property, theorem 62.22 in effect asserts that everything whatever possesses some property, i.e. 'exists'.

4. It would seem that we have inadvertently defined 'exists' not in

the narrow but in the wide sense, i.e. in the sense in which Pegasus exists as well as Socrates. That is not, however, the moral that Russell himself draws from the presence in his system of a theorem equivalent to 'For some φ, x φs'. (It was not Bertrand drunk but Bertrand sober who contributed to *Principia Mathematica*.) The Russellian justification of the law 'For some φ, x φs' would, rather, run more or less like this: In the system of *Principia Mathematica* the variables x, y, z, etc., are understood as standing for 'names' in an extremely strict sense of the word—in the sense of expressions which serve purely to identify individuals without describing them, so that if there is no individual really there to take a given label, then this label is not the sort of expression that the Russellian x stands for. The problem about Pegasus can therefore be disposed of by saying that the word 'Pegasus', as ordinarily used, is simply not a 'name' in the sense in which the x of the theorem 'For some φ, x φs' is a 'name'-variable. 'Pegasus' is at best a disguised 'description', i.e. it is an expression of the same sort as 'the man next door', 'the man in the moon', 'the author of *Waverley*', 'the present King of France', 'the property of non-self-inherence', not simply substitutable for the xs, ys, zs, etc., of Russellian formulæ, but requiring a more complicated treatment.

5. Though the point is a subtle one, it will be worth our while to look a little more closely at this alleged non-substitutability of phrases like 'The man next door' (or 'Pegasus', considered as a disguised expression of the same sort) for the x in the law 'For some φ, x φs'. The matter rests in the end on the syntactical relations of names and verbs. A good working definition of a verb is 'an operator by which we construct a statement out of a name' (e.g. we construct the statement 'Socrates smokes' by means of the verb 'smokes' out of the name 'Socrates'); and it might be thought equally fitting to define a name as an expression which forms a statement when a verb is attached to it. But this definition would yield a very odd sense of 'name'. For example, we may construct a statement by attaching a verb to the expression 'Not every man—'; but is 'Not every man—' a name? To say that it is, would be not merely odd, but extremely inconvenient. Consider, for example, the formula $V\varphi x$. If x is a name in the Russellian sense, it makes no difference whether we mentally bracket this as $V(\varphi x)$ and read it as 'If x φs then x φs', or

bracket it as $(V\varphi)x$ and read it as 'x φs-if-it-φs' (or 'x does-not-φ-without-φ-ing'). But if we allow 'Not every man—' to count as a name, then when we substitute this for x we must read $V(\varphi x)$ as 'If not every man φs then not every man φs', which is a logical law, but $(V\varphi)x$ must be read as 'Not every man φs-if-he-φs', which is not a logical law and is even the contradictory of one. But in our proof of the theorem $\Sigma\varphi\varphi x$, it is $V(\varphi x)$ which we obtain by substituting φx for p in the law Cpp or Vp, whereas what we obtain by substituting $V\varphi$ for φ in $C\varphi x\Sigma\varphi\varphi x$ is not $CV(\varphi x)\Sigma\varphi\varphi x$ but $C(V\varphi)x\Sigma\varphi\varphi x$; so that our deduction would fail if we could substitute for x such expressions as 'Not every man—'. And the point about what Russell calls 'descriptions', i.e. such phrases as 'The man next door', 'The man in the moon', 'The winged horse of Bellerophon', is that at this point they resemble expressions like 'Not every man—' rather than genuine names. On the Russellian view, 'The winged horse of Bellerophon φs' is short for 'Exactly one thing is a winged horse of Bellerophon, and every winged horse of Bellerophon φs'; so that '$V(\varphi$(the winged horse of Bellerophon))' expands to 'If exactly one thing is, etc., then exactly one thing is, etc.', which is true, but '$(V\varphi)$ (the winged horse of Bellerophon)' expands to 'Exactly one thing is the winged horse of Bellerophon, and every winged horse of Bellerophon φs-if-it-φs', and while the second conjunct of this is true the first is false, so that the whole is false. So if such expressions as 'The winged horse of Bellerophon' were names, the deduction of the theorem 'for some φ, x φs' would fail, just as it would if such expressions as 'Not every man—' were names.

6. Let me give one other parallel case, from a slightly different field. Just as a verb may be defined as an operator which constructs statements out of names, so a propositional operator may be defined as one which constructs statements out of statements. For example, the statement 'It is not the case that if grass is green then grass is green' may be regarded as constructed out of the statement 'If grass is green then grass is green' by means of the propositional operator 'It is not the case that'. It may also be regarded as constructed out of the simpler statement 'Grass is green' by means of the more complex operator 'It is not the case that if—then—'. That is, we may think of it either as $N(Vp)$ or as $(NV)p$, and it is a matter of no moment whether we think of it in the one way or in the other. But

can we include among 'statements' all expressions which form statements when attached to propositional operators? We would then have a third way of regarding the statement 'It is not the case that if grass is green then grass is green'—namely, as constructed out of the 'statement' 'It is not the case that . . . grass is green' by means of the operator 'If—then—'. The 'statement'-form 'It is not the case that . . . p' might be abbreviated to Tp, and introduced into the propositional calculus by the definition

$$DT: \varphi Tp = N\varphi p$$

But if there were any such form of statement as this, it would be an easy matter to deduce from any tautologous formula, or logical law, its own negation. We would do it thus:

1. Vp
      1 $p/Tp = 2$
2. VTp
      2 $\times$ DT $\varphi/V = 3$
3. NVp

The trouble here is simple. In the definition DT what is clearly intended is the equation of φT with $N\varphi$, i.e. its implicit bracketing is '$(\varphi T)p = (N\varphi)p$'. But when we treat VTp—derived by substituting Tp for p in Vp—as a case of the form φTp, our implicit bracketing of the left hand side is not $(\varphi T)p$ but $\varphi(Tp)$—for it is unquestionably $V(Tp)$ that we have proved—and with this sort of propositional fragment the difference is important. That very fact suffices to distinguish expressions of the form Tp from 'statements' properly so-called, just as the analogous fact serves to distinguish 'Not every man' from a genuine 'name'.

7. We have, then, the following argument against substituting 'Pegasus' for x in 'x exists', when this is defined as 'for some φ, x φs' and this in turn is established as a logical law (true for any x):

(a) We can only substitute for x in this formula an expression which preserves the equivalence of $\delta(\varphi x)$ and $(\delta\varphi)x$, where δ is any statement-forming operator on statements, such as V.

(b) Expressions of the form 'Exactly one thing φs, and if anything φs it—', when substituted for x, do not preserve this equivalence.

(c) Expressions of the form 'The φ-er' are short for 'Exactly one thing φs, and if anything φs it—'.

(d) 'Pegasus' is short for some expression of the form 'The φ-er', e.g. for 'The winged horse of Bellerophon.'

With (a) and (b) there can be no quarrel, but it is worth considering what happens if we deny (c) or (d). Mr P. F. Strawson has brilliantly developed the consequences of denying (c) while accepting something very like (d). They can only be described as appalling. The Russellian argument for (d) is that 'Pegasus' cannot function as a 'logical proper name', since this is a direct labelling of some actual object, so if it is not meaningless, a 'description' is the only thing it can be. Strawson goes further and obliterates, or anyway smudges, the Russellian distinction between logical proper names and descriptions, not only in difficult cases like that of 'Pegasus', but in all cases, and then proceeds to treat descriptions as Russell treats logical proper names. Just as Russell treats expressions of the form 'x smokes' as making no assertion when there is no individual that the name x labels, so Strawson treats, say, 'The present King of France smokes' as making no assertion when there is no individual that 'the present King of France' describes. And since no expression of the form 'Pegasus φs' makes an assertion, 'For some φ, Pegasus φs', or 'Pegasus does something', or (on the suggested definition of 'exists') 'Pegasus exists', makes no assertion either. (On the Russellian view, 'For some φ, Pegasus φs' is short for something like 'For some φ, exactly one thing is a winged horse of Bellerophon, and every winged horse of Bellerophon φs'; and though this is not of the form 'For some φ, φx', and does not assert anything that is true, it does assert something that is false.) In the Strawsonian position we see Bertrand not merely sober but dead sober, and most marvellously tongue-tied.

8. I want now to sketch a system which is in some ways the exact opposite of Strawson's, the 'ontology' of Leśniewski. Here (c) and (d) above are both denied, and 'For some φ, φ (Pegasus)' is affirmed (being a legitimate substitution in 'For some φ, φx', which is

provable as in Section 4), but is not equated with 'Pegasus exists', the form 'x exists' (or rather 'The x exists') being defined in a different way. In this system the variables x, y, z, etc., do not stand, or do not ordinarily stand, for 'names' in the strict Russellian sense, nor do they stand for Russellian 'descriptions', but for common nouns (like 'man', 'man next door', 'man in the moon', 'horse', 'winged horse of Bellerophon', and so on). And the system contains an undefined operator ε, such that $\varepsilon x y$ may be read as 'The x is a y', or if you like, 'The only x is a y'. Proper names may be introduced into the system by being treated as if they were common nouns. Thus the form $\varepsilon x y$ covers such examples as '(The) Socrates is a man', '(The) Pegasus is a horse', and also 'The man next door is (a) Socrates'. The form '(The) x exists' is taken to be short for 'For some y (the) x is a y', $\Sigma y \varepsilon x y$. This is not a logical law, as there are xs, e.g. Pegasus, for which it does not hold. Of Pegasus it is not true that for some y (the) Pegasus is a y; for no proposition of the form '(The) Pegasus is a—' is true, though there are true propositions of other forms into which the term 'Pegasus' may enter, e.g. the proposition 'It is said that Pegasus is a winged horse', and all the propositions whatever of the form 'It is not the case that Pegasus is a—'. (We still have 'For some φ, φ (Pegasus)'.)

9. Complex terms may be introduced into the Leśniewskian system, but only under certain special conditions. We can introduce, for example, the negative term 'non-y', but not by equating 'The x is a non-y' to 'It is not the case that the x is a y'. We equate it, rather, to the conjunction of this with 'The x exists'; 'The x is a non-y' means 'The x is not a y, but it is something'. In other words, 'The x is not a y, but is something' can be treated as a special case of the form 'The x is a y', obtainable from it by the substitution of 'non-y' for y; but 'The x is not a y' is not a special case of the form 'The x is a y', and is not obtainable from it by any substitution for y; though it is a special case of the form φx, obtainable from it by substituting for φ.

Again, we can introduce the complex term 'thing-said-to-be-a-y', but not by equating 'The x is a thing-said-to-be-a-y' to 'It is said that the x is a y'. We equate it, rather, to 'The x exists, and it is said that it is a y'. This latter is thus a special case of the form 'The x is a y', obtainable from it by substituting 'thing-said-to-be-a-y' for y;

but the mere 'It is said that the x is a y' is not a special case of the form 'The x is a y', and is not obtainable from it by any substitution for y; though it is a special case of the form φx, obtainable from it by substituting for φ.

Again, we can introduce the complex term 'thing that is a y if it is a y', but not by equating 'The x is a thing that is a y if it is a y' to 'If the x is a y it is a y'. We must equate it rather to the conjunction of this with 'The x exists'. This conjunction is a special case of the form 'The x is a y', obtainable from it by substitution for y; but 'If the x is a y it is a y' is not a special case of the form 'The x is a y', and is not obtainable from it by any substitution for y; though it is a special case of φx, obtainable from it by substituting for φ.

Hence, although $V\varepsilon xy$ and $C\varepsilon xy\Sigma y\varepsilon xy$ are both laws of ontology, we cannot obtain $\Sigma y\varepsilon xy$ as a law, as we cannot obtain $CV\varepsilon xy\Sigma y\varepsilon xy$ from our second premiss. If we introduce the complex term vy we can obtain $C\varepsilon xvy\Sigma y\varepsilon xy$ by substituting for the free y in $C\varepsilon xy\Sigma y\varepsilon xy$, but εxvy is not a law, for we cannot introduce this form as an equivalent of $V\varepsilon xy$ but only as an equivalent of $KV\varepsilon xy\Sigma y\varepsilon xy$. $\Sigma\varphi\varphi x$, however, is provable as usual.

10. Having thus filled Bertrand sober with a strong draught of new Polish wine, we can now consider seriously whether there is any defence for Bertrand drunk. Believers in two senses of 'existence' commonly distinguish the wider sense by calling it 'being'. We have seen that the form 'For some φ, φx' remains tautologically true even in ontology; this makes it unsuitable as a definition of 'x exists', but does it not make it eminently suitable as a definition of 'x is'? I can see nothing in principle against this, provided it be realised what a very broad sense of 'is' is now being suggested. It is not merely a question, for example, of affirming the 'being' of all *possibilia*, while affirming 'existence' of only some of them (those that have been 'actualised'). For the formula 'For some φ, φx' holds for *impossibilia* also. For example, if the variable x is used as in ontology, and (xx') is the complex term 'actual thing that is both x and non-x' (e.g. human and non-human), we may affirm 'For some φ, $\varphi (xx')$, e.g. 'For some φ, φ (human non-human)', or 'Human non-human is', in our new sense of 'is'. For there are plenty of true formulæ of the form' φ(human non-human)', e.g. 'No human non-human is either wise or non-wise'; 'No human non-human is anything at all',

ΠyN $\varepsilon(xx')y$; and of course 'If y is a human-non-human then y is a human-non-human', $V\varepsilon y(xx')$.

11. Moreover, if we are going to use the form 'x is' to mean 'For some φ, φx', with the meaning that that has in Leśniewski's ontology, it should be realised that 'is' is not now, strictly speaking, a verb; and that, whether we abbreviate it to 'x is' or not, the form 'For some φ, φx' is not now properly translatable as 'For some φ, x φs', or 'x does something'. For e is now an operator which constructs statements out of common nouns, and it is not verbs or verb-forms, like '—smokes' or '—is a smoker', which do this, but rather forms like 'The—is a smoker', 'Every smoker is a—', and so on. (In 'Man is an animal', 'Man' is not a common noun but the proper name of a species; and when we translate the forms of ontology by such sentences as 'Socrates is a smoker' rather than 'The Socrates is a smoker', this is only a concession to English idiom. It would not need to be made in Greek.)

12. We might put it this way: If the grammar of this mixture of English and Mathematics that we are now talking is going to be such that 'Human-non-human is' will count as a statement, and in fact as a tautology, then we might as well also allow as a tautology, say, 'Grass is green is'. I have here chosen my words, and my quotation-marks, carefully; I do not mean 'The greenness of grass is', and still less do I mean ' "Grass is green" is'. Not that I would not affirm these things too; indeed I would say that the greenness of grass, and the expression 'Grass is green', not only are but exist; but that is another story. 'The greenness of grass' and ' "Grass is green" ' are names or descriptions, and it is not at all surprising that the entities which they name or describe should be. But 'Grass is green' is not a name or description of a state of affairs or of a statement, but a statement; nevertheless grass is green is, if we use 'x is' in the sense, or rather in the collection of senses, indicated by the formula 'For some φ, φx'.

13. For the formula 'For some φ, φx' is provable, by the steps sketched in Section 4, no matter what types of expression x and φ stand for, provided that φx as a whole can stand for a statement, and the equivalence of $(V\varphi x)$ and $(V\varphi)$ x can be presumed. (The wise

philosophical toper will avoid DTs.) If x stands for a logical proper name, φ will stand for a verb, e.g. 'smokes', and 'For some φ, $\varphi(\ \ )$' will stand for a verb too, namely the verb 'does something' (or 'acts somehow'). If x stands for a common noun, such as 'human non-human', then φ will stand for a statement-forming operator on common nouns, such as 'No—is a Strawsonian', and 'For some φ, $\varphi(\ \ )$' will be an operator of this sort also. And if x stands for a statement, such as 'Grass is green', then φ will stand for a statement-forming operator on statements, such as 'It is not the case that—', and 'for some φ, $\varphi(\ \ )$' will be an operator of this sort also. If in all these cases we abbreviate 'For some φ, $\varphi(\ \ )$' to '$(\ \ )$ is', it is clear that this 'is' not only will not always be a verb, but will differ in its syntactical function with all differences in the syntactical functions of the expressions to which it is attached. The word will thus have all the 'systematic ambiguity' that the exponents of the theory of types, or doctrine of analogy, like to ascribe to it; in fact vastly more, since these writers make it a verb in all its senses.

14. A theory of types, or doctrine of analogy, is unobjectionable so long as it is sufficiently platitudinous; and it is platitudinous that 'is' is being used in different senses when it is being used for different parts of speech (just as it is platitudinous that 'hail' has not quite the same meaning in 'The hail was two inches thick' and 'It will probably hail tomorrow'). The theory ceases to be platitudinous, and in my view ceases also to be true, when it is alleged that 'is' has different senses in, say, 'The man next door is' and 'The property of living next door is'. These make different assertions, for the man next door is one thing and the property of living next door is quite another thing, and another kind of thing too; but both 'are' in the same sense of 'are'. How such a view as this may be maintained without paradox has been sufficiently shown by Quine in *New Foundations*; but Quine has missed the truth in the other, the 'platitudinous', theory of types. Not that Quine argues that the operator 'For some φ, $\varphi(\ \ )$' must be a verb no matter what kind of operator the variable φ can stand for. What must always be a verb, on Quine's view, is what goes into the blank of 'For some x, $(\ \ )$ x', no matter what kind of expression the variable x may stand for. Or rather, he seems to hold that there is only one kind of expression the x here can stand for; to bind a variable by a quantifier is (on his

view) *ipso facto* to treat it as a name-variable. What other interpretation can we put on his argument that although no belief in 'nameable' abstract objects is involved in the use of verbs, such a belief is involved as soon as we bind verb-variables by quantifiers? The view here adopted is, rather, that the syntactical function or category of the operator 'For some x, ( ) x', like that of the operator 'For some φ, φ( )' or '( ) is', varies as the syntactical function of x and φ varies. If x is a name-variable, then 'For some x, ( ) x' is an operator on operators on names, i.e. on verbs; but if x is something else, then 'For some x, ( ) x' is something else too.

15. We can, then, admit 'different but analogical' senses of 'is' if 'is' is so oddly used that its uses are different parts of speech. But we can also admit cases in which 'is' has different but analogical senses although it is in a way (but in a queer way) a verb both times. This is connected with another point, namely that we can find a sense in which 'Pegasus is' is tautologically true even within the strict Russellian framework, i.e. even when it is taken to mean '(Exactly one thing is a winged horse of Bellerophon and if anything is a winged horse of Bellerophon it) is'. But before returning to Pegasus, let us have a second look at the operator T of Section 6. In that section we found ourselves in grave trouble through regarding the form 'It is not the case that . . . p' as a form of statement, i.e. as a possible argument of such operators as 'If—then—'. But if we treat the operator 'If—then—' as the argument and Tp as a higher-order operator upon it, i.e. if we replace the DT of Section 6 by

$$\text{Df. T: } (Tp)\varphi = N\varphi p,$$

our troubles disappear. We cannot now replace p by Tp in the law Vp, as Tp is not a statement; VTp, in fact, is so far from being a logical law that it has not the form of a proposition. The fact that the form NVp, 'It is not the case that if p then p' can be thought of as constructed out of the operator 'If—then—' by means of 'It is not the case that . . . p', is not now expressed by equating it to VTp but by equating it to $(Tp)V$; and there is of course no substitution which will turn Vp into this. Further, if δ is any statement-forming operator on statements, $(\delta(Tp))\varphi$ will always be equivalent to $\delta((Tp)\varphi)$. In particular, $(V(Tp))\varphi$ is equivalent to $V((Tp)\varphi)$. And from this we may see that although $V(Tp)$ is not a form of statement, it is not without meaning—it is, like Tp itself, an operator on operators on statements. It means 'If it is not the case that . . . p, then it is not the case that . . . p'; and although it is not itself a tautology, it always forms tautologies (e.g. when attached to the argument 'it is not the case that', it forms the tautology 'If not not p then not not p').

16. Quite similarly, although we run into trouble if we treat 'Not every man' or 'The winged horse of Bellerophon' (as expanded by Russell), as names, on which verbs operate to form statements, we encounter no such trouble if we treat them as statement-forming operators which take verbs as arguments. And from them we can form, by the attachment of V, the tautology-forming operators on verbs 'If not every man—, then not every man—' and 'If the winged horse of Bellerophon—, then the winged horse of Bellerophon—', it being understood that the same verb, e.g. 'smokes', is to go into both blanks. By means of these special cases of φ, we could prove, in the manner of Section 4, the theorem 'For some φ, φ(smokes)', or 'Smokes is', in our wide sense of 'is'. This does not assert that some individual smokes—that assertion would be, rather, 'For some x, (smokes) x', and of course is no logical law, though it is true enough. 'For some φ, φ (smokes)' is not translatable from English-and-Mathematics into plain English ('Smokes is' is not plain English, at all events not yet); but it is equivalent to the assertion that some statement in which 'smokes' occurs, e.g. 'If anyone smokes he smokes,' is true. (It is not the same as this assertion, for it says nothing about the word 'smokes', any more than 'Socrates acts somehow' says anything about the word 'Socrates', though it is equivalent to the assertion that some statement in which 'Socrates' occurs, e.g. 'Socrates smokes if he smokes', is true, i.e. it is true if and only if some such statement is true.)

17. 'The winged horse of Bellerophon', then, in its Russellian sense, is not a name but an operator on operators on names. There are also operators on operators on operators on names; and grammatically these often have the same form as operators on names, i.e. as verbs. For example, the verbal form 'If—smokes then—smokes' could represent an operator on operators on verbs, i.e. it could have

for its argument such expressions as 'not every man' and 'the winged horse of Bellerophon'; or it could represent a verb, being then equivalent to '—smokes-if-it-smokes'. Considered as a verb, it yields a falsehood when 'The winged horse of Bellerophon' is attached to it, and a contradiction when 'Not every man' is attached to it. But considered as an operator on operators on verbs, it yields a tautology in both cases. And in this latter sense of it, '$(V\varphi)$(not every man)' and '$(V\varphi)$(the winged horse of Bellerophon)' are equivalent to '$V(\varphi$(not every man))' and '$V(\varphi$(the winged horse of Bellerophon))'. Hence we can prove, by the method of Section 4, 'For some φ, φ (the winged horse of Bellerophon)', or 'The winged horse of Bellerophon is', and for that matter 'Not-every-man-is', provided that our φ, and consequently our 'is', be of the right sort. This 'is', we might say, is a verb in the sense, but only in the sense, in which 'It is not the case that . . . grass is green' is a statement. So long as this be understood, we can claim that 'Pegasus is' is a tautology even in the system of *Principia Mathematica*. Even Bertrand sober, it would seem, is not as sober as he pretends to be.[1]

---

[1] This paper was originally to have appeared in 1955. I withdrew it from publication for reasons which then seemed good to me but now [1962] do not seem to me to have any force. I ought to say, though, that I no longer agree with the 'Platonism' expressed in some asides in Sections 11, 12 and especially 14. The main position of the paper, which I still adhere to, is equally consistent with that 'Platonism' and with the view that 'is' has different senses in 'The man that lives next door is' and in 'Living next door is', and that the change of 'lives next door' into 'living next door' plus the addition of 'is' amounts to precisely the non-verbal sense of 'is' in the sentence 'Lives next door is' of the language that the paper proposes. The second paragraph of Section 9 now seems to me, for other reasons, a little *simpliste*.

13. *What is Logic?*

The precise problem which I wish to raise might be put like this:
Consider the following three sets of statements;

A (1) If Polly is an animal then Polly is an animal.
  (2) If Polly is a feathered animal then Polly is an animal.
  (3) If all feathered animals breathe air then what does not breathe air is not a feathered animal.

B (1) If Polly is a feathered animal she breathes air.
  (2) If Polly has feelings, I am obliged to treat her kindly.
  (3) If Polly isn't my parrot, she's Peter's.

C (1) If there are parrots, there will always have been parrots.
  (2) If I know that Polly breathes air, she does breathe air.
  (3) If I am obliged to treat Polly kindly, then I am not obliged not to treat Polly kindly.
  (4) If it is not possible for Polly not to be a parrot, then it is possible for her to be a parrot.

Between A(1)–(3) on the one hand and B(1)–(3) on the other there is a difference which I think all of us immediately feel, and which is often expressed by saying that A(1)–(3) are *logically true*, while B(1)–(3), if true at all, are not logically true but only factually true. In the case of C(1)–(4) it is not so clear what we ought to say. Some may be inclined in particular cases, e.g. C(4), to plump definitely this way or that; but there is enough doubt about at least some members of this group for us to wish for some clear definition or criterion of logical truth which will enable us to make up our minds. That is what I want now to look for; and it will be sensible to start by considering some of the main things that other people have had to say on the subject.

122

In the first place we can hardly ignore the theory that logically true statements are ones which owe their truth entirely to the way in which we have chosen to speak, while factually true statements are true because that is how things really are. This account of the matter seems to me a muddle: I cannot see how any statement whatever can be made true simply by using language in a particular way, except, of course, the statement *that we are* using language in the way in question, and nobody would contend that a statement to this effect would be logically true—it is not logically necessary that we should speak in such and such a way.

What we have in this story seems to me a muddied reflection of quite a different distinction, namely that between a statement and a proposal. To make a statement about birds is one thing, and to propose that nothing be called a 'bird' unless it has feathers is quite another thing. In particular, statements about birds are true or false, but any proposal, such as the proposal to call nothing a bird unless it has feathers, can only be odd or ordinary or useful or tiresome, never true or false. Nor is any such proposal in itself sufficient to make *anything else* true or false. If we agree to call feathered animals and only feathered animals 'birds', this will turn the statement 'All birds breathe air' into a way of saying that all feathered animals breathe air, which is true, but not in the least because we have agreed to call feathered animals 'birds'. And similarly, if we agree to use the word 'bird' in this way, this will turn the statement 'All birds are animals' into a way of saying that all feathered animals are animals; which again is true, and this time logically true, but not in the least because we have agreed to call feathered animals 'birds'. That all feathered animals are animals would be just as true, and logically true too, if the word 'bird' had never been invented.

Nor, so far as I can see, is the truth of 'All feathered animals are animals' due solely to the way we have agreed to use the word 'all', or the truth of 'If Polly is an animal then Polly is an animal' due solely to the way we have agreed to use the word 'if'. Certainly if we used the word 'if' differently the truth-value of the latter sentence might be altered, but so might the truth-value of 'I have toothache' be altered if we used the word 'toothache' to mean 'brown eyes', though nobody would say that whether I have toothache or not, or whether I have brown eyes or not, depends at all on linguistic usage. I might, indeed, explain the meaning of the word 'If', that is *my* meaning of it, to another person, by saying that I am using it in such a way that anything of the form 'If *p* then *p*', together with statements of certain other forms, is true. But this explanation will fail to explain unless there *is* a way of using the word 'If', and one which the other person knows about, which is such that statements of the form 'If *p* then *p*' are always true. And of course I can give this sort of explanation, with the same proviso, of other words too, even nonlogical words like 'toothache'.

Further, even if one did not have to make this proviso, in deducing the truth of 'If Polly is an animal then Polly is an animal' from my explanation of the word 'If' I have to apply the principle of the syllogism; I have to argue that since anything of the form 'If *p* then *p*' is true by my convention, and the statement about Polly is of this form, this statement is true; and I must similarly use the principle of syllogism in any case in which I give a *general description* of what statements I am making true and not a *complete list*. Hence the truth of the principle of syllogism cannot itself be explained along these lines.

There is, indeed, a negative truth in the contention that 'If Polly is an animal Polly is an animal' is true solely because of the way we use the word 'If'. It is true at least that there is no *other* word on whose meaning it depends. Its truth does not depend, for example, on what particular creature we are calling 'Polly'. And this leads us to another account that has sometimes been given of logical truth. So far as the statement that if Polly is an animal then Polly is an animal is about anything, it is about Polly; but we do have some disposition to say that it is *not* about Polly. It is at least not *distinctively* about Polly; it tells us nothing about Polly that could not be said with equal truth about any other creature; it is, to use the current technical term, only *vacuously* about Polly.

But this is not in itself enough to make our example a *logical* truth about Polly. For example, our statement B(1), that if Polly is a feathered animal then Polly breathes air, is only vacuously about Polly, for it is a fact of nature, so far as I know, that if *anything* is a feathered animal it breathes air—there are no feathered animals that *don't* breathe air. Yet I don't suppose anyone wants to lift this statement from the B list into the A list. The point about A(1), by contrast with B(1), is that with A(1) it not only doesn't matter what creature we are calling 'Polly'; it doesn't matter what it is to be an animal either; only the 'If', and of course the identity with one another of the antecedent and consequent, must not be tampered with. So now what we want to say is that a truth is a logical truth if all the words used in its statement occur vacuously except the logical words. But this is obviously no more than a buck-passing solution—what is a *logical* word?

Perhaps, though, an answer can be given to this question—the question what a logical word is—without referring back to logical truths. It might be thought, for example, that logical words are words of a certain degree of abstraction. No proper names, it might be said, are logical words; nor are any verbs, that is, expressions which construct statements out of proper names. But expressions like quantifiers which construct statements out of verbs, or ones like 'if' which construct statements out of other statements, are logical words. This will not do, however. For the expressions

Aristotle thought that—
That—is more surprising to me than that—

construct statements out of other statements, but are certainly not expressions belonging to logic; while on the other hand the expression

—does whatever—does,

or in other words

—is identical with—,

almost certainly *is* a logical expression, although it is an operator forming statements out of names, in other words a verb.

Sometimes—to turn to another proposed solution—it is said that a logical truth is one which does not function in inference as a *premiss from which* a conclusion is drawn, but only as a *principle according to which* the conclusion is drawn. This distinction is certainly important; as Lewis Carroll has shown, if we don't make it we shall never be able to find premisses enough for any inference at all. But it is one thing to distinguish, in any given argument, between the premisses and the principle of the inference, and quite another thing—and a much more dubious thing—to say that there are some truths which can only be used in inference as premisses and others which can only be used as principles. In the first place, logicians are constantly inferring a logical truth from one or more other truths; there are in fact innumerable complicated logical truths of which we should never have known had they not been deduced in this way. Moreover we infer logical truths in accordance with the very same principles, such as the principle of syllogism, which we use in everyday argument from perfectly contingent premisses. And on the other hand, I see no reason why the inference 'Polly is a feathered animal, therefore Polly breathes air', should not be considered a perfectly complete and valid argument proceeding in accordance with the principle that all feathered animals breathe air. If we deny this, we can only explain our denial by saying that the only truths which we count as principles of inference are *logical* truths: but this deprives of the right to explain what a logical truth is by referring to the premiss-principle distinction.

C. S. Peirce, indeed, has a curious device which purports to establish a clear distinction between what he calls 'logical leading principles' and other leading principles. Take the argument

> Polly is a feathered animal
> Therefore Polly breathes air,

which proceeds in accordance with the principle that if anything is a feathered animal it breathes air. We could, if we wished, use this last truth as a further premiss, and infer in accordance with the principle of syllogism. But suppose we make *this* a premiss, and argue thus

> Any object and pair of properties such that whatever has the first property has the second and the object has the first property, are such that the object has the second property;
> Polly, feathered animality and breathing air are an object and a pair of properties such that whatever has the first property has the second and the object has the first property;
> Therefore Polly, feathered animality and breathing air are such that the object has the second property.

Then the principle used here is once again the principle of syllogism. Peirce argues that as soon as we find ourselves doubling back on ourselves in this fashion when we turn a principle into a premiss, we know that what we have is a 'logical' leading principle. So far as I can see, however, this dodge gives us *only* the principle of syllogism; that is what we get back to in the end this way, simply because inferring in accordance with a principle is one kind of application of a rule, and the principle of applying rules to cases falling under them *is* the principle of syllogism.

We might, nevertheless, find a suggestion here of a better criterion; and one which was used by Peirce in practice. So far as I can see, a truth which is being used as a principle of inference *must* be a universal implication—it must be that in order to function as a *rule* at all. Universality and implicativeness, therefore, are common to all principles of inference, however 'material' or 'non-logical' they might be; so we might define logical truths as ones in whose statement all signs occur vacuously except signs of universality and implication. This does give us something pretty comprehensive. If 'implication' be used in the minimum sense, we can introduce negation as a complex of implication and universality; 'It is not the case that p' amounts to 'If p then anything at all'. Now the whole logic of truth-functions can be developed in terms of implication and negation; and with universality and negation we have the whole theory of quantification.

What sort of ruling would this give us for some of our doubtful cases—my examples of type C? We might try to exhibit some of them as just special cases of the laws of truth-functional and quantificational logic. For example, my first one, 'If there are parrots, there will always have been parrots', might be said to be just a way of saying

'If there are parrots at this present time x, then for any time y which is later than x, there is some time, than which y is later, at which there are parrots',

or in symbols

$$C\varphi x\Pi y C\psi yx\Sigma x K\psi yx\varphi z.$$

In other words, it is of exactly the same form as

> 'If Sally is a housemaid, then anyone who loves Sally has someone whom he loves who is a housemaid.'

That is, all signs occur vacuously in this except the quantifiers and truth-functional connectives, all ultimately definable in terms of universality and implication.

I admit that you *might* deal with this example in this way, but I think there are objections. For the same method of analysing statements with tenses would justify us in saying, on the basis of propositional logic and quantification theory alone, that

> 'If there are parrots, there have always been going to be parrots'

is a logical truth, and I personally don't think this is necessarily true at all. Before God, or whoever it is that is responsible for these things, had decided to make parrots, 'There are going to be parrots' wasn't true at all, I think, but at best neuter in truth-value. And no logic of tenses which takes the difference between past and future seriously can be reduced to propositional calculus and quantification theory.

Some writers have attempted to represent modal logic also as a kind of disguised quantification theory—perhaps with quantification over 'possible states of affairs'. I don't myself think that this will do either, though I won't develop my objections to it now. And quite certainly the logic of obligation and the logic of knowledge cannot be represented in this way.

So what I am inclined to say is that the term 'logic' admits of a strict and a loose sense. In its strictest sense, logic studies the properties of implication and universality; in a looser sense, it concerns itself with principles of inference generally, in all sorts of fields. But there is a difficulty in this account. As I mentioned earlier, even the truth that all feathered animals breathe air *can* be used as a principle of inference, so ought we to talk about not only a logic of time, a logic of obligation, a logic of knowledge, and things like that, but even a logic of organic life? Well, in principle I don't see why not—Professor Toulmin sometimes talks rather like that, and there's something to be said for it. One of the main jobs of biologists is to discover which properties of living things have plenty of consequences, in other words which properties of living things can be safely used in making inferences about them, and which can not, and this surely *is* learning a logic of a sort.

I do not want to be able to say, though, that there is some kind of a gradation in these things—that there is somehow *more* point, for example, in talking about a logic of time and tenses than there is in talking about a logic of organic life. The truth that if there are parrots there will always have been parrots, even if it is *not* reducible to a special case in quantification theory—and I don't myself think it *is* so reducible—is nevertheless *more* like a logical truth (or even, more of a logical truth) than the truth that all feathered animals breathe air. But I don't think that there's anything better to be said here than that some subjects do in fact have more order, more structure, more form, than others—that some subjects are more capable than others of being handled by means of a formal symbolic calculus—and in these cases it is more proper than in others to speak of a 'logic' of the thing. It is certainly profitable to construct a calculus for handling times and tenses; it seems profitable also to construct a calculus for handling some truths about obligation, though not very concrete ones; we are also beginning now to get formalisations of classical and relativity physics and of parts of economics; about a logic of biology I am rather more sceptical, though Woodger has attempted it. In any case the important point is that these things are a matter of degree, and the only way to discover whether a given field can be handled as a logic, that is as the subject of a calculus, and how far it can be so handled, is to try it out and see what happens. You can't settle the question *a priori*.

14. Some Problems of Self-reference in John Buridan

In all the periods in which their subject has been in a flourishing condition, logicians have devoted considerable attention to paradoxes involving self-reference. In this preoccupation, it is easy to accuse them of pedantry and even of frivolity; but such accusations are a mistake. Some of the paradoxes of Buridan even have a certain grim relevance to our practical predicaments in this nuclear age, and as it were bring together the Russell who gave us his part of *Principia Mathematica* and the Russell who worries about world peace. But even apart from that, paradoxes about self-reference present exceptions or apparent exceptions to logical generalisations of great persuasiveness, and any logician with a scientific conscience is bound to take them seriously.

The puzzles of this sort which I shall be considering in this lecture come from the eighth chapter of Buridan's *Sophismata*.[1] This treatise, like medieval logical treatises generally, is rather unsystematic by modern standards, and we have to gather what Buridan's leading principles are as we go along; its acuteness lies in its details, and in Buridan's eye for ingenious objections to inadequate solutions. The skill of modern logicians, and indeed of some ancient logicians, in developing not only particular proofs and disproofs but large deductive systems, is something which seems to me wholly admirable; but it is useful, and I think it even makes for the construction of better systems in the end, if this activity is continually interrupted by bouts of the philosophic niggling at which the schoolmen were masters, and Buridan perhaps one of the greatest masters.

[1] I should like here to thank Mr Peter Geach for not only drawing my attention to this chapter but sending me a copy of it when I was working on these problems in some isolation in New Zealand.

Chapter 8 of the *Sophismata* contains some twenty 'sophisms' or debatable sentences or arguments, which fall successively into a few broad groups. There are to begin with one or two which involve the notions of logical consequence and possibility; for example, he inquires into the validity of the inference 'No proposition is negative, therefore some proposition is negative'. This hinges on the question whether it is possible that no proposition should be negative, the argument against it being that if the proposition 'No proposition is negative' were ever true it would be false, since it is itself a negative proposition. Then there is a small group about propositions which occur as parts of other propositions, as in 'I say that a man is a donkey'—if a man thus says, not that a man is a donkey, but only *that he says that* a man is a donkey, is he right or wrong? After this group we have Buridan's variations on the ancient paradox of the Liar. He asks whether the proposition 'Every proposition is false' would itself be true or false if enunciated when all *other* propositions were certainly false; and again, whether Socrates and Plato speak truly or falsely if Socrates says 'What Plato says is false', and nothing else, and Plato says 'What Socrates says is false', and nothing else; whether Plato speaks truly or falsely if under the same conditions he says 'What Socrates says is *true*', and says nothing else; whether a man speaks truly or falsely if he says 'There are exactly as many true propositions as false ones' when the only other propositions are two obviously true ones and one obviously false; whether a man utters a falsehood or a truth if he simply says 'I am uttering a falsehood' and says nothing else (this is, of course, the original 'Liar' paradox); and finally, whether the conjunctive proposition 'God exists and some conjunctive proposition is false' is true or false if it is the only conjunctive proposition there is. After this we have a group involving the notions of knowledge, doubt and belief. Suppose we say that a proposition is in doubt with a person if and only if he neither knows that it is true nor knows that it is false. Then we can suppose that the proposition 'Socrates knows that the proposition written on the wall is in doubt with him' is written on a certain wall, and nothing else is written there, and Socrates sees it and wonders whether it is true or false, and knows that he is doing this. Buridan asks whether in this case the proposition on the wall would be true or false.

After some further examples of this last sort, Buridan has a final section in which he considers puzzles arising not with statements but with questions, wishes, promises, &c. He asks, for example, what we are to make of the answer 'No' to the question 'Will you answer this question negatively?' Then he considers a situation in which Plato promises to let people over a certain bridge if and only if the first thing they say to him is true, and to throw them in the river if and only if what they say to him is false, and Socrates says to him, 'You will throw me in the river'. This is a puzzle of some literary interest, since there is a very similar one in *Don Quixote*— Sancho Panza, as governor of an island, is asked to adjudicate in a case where people who cross a certain bridge are hanged if they state their purpose falsely, and let go if they state it truly, and a man announces as *his* purpose that he has come over to be hanged.[1] To finish up with, there are three puzzles about conflicting conditional wishes. For example, Socrates wishes to eat if and only if Plato wishes to eat, but Plato wishes to eat if and only if Socrates does *not* wish to eat. This is where we begin to be reminded of contemporary problems of high politics.

I shall not be discussing this last group of puzzles here, but will concentrate on some of the more elementary ones. And before examining some of Buridan's solutions in detail I want to jump the centuries and, for comparison's sake, briefly survey the treatment that such self-reflective paradoxes have received in our own time. In the preface to the first edition of Whitehead and Russell's *Principia Mathematica* some seven 'contradictions' of this sort are listed, and there is said to be in all of them 'a common characteristic, which we may describe as self-reference or reflexiveness'.[2] F. P. Ramsey, in his 1925 paper on *The Foundations of Mathematics*, divided these into two sharply demarcated groups, of which the first 'consists of contradictions which, were no provision made against them, would occur in a logical or mathematical system itself', while those in the second group 'all contain some reference to thought, language or symbolism'.[3] Typical of the first group is Russell's

---

[1] Miguel de Cervantes, *Adventures of Don Quixote de la Mancha*, ch. li (cited in Alonzo Church, *Introduction to Mathematical Logic*, Exercise 15. 10).

[2] Alfred North Whitehead and Bertrand Russell, *Principia Mathematica*, 1st ed., vol. i (1910) pp. 63 ff.

[3] F. P. Ramsey, *The Foundations of Mathematics and Other Logical Essays* (1931), p. 20.

paradox of the class of all classes which are not members of them-selves—this class being, on the face of it, a member of itself if it is not, and not a member of itself if it is. Typical of the second group is the paradox of the Liar—the man who says 'What I am saying is false', and says nothing else, his statement being, on the face of it, true if it is false and false if it is true.

The 'provision' which Ramsey had in mind for preventing our logic and mathematics from being disfigured by paradoxes of the first sort, was the so-called 'simple theory of types'. Here the paradoxes are resolved by denying that classes of classes are classes at all in the sense in which classes of individuals are. This view is usually associated with the view that classes are in any case 'logical fictions', talk about classes being only an oblique but often handy way of talking about individuals. Thus understood, the theory of types is basically a theory of 'syntactical categories' or, in a broad sense, 'parts of speech'. To say that x is a member of the class of smokers is not really to relate two objects, x and the class of smokers, but is simply to say, approximately, that x smokes, where 'smokes' is not a name but a verb, that is an expression which forms sentences out of names. To say (no doubt falsely) that the class of smokers is a member of the class of 6-membered classes is again not to relate two objects, or even any objects, but simply to say, approximately, that exactly six individuals smoke, where the prefix 'Exactly six indi-viduals' is neither a name nor a verb but a higher-type expression, a numerical quantifier in fact, which forms sentences out of verbs. Talk of classes being members of themselves then expands to a form in which we make some verb its own subject—a form with a bit in it like 'smokes smokes'—which just does not construe, or as the logicians say is 'ill-formed'.

This may seem an awful lot of grammar for dealing with para-doxes of Ramsey's *first* type, but remember that what is being straightened out here is our talk about individuals and classes and numbers; what has to be straightened out to get rid of the other group of paradoxes is our talk about talk. And their solution is usually understood to require not merely a hierarchy of syntactical categories or parts of speech, but a hierarchy of languages. Sen-tences which are true or false are always true or false in some language, and *that* they are true or false is not itself true or false in that language but in some higher one. These might not be different languages in any ordinary sense, but rather different levels or stages of a single one, but the point remains that an assertion *about* the truth or falsehood of a sentence cannot itself be true or false in the language or level or stage of a language to which the sentence itself belongs. For this reason no sentence can directly or indirectly assert its own falsehood, or for that matter its own truth. This hierarchy of languages is a very fundamental conception in, for example, Tarski's well-known monograph on Truth.[1]

Even before Ramsey wrote his paper there were known to be alternatives to the theory of types as a method of handling the strictly mathematical or logical paradoxes, and some of these alternatives have been very fully developed since. In particular it is perfectly possible to treat classes of individuals, classes of classes, &c., as nameable objects in exactly the same sense as individuals are, provided that we do not over-simplify the relations between objects of these various sorts. One may, for instance, refuse to equate simply φ-ing with being a member of the class of φ-ers, and one may hold, e.g. that the class of classes which are not members of themselves is-not-a-member-of-itself and yet is not a member of the *class* of classes-which-are-not-members-of-themselves. Zermelo's set theory and the modifications of it which have been made by von Neumann and Quine are well-known systems of this broad type.[2]

On the side of the puzzles which Ramsey has classified as linguistic rather than logical or mathematical, the most important development since his time has been the clear demonstration by Gödel, Carnap and others that there is a great deal that *can* be said within a given language or language-level about that language or language-level itself, e.g. we can talk within a language about that language's grammatical structure. What is still generally disallowed, in order to eliminate contradictions, is talk within a language about its relation to the rest of the world, and in particular about questions of the meaning and truth of expressions within it. Taking one of Buridan's examples, a modern logician would insist that the proposition that the proposition 'No proposition is negative' is *true* must belong to a higher language-stratum than that proposition itself, but the proposition that it is *negative* is one that *can* be framed

[1] Alfred Tarski, 'The concept of truth in formalised languages', Item VIII in *Logic, Semantics and Metamathematics* (1956).
[2] See, e.g. W. V. Quine, *From a Logical Point of View* (1953), Item V.

within the very language-stratum in which the proposition itself is framed.

There has also been considerable interest in recent years in what are called 'pragmatic' paradoxes, involving personal attitudes like belief and knowledge. Particular attention has been given, under this head, to a puzzle which appears in the literature in a variety of dramatic guises, e.g. the story is told of a prisoner who is sentenced to be hanged on some one of a number of days, but who is told when he is sentenced that he will not know which day it is until the time comes. He works out that it cannot be the last day because then, all the other days having passed, he would know beforehand that it was going to happen that day. He then successively eliminates the other days in the same way, but is nevertheless hanged on one of them, and unexpectedly too. There is no general agreement as to how paradoxes of this sort are to be solved or classified.

It seems to me useful to bear in mind these broad features of current work when examining Buridan's treatment of the same and allied topics, but we would be wise *not* to take it for granted that we know all the answers better than he did; and with a little open-mindedness I think we can find in him not only the material for new formal exercises but also suggestions towards new solutions of our problems. And I shall devote a good deal of time to simply *discussing* Buridan's theories as if he were present and one of us—on the general principle that there is much less to be learnt from the history of philosophy as history than there is from the people we meet in it.

One of the most striking contrasts between Buridan's discussion and, for example, Russell's is the complete absence from Buridan's chapter of any puzzles falling into Ramsey's first or logico-mathematical group. In an earlier chapter of the same work there is indeed something that could be construed in this way. This is the fourth *sophisma* in Chapter 3, to the effect that there is a wider *genus* than the widest one, for the term *genus* itself covers both the widest *genus* and all the less wide ones besides. A distinction between classes of individuals and classes of classes seems clearly called for here, but Buridan's own solution is very brief and not very satisfactory—he seems to think that the secret lies in the distinction between the *word* 'genus' and what the word signifies. Ramsey could have put him right here.

In the eighth chapter, all the puzzles considered do fall into Ramsey's second or linguistic group, apart perhaps from the ones near the end about doubting, &c., which modern writers would classify as 'pragmatic'. It is significant here that Buridan almost invariably uses the term *propositio* to mean simply a bit of language, a spoken or written sentence—a particular noise or inscription. And he never forgets that the very existence of 'propositions' in this sense is a contingent matter, and speaks quite freely of the *annihilation* of propositions (asking what would be the case, for example, if all negative propositions were annihilated). There is just no trace in him of the use of the term 'proposition' to mean, not a sentence, but a supposed abstract entity of which the sentence, or the corresponding 'that' clause, is a name. Nor does he appear to believe that there *are* entities of this sort. There is, indeed, a passage in the discussion of his seventh *sophisma* in which he might seem to hold that *true* sentences do name such abstract entities but *false* sentences do not, and he even at this one point uses the word *propositio* for what does not exist when a sentence is false. He makes in this passage the strange remark *hominem esse asinum nihil est*, and the context makes it clear that he would have equally said *hominem esse animal aliquid est*. It is quite clear from what he says elsewhere, however, particularly under his sixth *sophisma*, that he would *not* have meant by this that there is an abstract entity of which the expression 'that a man is an animal' is a name. The *aliquid* that the expression *hominem esse animal* and even the sentence *homo est animal* stands for is not an abstract entity but simply a *man*, a man being an animal, and *hominem esse asinum* or *homo est asinus* in this sense stands for nothing because there is no such object as a man being a donkey.

What is really illuminating in Buridan, however, is not this rather curious material about what sentences 'stand for' but his treatment of the question as to what they *mean* or signify. What he does is not so much to answer this question as to transpose it. The transposition comes out most clearly in his account of what it is for a sentence to be true. A sentence is true if and only if *sicut significat, ita est*, or as he sometimes says if *qualiter significat, ita est*; this, though, is only a first approximation—the final version is: *qualitercumque significat, ita est*. This is not easy to put into English, but the important point is that Buridan does not say that a sentence is true if and only if *what* it signifies, or *whatever* it signifies, is so or is the case; what he says is rather that a sentence is true if and only if *however* it signifies that things are, *thus* they are. He gets rid of the suggestion of *objects* that are signified by sentences by beginning his definition not with a generalised noun but with a generalised adverb, *qualitercumque*.

What this means, in modern terms, is that the hierarchy of parts of speech is relevant not only to our talk about classes and the like, but also to our talk about meaning. Modern writers have seen this also; for example, Russell in his 1924 paper on 'Logical Atomism' says this: 'When two words have meanings of different logical types, the relations of the words to what they mean are of different types; that is to say, there is not one relation of meaning between words and what they stand for, but as many relations of meaning, each of a different logical type, as there are logical types among the objects for which they are words.'[1] By current standards even this, with its easy talk of 'objects' of different logical types and of 'relations' of meaning which hold in each case, is extremely loose and a little misleading, but I think we can put what Russell is getting at in the following way: In spite of some recent objections, I think it can be argued that what a proper name means is simply the object that it names—'Fido', the name, means or names Fido the dog. But a verb cannot have this sort of meaning, for verbs do not name anything, and if we wrote, for example, ' "Runs" means runs' this would just be a senseless sentence, with two verbs and only one subject. In English and other languages we invent abstract nouns to meet this difficulty, and we could say that 'runs' means or signifies the activity of running, or more shortly that 'runs' means running. But we misunderstand the function of abstract nouns if we think that there is an object called 'running' which the verb 'runs' names, or even does something else to ('connotes' it or what have you). The fact of the matter is that here the word 'means' has no meaning in itself but is just part of the expression 'means (blank)-*ing*', which constructs a sentence not out of two names but out of a name and a verb. When we come to the meaning of *sentences*, the word 'means' is again without meaning on its own, but is part of the expression 'means *that*', which constructs a sentence not out of two names but out of a name and a sentence—'A man is a donkey' *means that* a man is a donkey. So we need not ask what is named by the clause 'that a man is a donkey'; the word 'that' does not belong here but with the

[1] Bertrand Russell, *Logic and Knowledge*, pp. 332–3.

'means' that precedes it, and what is left, 'a man is a donkey', names nothing because it is not a name but a (subordinate) sentence.

After this excursion into grammar, we can re-state Buridan's definition of truth as follows: A sentence x is a true one if and only if for any p, if x means that p, then it is the case that p; or more shortly, if for any p, if x means that p, then p. This is much simpler than any of Tarski's definitions of truth for the various languages that he considers. It ought in fairness to be added that part of Tarski's aim was to avoid the use of 'intensional' conceptions like that of 'meaning'; but it is certainly worth noting that if we do not restrict ourselves in this way, and get our grammar straight, it *is* possible to define 'true' very straightforwardly.

Does Buridan's definition, however, avoid the necessity of a language-hierarchy? On the face of it, it does not, but merely traces the systematic ambiguity of 'true' to a similar ambiguity in the more basic conception of 'meaning'. And I am not now referring to the different syntactical types involved in the meaning of different types of expression, but to the ambiguity which still seems to remain when we confine our attention to the meaning of *sentences*, i.e. to the sort of meaning that is always a meaning *that* something-or-other. For suppose I utter the sentence 'The sentence I am uttering is false', and utter no other sentence; then it would appear that what this sentence means, and all that it means, is *that* the sentence I am uttering is false, and this is therefore true, by the definition of 'truth' just given, if and only if the sentence I am uttering *is* false, and we are back with the 'Liar' paradox. It therefore seems necessary to say that 'meaning that p' must always be 'meaning in a language L that p'; and *that* a sentence means in a language L that p, cannot itself be said by a sentence of the language L.

Buridan, as we have seen, was as familiar with the 'Liar' paradox, and variations upon it, as anyone has ever been, and indeed it is precisely in this context that his definition of truth appears. Language-hierarchies of the systematic type that we meet with in such writers as Tarski are a comparatively modern invention, but Buridan does consider and reject certain solutions which it would be easy to put into the language-hierarchy form. For example, when considering the proposition 'Every proposition is false', supposed to have been put forward by Socrates after all other propositions had been annihilated but false ones, he says that we might understand the proposition of Socrates simply as a comment on everything that was being said in the time just preceding its own appearance on the scene, and then it would be quite straightforwardly true. But, he very properly asks, what happens if we *don't* understand it in this way, but understand it as referring to all propositions in being *at the time*, itself included? He tells us that according to some it just cannot be so understood, because in a proposition which contains terms which themselves stand for propositions, these terms cannot stand for that proposition itself but only for all others. This, however, Buridan says, won't do, for *quod aliquis intelligit, de illo potest loqui*, and as it is certainly possible for someone to think about all propositions whatsoever (past, present, and to come), what he thinks about them can be expressed in a proposition, which will inevitably be itself among those intended.

What else, then, can we do about these paradoxes? Buridan mentions, but rejects out of hand, the solution that some propositions can after all be true and false at once. He then mentions another, which he says that he himself formerly thought satisfactory, to the effect that every proposition, whatever else it may signify or assert, signifies or asserts, by its very form as a proposition, that it is itself true. Any proposition, therefore, which asserts or implies its own falsehood asserts both its falsehood and its truth, and is bound to be in fact false, since at least *something* that it asserts to be the case is not so. We cannot pass back from its falsehood, thus established, to the conclusion that it is after all true, since it says that it is false and things are as it says they are; for things are not *entirely* as it says they are, part of what it says being that it is true.

To this former view of his own, Buridan now objects that propositions do *not* in general signify in virtue of their very form that they are themselves true, because if you take, say, the proposition 'A man is an animal', its terms are 'of first intention', i.e. non-linguistic, while the proposition 'The proposition "A man is an animal" is true' contains terms 'of second intention', i.e. terms referring to pieces of language. Buridan is led by these considerations to distinguish between what a proposition 'formally' signifies and what it 'virtually' signifies. What it 'virtually' signifies is what follows from the proposition itself together with a proposition correctly describing the circumstances of its utterance. In particular, from a proposition *x* together with the proposition 'The proposition *x* exists' we may infer the proposition 'The proposition *x* is true'. And a proposition is only true if all that it signifies, formally *or* virtually, is so. From this point on the argument is very much as before, but I shall not follow it out in detail because this later position of Buridan's seems open to a quite fundamental objection. Since he employs this term 'formal signification' in such a sense that 'What I am now saying is false', for example, formally signifies that what I am now saying is false, and nothing else, we can re-state the paradox in terms of formal signification without bringing in truth and falsehood at all. We simply suppose a person to say 'What is formally signified by this sentence is not the case', and ask about this sentence, not whether it is true or false, but whether things are or are not as it formally signifies that they are, and the answer is that they are if they aren't and they aren't if they are.

This is a transformation of the paradox which suggests itself more readily to a modern logician, accustomed to the use of abstract symbolism, than it would to a medieval one. Suppose I write 'It is φ that *p*' for *any* sentence formed from the sentence '*p*', for example 'It is not the case that *p*', 'It is possible that *p*', 'It is signified by the sentence *x* that *p*', 'It is feared by the person *y* that *p*', &c., I can then construct the following formula:

It is φ that , for any *p*, if it is φ that *p*, then it is not the case that *p*; and for no other *p* is it φ that *p*.

From anything of this form it is possible to deduce contradictory consequences, by quite elementary logical processes. There can therefore be no φ which will turn a complex of this form into a true sentence. For example, none of the following can possibly be true:

1. It is being brought about by James that whatever is being brought about by James is not the case; and nothing but this is being brought about by James.
2. It is feared by James that nothing that is feared by James is the case; and nothing but this is feared by James.
3. It is apparently feared by James that nothing that is apparently feared by James is the case; and nothing but this is apparently feared by James.
4. It is signified by *x* that nothing that is signified by *x* is the case; and nothing but this is signified by *x*.

5. It is signified by x (so far as x signifies anything at all) that whatever is signified by x (so far as x signifies anything at all) is not the case; and there is nothing else that is signified by x (so far as x signifies anything at all).

6. It is conventionally (normally, formally) signified by x that nothing that is conventionally (normally, formally) signified by x is the case; and nothing that is conventionally (normally, formally) signified by x.

At least, none of these is true if the expression substituted for 'φ' is used in the same way throughout the sentence. (If, for example, 'signified' means 'signified in L' in one occurrence and 'signified in M' in another, it is quite a different story.) And any semantics which is to avoid inconsistency must have some means of blocking the introduction of φs with which sentences of this general form are constructible and provable. Buridan's later theory, so far as I can see, fails to meet this requirement.

But what of his *earlier* theory? This it seems to me, *is* logically workable; it is, at all events, not immediately open to the above objection, since it involves no sense of 'it is signified by x that' for which a sentence of the above form would be provable. Its method of preventing this has its own repercussions, some of them perhaps not too palatable; but I fear we must reconcile ourselves to the fact that, however it is conducted, Semantics is a mess. (A theologian of some logical competence once described this as 'a sign of our creaturely status', but even God's language, if such there be, and if it is consistent, must be subject to the same limitations.) It is of some interest that the solution now proposed (the younger Buridan's) has been defended in our own period by a very great logician indeed, namely Charles Sanders Peirce.[1] Peirce did not attempt a detailed formalisation of the position, and I have myself only looked at the beginnings of such a development, but I am fairly confident it can be done. In other words, a language *can* contain its own semantics, that is to say its own theory of meaning, provided that this semantics contains the law that for any sentence x, x means that x is true. To set the whole thing out in a fully formalised way, we would need to introduce a symbol, say 'M', for 'means that', and write 'Mxp' for 'x means that p', and then with

[1] *Collected Papers of C. S. Peirce*, 5. 340.

this and ordinary logical symbols we could formulate, and assert as a law of the system, the sentence 'x means that for all p, if x means that p, then p', i.e. 'x signifies that, however x signifies that things are, thus they are', or 'x means that x is true'. This law is not intended as a definition of 'means that', and as such would be circular and absurd, nor does it assert that *all* that a sentence x means is that x is true, but it does say that any sentence x means this, whatever else it may mean besides. The Liar paradox could then be disposed of exactly as the younger Buridan did dispose of it.

What I am really suggesting now is that the fault of Buridan's later theory, and the source of its inconsistency, is just its half-heartedness. When Buridan, in objecting to his own earlier theory, makes so much of the distinction between sentences which do and sentences which do not contain terms of second intention, he has already sold the pass to the proponents of language hierarchies; a man who is really determined to abandon these—a whole-hearted Presbyterian in semantics, as we might say—will not attach much weight to such arguments, drawn as they are from the armoury of linguistic Prelacy. The fact seems to be that if any sentence *could* be about the semantics of its own language, then all sentences of that language to a certain extent *must* be about its semantics, though in general they will be about other things as well.

Let us not, however, be over-violent here, and replace linguistic feudalism by a new totalitarianism. We must live and let live. It would be foolish to deny that the word 'means' must be relativised to a language—words don't just 'mean' on their own; 'meaning' *is* always 'meaning in a language L'. And the language L in question *could* be one which does not itself contain the expression 'means in L', and which thereby gains various simplicities. But it could also be one which does contain this expression; for this a price must be paid, but it can be a price less than inconsistency.

I would envisage such a 'Buridanian' language as having a syntax of a broadly Russellian type, with a sharp distinction made between genuine proper names and definite descriptions. In particular, the enclosing of a sentence in quotation-marks should not be thought of as forming a genuine proper name of that sentence, but rather as an abbreviated description. ('The sentence "Grass is green"' would abridge something like 'The sentence formed by writing a Gee followed by an Ar followed by an Ay', &c., &c.) A genuine proper name would have no internal logical structure. But a 'Buridanian' language *would* contain genuine proper names of its own expressions; in fact, in the law '*x* means that *x* is true', the variable must be thought of as one keeping a place for precisely such a proper name. (The law might, incidentally, have to be enunciated in the qualified form 'If *x* means-that anything'—i.e. 'For any *p*, if *x* means that *p*' —'*x* means that *x* is true'; since a proper name is not by its very form a name of a sentence rather than of some other object.) Such a proper name could, moreover, be a name of a sentence in which this name itself occurs, e.g. 'A' could be a name of the sentence 'A is false'. If A were not a genuine proper name but just an abbreviation of the description. 'The sentence "A is false" ' this would not be possible, as we would never be able to give the fully expanded form of this description; but a mere proper name would not require any such expansion.

Buridan himself frequently used letters as proper names of sentences, and described them as precisely that. He made it clear, and a modern refurbishing of his semantics would also have to make it clear, that these are proper names not of sentence 'types' but of particular utterances and inscriptions. If 'A', for example, is the proper name of the following inscription: *A is false*, then it is not the name of the following exactly similar (or as is often said 'equiform') but numerically different inscription: *A is false*. And if it is in *this* sense of 'sentence' that all sentences signify their own truth, it follows that even a pair of equiform sentences are never *quite* synonymous. '2 and 2 are 4', for instance, means that 2 and 2 are 4 and that *that* inscription back there is a true sentence; while the following: '2 and 2 are 4', means that 2 and 2 are 4 (this much meaning the two inscriptions have in common) and that *this other* inscription (the nearest one to here) is a true sentence. Further, two equiform inscriptions may not always even have the same truth-value (a consequence which Buridan quite boldly drew). For example, if 'A' is the proper name of this inscription: *A is false*, then A in fact *is* false, but precisely because of this the following inscription: *A is false*, is true. For the first inscription asserts its own falsehood (and, of course, like all inscriptions, its own truth), but the second inscription asserts, not *its own* falsehood, but the falsehood of the *first* inscription (together with *its* own truth; but now there is no contradiction, only a difference in truth-value between equiform inscriptions).

So-called structural-descriptive names of sentences (like 'The sentence formed by writing a Gee followed by an Ar', etc., etc.) will in consequence not be even genuine *descriptions* of sentences, in the sense of 'sentence' intended, but will refer rather to classes of equiform sentences; and the rules which give the meaning of particular sentences will be somewhat complicated. In many cases, nevertheless, equiform inscriptions *will* have the same truth-value, e.g. all inscriptions equiform with this one: *No proposition is negative*, are false; and their differences in meaning can in many contexts be ignored, so that no harm is done by talking about, say, 'The sentence "No proposition is negative" ' when what is really intended is 'All sentences equiform with the sentence "No proposition is negative" '. (And I shall myself indulge in this harmless laxity below.)

With this particular example, we do run into a difficulty, though not an insuperable one, in connexion with the problem which we have already found Buridan raising about it. Buridan insists that the proposition 'No proposition is negative' must be classified as a 'possible' one because things could be as it signifies, even though it could not possibly be true. It cannot possibly be true because it will only be true if it exists, and if it exists there will be at least one negative proposition, namely itself. But if God were to annihilate all negative propositions there would in fact be no negative propositions, even if this were not then being *asserted* in any proposition at all. In short, *it can be that no proposition is negative, though it cannot be that 'No proposition is negative' is true*. Up to this point Buridan's reasoning seems to me quite conclusive and extremely important. Numerous modern writers have insisted that 'possibility' is in the first instance a property of sentences; there are, they say, no possibilities in things themselves, which are simply so or not so; and to say that some state of affairs is possible (that is, to say with respect to some p that it is possible that p) is just to say that the sentence which expresses this state of affairs (that is, the sentence x such that x means that p) has some property or other. What this property is supposed to be is a little obscure, but Buridan's example at least shows that it cannot plausibly be possible-truth. Buridan is still prepared, nevertheless, to use 'possible' as an adjective predicable of sentences, and attempts what one would have thought to be a more hopeful task than the converse modern one, the definition of this 'possibility' of sentences in terms of the possibility of states of affairs (not *vice versa*). A sentence *x*, he says in effect, is possible not only if it could be true, but also (even when it *couldn't* be true) if things could be as *x* says they are, or in modern formal terms, if for all *p*, if *x* means that *p*, then it could be that *p*.

If, however, we adopt the semantics of the younger Buridan, this account of 'possibility' in sentences won't quite do. For according to this semantics, one thing that is meant by any sentence *x* is precisely that *x* is true; and in particular, one thing that is meant by the proposition 'No proposition is negative' is precisely that the proposition 'No proposition is negative' is true. If we adopt Buridan's later distinction between 'formal' and 'virtual' signification, we can escape this difficulty by saying that a sentence is possible if everything that is *formally* signified by it could be the case, and since the proposition 'No proposition is negative' formally signifies only that no proposition is negative, and *not* that the proposition 'No proposition is negative' is true, we can classify this proposition as 'possible' because it could be that no proposition is negative, even if the other thing could not be. But we have already seen where this notion of 'formal signification' leads us—either back to the paradox of the Liar, or, as the only means of escaping this, back into the Babylonish captivity of a hierarchy of languages.

There are, however, ways out of this predicament which are quite simple and I think quite satisfactory. In the first place, I don't see that there *has* to be a sense of 'possible', as an adjective predicable of sentences, which is distinct from 'possibly true'. We can still say that it could be the case that no proposition is negative, *without* saying that the proposition 'No proposition is negative' is thereby classifiable as a 'possible proposition'. But if we do insist on using this language, we can define 'possible' as applied to sentences in a more indirect way, namely by saying that a sentence *x* goes into the 'possible' class if and only if the sentence formed by prefixing 'It could be that' to this sentence *x* is a true one. This does give the distinction that Buridan wanted to make. The proposition 'No proposition is negative' is 'possible' in the sense that the proposition 'It could be that no proposition is negative' is true. This longer proposition, it must be admitted, signifies not only that it could be that no proposition is negative but also that the proposition 'It could be that no proposition is negative' is true; but to say that the proposition with 'It could be' in it *is* true is a different thing from saying that the proposition without that addition *could be* true; so Buridan's distinction is still preserved.

The semantics which I have sketched might prove to be in its details (despite the Russellian character of the associated syntax) not unlike the Zermelo-Quine alternative to the theory of types, and I cannot help feeling that it is much more called for. For the simple theory of types, especially in the forms in which it is now propounded by Polish logicians such as Suszko and Borkowski, seem to me not at all burdensome, and anyway even the Zermelo-Quine logic itself has to have *some* distinctions of syntactical categories—a name, for example, is still something different from a sentence. The only gain which this logic brings is a rather technical one, a limitation of the kinds of variables that need to be bound by quantifiers, and I don't think even this advantage can be plausibly carried over into non-mathematical contexts. But a hierarchy of languages, as opposed to a hierarchy of parts of speech, really *is* a lot for us to have to carry around, and if the theories of the younger Buridan promise a way out of it, they are certainly worth looking into.

15. *Oratio Obliqua*

We have, in English, at least two ways of reporting an utterance. The following will do as an example:

(1) James says, 'Man is mortal'
(2) James says that man is mortal.

In the first, the so-called direct speech, we enclose the reported utterance in quotation-marks; in the other, we use a subordinate clause beginning with 'that'. In certain cases the change from quotation-marks to a 'that' clause is accompanied by other changes, e.g. of tenses and personal pronouns, but I do not propose to concern myself with these in the present paper. It is commonly assumed—and this assumption I shall not here question, though I think it is questionable—that we can give a reasonably satisfactory account of the first form by saying that it expresses a relation between a speaker and a form of words, the form of words being named by being enclosed in quotation-marks. The second way of doing things, on the other hand, is commonly assumed—and this assumption I do propose to question—to be extremely problematic as it stands, and various attempts have been made either to reduce it or to assimilate it to the other form. The reductionist theory is that the *oratio obliqua* form is at least indirectly about a form of words, e.g. our (2) may be said to mean that James either stands to the form of words 'Man is mortal' in the relation expressed by our (1), or stands in that relation to some other form of words which is synonymous with it. The theory which does not reduce but assimilates (2) to (1), is to the effect that (2) expresses a relation, not between James and a form of words, but between James and a more obscure object called a 'proposition', this object being named by the clause introduced by the word 'that'.

147

There are objections to both of these theories which I do not wish to rehearse here; the advocates of each have sufficiently developed the objections to the other, and they can all be easily found in the literature, and anyhow the main point I want to make is that it is not necessary to adopt either of them. It may be observed at this point, however, that the second or *oratio obliqua* form occurs not only with 'says' as its principal verb but also with any one of numerous other verbs, such as 'thinks', 'hopes', 'fears', 'wishes', 'brings it about', and that with these the reductionist theory is so unplausible that it has hardly ever been brought forward. We can no doubt extend it to 'thinks' by means of a bit of patter about thought being 'the conversation of the soul with itself', but the 'form of words' story wears thinner and thinner as we proceed to the other members of the series. 'James brings it about that X is Y' is quite obviously not about a form of words at all, even indirectly, and this seems equally obvious with 'James wishes that X were Y'. At this point the friends of 'propositions' do seem to have the best of the argument.

To come back, however, to my main contention: it is simply that the second form, 'James says that man is mortal', is perfectly in order as it is. This, in a way, the friends of 'propositions' also admit; but they go on, with a glance over their shoulder at Form (1), to parse Form (2) as 'James says/that man is mortal', and this is their fundamental mistake. I want to suggest that the word 'that' doesn't go with the sentence that follows to turn it into a name; it goes, rather, with the verb that precedes to turn it, or at all events that end of it, into a sentential connective. The proper parsing is 'James says that/man is mortal', in which a sentence is constructed, not out of a name, but out of another sentence, and the whole is no more *about* that sentence than, for example, 'It is not the case that man is mortal' is about that sentence. The full sentence *is* of course about James, and 'says that man is mortal' is as a whole a genuine verb or predicate (this is true on *any* reading of what comes after 'says'); but 'thinks that' is not a two-place predicate—it does not express a *relation* between James and anything whatever, for what goes on to the other end of this expression isn't a name—neither the name of a form of words nor the name of a 'proposition'—but another sentence. Seeing it in this way, we may compare the expression '—says that—' not only with '—brings it about that—'

but also with something quite flat and 'extensional' like '—is a man and—', where we can fill in the first blank with a name and the second with a sentence to get, say, 'James is a man and man is mortal'.

I don't claim any originality for the point of view that I am developing here; it is simply an expansion of a hint of F. P. Ramsey's.[1] The same view has been more recently advocated, though somewhat half-heartedly, by W. V. Quine. At the end of Section 44 of *Word and Object*, after considering and rejecting a number of other possibilities, Quine says, 'A final alternative that I find as appealing as any is simply to dispense with the objects of the propositional attitudes . . . The verb "believes" . . . ceases to be a term and becomes part of an operator "believes that", . . . which, applied to a sentence, produces a composite absolute general term whereof the sentence is counted as an immediate constituent'. In the following section, however, headed 'The Double Standard', he suggests that this procedure is only legitimate in a rather inferior language-game in which we are being 'dramatic' rather than 'scientific'; but the 'scientific' conscience which is here asserting itself seems a rather narrowly behaviouristic one. In an earlier paragraph he has an objection of a more solid sort to this refusal to take 'believes' seriously as a transitive verb, i.e., as the expression of a relation between objects; if we take this line, he says, we will not be able to make sense of statements like 'Paul believes something that Elmer does not'. But he edges out of this by suggesting that such statements are 'perhaps expendable'; 'such quantifications tend anyway to be pretty trivial in what they affirm, and useful only in heralding more tangible information'. This is what Bosanquet tried to maintain about existential quantification generally,[2] and I doubt whether Quine is *much* happier about it than I am. But his worry here seems to me to be quite unnecessary; like many other difficulties of his, it only arises through his insistence that all quantification must govern variable *names*. I see no reason why we

---

[1] *Foundations of Mathematics*, p. 143. Ramsey, like other writers of the period, uses the grammatically dreadful forms 'he asserts p' and 'p is true' (without either a 'that' or quotation-marks), but it is clear enough what he is after.

[2] *Essentials of Logic*, pp. 116–17. There is a good critical discussion of Bosanquet's view in Keynes's *Formal Logic*, 4th ed., pp. 101–2, and of similar views about negation on pp. 122–4.

should not—still following Ramsey—quantify our *sentential* variables and concoct such complexes as 'For some *p*, Paul believes that *p* and Elmer does not believe that *p*', without thereby being 'ontologically committed' to the view that there are objects which sentences *name* (I doubt whether any dogma, even of empiricism, has ever been quite so muddling as the dogma that to be is to be a value of a bound variable).

Quine is also undoubtedly worried by the fact that, while his suggestion removes the necessity for 'intensional abstracts', the 'operators' into which the 'that' of intensional abstraction is absorbed remain themselves 'intensional' in another sense, namely, in the sense of violating the law that if a pair of sentences are the same in truth-value then any sentences constructed out of them by the same 'operator' must be the same in truth-value too. But so far as I can see there is no more reason for accepting this 'law of extensionality' as true than there is for believing that the earth is flat, and it is in one way a rather similar belief. What we say by our sentences (or better, how we say things are) may vary in innumerable other 'dimensions' than that of truth-value; for any given *p*, it may not only be or not be the case that *p*, but may also be believed by Paul or by Elmer or by everybody or by nobody that *p*, it may be possible or impossible or necessary that *p*, it may be desirable or undesirable or a matter of indifference whether *p*, and so on, and for a given *f*, whether it is or is not the case that *f*(*p*) *may* depend solely on whether it is or is not the case that *p*, but it may on the contrary depend on a variety of these other factors in the situation. Nor need we say in these cases that there are other truth-values 'between' the usual two; in *that* dimension of variation, truth and falsity (being the case and not being the case) *are* the only alternatives there are; but why should this be the only dimension? In a sound, to take a different case, being high-pitched isn't something 'between' being loud and being soft, but that doesn't prevent a loud or soft sound from being high-pitched too. The so-called law of extensionality was an interesting early effort at generalisation in a scientific logic, and no doubt does hold within the first area to be thoroughly examined—the functions required in the foundations of mathematics—but in no other science that I've heard of do the practitioners cling to the first guesses of their teachers, in the face of the most obvious counter-examples, with the fervour of religious devotees.

Possibly the attachment of some logicians to this principle arises from a mistaken assimilation of it to the principle that if x and y are one and the same individual object, then whatever is true of x is *ipso facto* true of y. This latter principle, sometimes called 'Leibniz's Law', or 'the indiscernibility of identicals', I am not now disputing, and in fact I think it true. I would not deny, either, that there is a sentential connective which is the analogue, at its own level, of the two-place predicate '—is the very same object as—', and for which an analogous law holds. When we assert or deny, as we sometimes may do, that the proposition that p is the very same proposition as the proposition that q—for example, when we assert that the proposition that for all x, x is red, is the same proposition as the proposition that for all y, y is red, and when we deny that the proposition that grass is green is the same proposition as the proposition that it is not the case that it is not the case that grass is green—we are employing such a connective, and there is no need to take the component phrase 'the proposition that p' at all seriously as a name of an object; the phrase 'the proposition that—' is merely part of the connective, just as it is merely part of a connective when we say 'The proposition that p is materially equivalent to the proposition that q', i.e., 'p if and only if q' (in one sense of 'if').[1] But this last is a *different* connective from the one first mentioned, and it is the mistake of 'extensionalism', in propositional logic, to identify them. If the proposition that p really *is* the same proposition as the proposition that q, then of course it follows, not only that if it is (or is not) the case that p then it equally is (or is not) the case that q, but also that if James says, thinks, wishes or brings it about that p he *ipso facto* says, thinks, wishes or brings it about that q; but this last does not follow from the mere material equivalence—or, I would add, from the strict equivalence, or from the mutual entailment—of the proposition that p and the proposition that q. To equate propositional identity with any of these other things has

[1] This view of propositional identity is aired, and I think a little too hurriedly put on one side, in P. T. Geach's contribution to the symposium on 'Entailment' in *Arist. Soc., Supp.* 1958. I have discussed it more fully in a paper 'Is the concept of referential opacity really necessary?', in *Acta Philosophica Fennica*, vol. 16.

about as much justification as equating the identity of individuals with, say, having the same barber.

Returning now to the intensional 'operators' which link, not other sentences, but names, with sentences: we have noted that when the second gap in an expression like '—says that—' or '—brings it about that—' is filled by a specific sentence, the resulting complex is something perfectly familiar, a one-place predicate that can be attached to an ordinary name. Further, if the sentence that we tack on itself contains an ordinary name, we can knock this name out and the result will be an ordinary *two*-place predicate, expressing a relation between two objects. Suppose, for example, that Paul says that, or thinks that, or hopes that, or brings it about that, Elmer is a fellow-traveller. Then what we have to do with here *is* a relation, not indeed between Paul and a sentence or between Paul and a 'proposition', but between Paul and Elmer. Often, in fact, we employ turns of speech in which the relational character of what is asserted is clearly brought out, and the mode of construction glossed over, as when we say 'Paul has *accused* Elmer of being a fellow-traveller', and convert it to 'Elmer has been accused by Paul, *etc.*'

Although, however, there are these cases in which what is expressed by *oratio obliqua* does boil down to a relation to *some* object or other, there are a large number of cases in which it does not. Suppose, for example, that Paul believes, not that Elmer is a fellow-traveller, but merely that someone is, i.e., he believes that there are fellow-travellers, though he does not personally know of any and there is no particular person whom he even suspects of being one. This belief, so far as I can see, does not consist in a relation between Paul and anyone or anything whatsoever.

Further, there are cases in which even the quasi-relation of the believer to a 'proposition' is fuzzed up by the intervention of a quantifier in a similar way. Let me switch at this point from Quine's Paul and Elmer to a certain Mrs Murphy, who believes that everything that a certain Father Gordon says is true. From this, it should be noted, it does not follow that Mrs Murphy believes everything that Father Gordon says. In the stylised language which I am recommending, my initial statement comes out as

(3) Mrs Murphy believes that, for all p, if Father Gordon says that p, then p,

while the quite different statement that I am distinguishing from
it is that

(4) For all p, if Father Gordon says that p, then Mrs Murphy
believes that p.

It is easy to construct circumstances in which (4) is falsified without
prejudice to Mrs Murphy's implicit faith in Father Gordon. A
simple case would be that in which Father Gordon says something
which Mrs Murphy doesn't happen to hear. Slightly more subtle is
the case in which Father Gordon says in Mrs Murphy's hearing
something, for example that there is a Necessary Being, or that there
are Three Persons in One God, which Mrs Murphy doesn't understand. Does it really count as believing in the existence of a Necessary Being, or in the Trinity, if these doctrines are propounded in
one's hearing by an authority which one believes to be infallible,
when one does not understand what it is that is being propounded? I should have thought not, but there is a further problem
here.

It seems clear that if Mrs Murphy does believe that everything
that Father Gordon says is true, and if she can do what the natural
deducers call U.I. (and can also do *modus ponens*), then *if* she
believes that Father Gordon says that there is a Necessary Being,
she *must* believe that there is a Necessary Being. And how can she
not believe that Father Gordon says this, if she actually hears him
say it? If, however, she doesn't know what 'There is a Necessary
Being' means, she can quite easily hear Father Gordon utter these
words and yet not *believe that Father Gordon says that* there is a
Necessary Being; for she may believe, and even know, that he has
uttered these words, but *what he has said*, in the sense of 'the p such
that he has *said that p*',[1] she does not know, if she does not know
what he means by these words. She does of course believe that for
any p, if he has said by these words that p, then p, i.e. she believes

---

[1] This phrase is of course no more a genuine name or even description of an
object than 'the proposition that p' is in the contexts discussed earlier 'x knows
which p is the p such that y has said that p' expands to 'For some p, (1) y has
said that p, (2) y has said nothing except that p, and (3) x knows that (1) and (2)'.
(2) in turn expands to 'For all q, if y has said that q, then the proposition that q
is the same proposition as the proposition that p.'

that whatever he has said on this occasion is true; and she may
believe that for some p he has said that p, i.e. that he has said
something, but there is no specific thing that she *believes him to have
said*, no p such that she believes him to have said that p.

But how far can this 'not understanding' go? I have in mind now
an example that is not at all theological. Suppose Father Gordon
says in Mrs Murphy's hearing that Johnny Jones has measles, but
Mrs Murphy hasn't the foggiest idea who Johnny Jones is. Can she
then be said to believe that Johnny Jones has measles? It is again
clear that if she believes that everything that Father Gordon says is
true, and if she can do U.I. (and *modus ponens*), then *if* she believes
that Father Gordon has said that Johnny Jones has measles, she
must believe that Johnny Jones has measles. But will she, in the case
envisaged—i.e. if she hasn't the foggiest idea who Johnny Jones is—
even believe that Father Gordon has said that Johnny Jones has
measles? Here again she may well believe, and even know, that he
has uttered the words 'Johnny Jones has measles'; and in this case
we can go further, since the words are not *completely* unintelligible to
her, and she will believe, and even know, that *there is someone of
whom Father Gordon has said* that he has measles. But there need be
no one—neither Johnny Jones nor anyone else—to whom she stands
in the relation of believing that Father Gordon has said of *him* that
he has measles.

I would not wish to say that, simply because she doesn't know
who Johnny Jones is, Mrs Murphy cannot stand in any relation to
him whatever. Quite trivially, they may for example be co-religion-
ists; or perhaps he lives in the next street; in fact we all stand in
innumerable relations, e.g. spatial ones, to individuals whom we
cannot identify. And what is more to our present point, Johnny
Jones may stand to Mrs Murphy in the relation of being the *verifier*
of her belief, in a sense that can be quite easily made clear; that is,
it may be *his* being said by Father Gordon to have measles which
verifies *her* belief that there is someone of whom Father Gordon has
said this. But this relation between Mrs Murphy and Johnny Jones
is as it were a blind one; it holds, so to speak, behind her back, like
his living in the next street. Her belief is no more a belief *about*
Johnny Jones than Paul's belief that someone is a fellow-traveller is
about Elmer, though the fact that Elmer, among other people, is a
fellow-traveller will serve to make this belief true.

Something else is possible also. If Mrs Murphy doesn't know who Father Gordon is talking about when he says 'Johnny Jones has measles', her hearing him say this is not sufficient for her to know or even believe that he has *said that* Johnny Jones has measles. But not only is it not sufficient—it is not necessary either, at least for the belief. For she might personally encounter Johnny Jones, and believe him to be the boy referred to by Father Gordon when the latter said, on another occasion, 'David Davies has measles'. She then really would stand to Johnny Jones in the relation of believing him to have been said by Father Gordon to have measles, and she would in that sense believe that Father Gordon had said that Johnny Jones had measles, though she would not of course express this belief in these terms—what she would *say*, to express this belief that Father Gordon had said that Johnny Jones had measles, would be 'Father Gordon has said that *this boy*'—or 'that David Davies'— 'has measles'.

It must be admitted that when I express *my* meaning in this way I am straining a little the ordinary use of expressions like 'Johnny Jones'—I am using 'Johnny Jones' as if it were what Russell calls a 'logical proper name'. And I do think that grammatical proper names sometimes can be, and sometimes are, so used; but I admit, as indeed Russell admitted, that they very often are not. And to get at the other use that they may have, or one of the other uses, let me state and discuss a possible objection to the way I have been describing this case of Father Gordon and Mrs Murphy and Johnny Jones. Is there not a sense in which, if Mrs Murphy hears Father Gordon say 'Johnny Jones has measles', she necessarily does know who it is that Father Gordon says has measles? She knows at least that it is the person referred to by Father Gordon as 'Johnny Jones'. But this is surely a Pickwickian sense of 'knowing who it is'. She 'knows who Father Gordon is talking about' only in the sense of knowing that he is the person that Father Gordon is talking about; and this is hardly enough. It must be admitted, however, that in a very large number of cases this, with further information of the same sort, is the only knowledge of who a person is that we have. For a tremendously large number of our beliefs are beliefs on hearsay, and are about people whom we only encounter as figuring in what we hear said, or in some equally indirect way. I am not here questioning the *reliability* of belief on hearsay—that is another problem altogether—but I am raising as sharply as I can a question as to its *content*.

Take, for example, the belief that we all have that Julius Caesar crossed the Rubicon. We know who Julius Caesar was only in the sense of knowing that he was the person that the records are about; is this enough to turn our belief in the truth of the records into a relation between ourselves and Julius Caesar? If we answer this question affirmatively, we are on a slippery slope which cannot end short of the position that if we hear someone utter the words 'Abracadabra is arbadacarba' and believe that what he says is true, this counts as believing that abracadabra is arbadacarba. (I have now reached the point of talking nonsense myself, for as Mr Geach has rightly insisted,[1] if the sentence 'Abracadabra is arbadacarba' is nonsense, the phrase 'believing that abracadabra is arbadacarba' is nonsense also; but it was, I hope, helpful nonsense.)

If we are to avoid this slide, I would suggest that we must adopt some such position as the following: When we describe our ordinary historical belief as a belief that Julius Caesar crossed the Rubicon, and even when we speak of a belief that *the records say that* Julius Caesar crossed the Rubicon, the words 'Julius Caesar' do not have *reference* but only *cross*-reference. Proper names may acquire intelligibility either through our being introduced in some way to their bearers, or by being incorporated into a *story*—'Once upon a time someone lived in Rome who was called "Julius Caesar", and this Julius Caesar conquered Gaul, crossed the Rubicon, and so forth.' We believe that Julius Caesar crossed the Rubicon in the sense that we believe the relevant part of this story; there is no one to whom we are related as believing the whole story of *him*, but we identify the subject of the later part of the story, ultimately, as simply the 'Someone' with whom the story begins. It would be quite misleading to say that the utterance 'Julius Caesar crossed the Rubicon', used in this context (i.e. in the normal context) is only about the *name* 'Julius Caesar', or even that it is about that name at all; it isn't strictly speaking 'about' anyone or anything, i.e., there is no one of whom I say that *he* crossed the Rubicon; but I do *say that someone* crossed the Rubicon, and I have previously said (among much else) that this same someone was called 'Julius Caesar'. And even a word like 'abracadabra', or let us say 'pi-meson', can acquire

[1] P. T. Geach, *Mental Acts*, p. 10.

'cross-reference' and so a place in intelligible discourse, in a similar way.

Genuine reference, moreover, is in general a transitory phenomenon. I do not mean that its objects are transitory—'Johnny Jones now', and the like. I see no reason why we should not sometimes indicate, and speak and think directly about, the persisting object Johnny Jones. Certainly we may be related in other ways—e.g., we may live next door to—such persisting objects; so why not in this way? But when the introduction is over, and Johnny Jones is out of sight, then what we describe as saying, thinking, fearing, etc., that Johnny Jones is or does so-and-so, will in fact be saying, thinking, fearing, etc., that *someone who has been introduced to us as 'Johnny Jones'* is or does so-and-so. As Peirce puts it, a proper name is a 'genuine Index', 'existentially connected with some percept or other equivalent individual knowledge of the individual it names', when and only when 'one meets with it for the first time'. After that, it is not an Index, but 'an Icon of that Index'.[1]

How does all this fit into my main group of contentions? I have argued, first, that the verbs which occur as principal verbs in indirect-speech constructions—verbs like 'says', 'thinks', 'believes', 'wishes', 'fears'—are not genuine transitive verbs or two-place predicates; that is, they don't express relations between one individual object and another; rather, they go with a following 'that' to form an expression of a different syntactical sort, which is like a predicate at one end (because at that end it hitches on to a name) and like a sentential connective at the other end (because at that end it hitches on to a sentence). That is my *main* contention. But I have qualified it by saying that in some cases these expressions can *enter into* genuine two-place predicates, that is they can form *part of* the expression of a relation between individual objects. For there are cases in which X says or believes something *of* Y, i.e. stands to Y in the relation of believing that Y is or does this, that and the other thing. This is not my main contention but is a kind of concession— the people who speak of belief, etc., as relations, are right at least to the extent that relations do sometimes come into it, though in this indirect way. But what all this about Julius Caesar and Johnny Jones brings out is that it is only *very rarely* that a genuine relation is involved even in this oblique way; or anyhow many cases which

[1] *Collected Papers of C. S. Peirce*, 2. 329.

look as if they might be examples of this, turn out to be nothing of the kind—they turn out to be examples rather of the *other* sort of case, in which there is no object to which we stand in the relation of believing that *it* is or does such-and-such, but we merely *believe that there is* an object that is or does the thing in question.

16. Conjunction and Contonktion Revisited

1. It is one thing to define 'conjunction-forming sign', and quite another to define 'and'. We may say, for example, that a conjunction-forming sign is any sign which, when placed between any pair of sentences P and Q, forms a sentence which may be inferred from P and Q together, and from which we may infer P and infer Q. Or we may say that it is a sign which, when placed between any pair of sentences P and Q, forms a sentence which is true when both P and Q are true, and otherwise false. Each of these tells us something that could be meant by saying that 'and', for instance, or '&', is a conjunction-forming sign. But neither of them tells us what is meant by 'and' or by '&' itself.

2. Moreover, each of the above definitions implies that the sentence formed by placing a conjunction-forming sign between two other sentences already *has* a meaning. For only what already has a meaning can be true or false (according as what it means is or is not the case), and only what already has a meaning can be inferred from anything, or have anything inferred from it.

3. By 'may be inferred', above, I mean 'may be validly inferred', in the sense of Stevenson.[1] 'Inference' in the sense of a permitted transformation of wffs in a purely symbolic game neither pre-supposes meaning nor gives it. For here the permitted moves are framed entirely in terms of the design of the symbols, independently of their interpretation. In the meta-theory of such a game we can indeed define terms like 'conjunction-forming sign', either directly in terms of the design of the symbols (e.g. ' "&" is a conjunction-forming sign'), or in terms of the permissions to transform. But to

[1] J. T. Stevenson, 'Roundabout the runabout inference-ticket', *Analysis* 21.6, June 1961.

believe that anything of this sort can take us beyond the symbols to their meaning, is to believe in magic.

4. In exactly the same way, it is one thing to define 'contonktion-forming sign', and quite another to define 'tonk'. We may say, for instance, that a contonktion-forming sign is one which, when placed between any two sentences P and Q, forms a sentence which may be inferred from P and from which Q may be inferred; or we may define it as one which, when placed between any two sentences P and Q, forms a sentence which is true if P is true and false if Q is false (and therefore, of course, both true and false if P is true and Q false). Each of these tells us something that could be meant by saying that 'tonk' is a contonktion-forming sign; neither of them tells us what 'tonk' means; and both imply that a sentence formed by placing a contonktion-forming sign between two other sentences already has a meaning.

5. Moreover, in the meta-theory of a purely symbolic game we can define a contonktion-forming sign, either directly in terms of the design of the symbol (e.g. it might be defined as one that looks like this: TONK), or in terms of the game's permitted transformations, e.g. as a sign such that from any wff we may move to a wff consisting of the first one followed by the contonktion-forming sign followed by any other wff, and from this to the other wff. Nor is there any reason why a purely symbolic game should not contain contonktion-forming signs in this second sense, except that such a game would be rather less interesting to play than noughts-and-crosses.

6. While the definitions of 'conjunction-forming sign' and 'contonktion-forming sign', coupled with the information that the signs 'and' and 'tonk' fall respectively into these two classes, do not *tell* us what 'and' and 'tonk' mean, they might nevertheless put us on the track of it. For we might know of senses which, if assigned to these words, would put them in these classes, and we might guess that these were the senses that our informant intended. This way of putting people on the track of the meaning of a word is often the best we have; and if understood thus modestly, is not to be despised. Both 'inferential definitions' and truth-tables *can* help us in this way to fix the meaning of a word. (Unlike Stevenson, I can see no

difference in principle between these devices.) So can even the rules of a symbolic game in which the word is used as a counter, if we are given the information that its sense is such that when the wffs of the game (in which the word plays a part) are interpreted as meaningful sentences, the rules will never lead us from truth to falsehood.

7. But these indirect and informal ways of fixing the sense of a word, however indispensable they may sometimes be, have definite limitations. In the first place, a definition of a class of signs, as opposed to the definition of a particular sign itself, may mark off a class which turns out to be empty. There are in fact *no* contonktion-forming signs in either of the senses given to this phrase in Section 4; and the information that 'tonk', or anything else, is such a sign, is simply false.[1] 'Contonktion-forming sign', like 'present King of France', is a perfectly clear description which applies to nothing whatever.

8. The definitions of 'conjunction-forming sign' in Section 1, considered as informal pointers to the meaning of the conjunction-forming sign 'and', do not suffer from this defect, but they do suffer from another. In any language rich enough for the formulation of the propositional calculus it will be possible to introduce not one but an infinite number of non-synonymous conjunction-forming signs in either of the senses given above. For let 'and', say, be one such sign. Then we may introduce, say, the form 'P & Q' as an abbreviation for 'Not (P and not-Q) and not (not-P and Q) and not (not-P and not-Q)'; and after that 'P et Q' as an abbreviation for 'Not (P & not-Q) & not (not-P & Q) & not (not-P & not-Q)', and so on *ad infinitum*. It is easy to show (e.g. by truth-tables) that '&', 'et', etc., are all conjunction-forming signs in either of the given senses. But they can hardly be synonymous, since the understanding of '&' requires us to understand *both* 'and' and 'not'; and each member of the series differs in logical form from all the others. Belnap[2] has seen the importance of synonymy in this discussion, but his criteria for it are surely too weak. I cannot see how the sense of

---

[1] At all events, this is true of any language that contains both true and false sentences. In a one-valued logic, *all* connectives would be contonktion-forming. And a one-valued logic, as a symbolic game, is at least interesting as a limiting case.

[2] Nuel D. Belnap, 'Tonk, plonk and plink', *Analysis* 22.6, June 1962.

6

a sentence can ever be identical with a logical complication of itself.

9. We can, of course, arbitrarily attach to a symbolic complex containing a sentence as a part the very same sense that we have given to this sentence itself, provided that we have not already assigned to the symbolic complex a sense of its own. It could be argued, for instance, that conjunctions are only intelligible if they have different conjuncts, so that the form 'P and P' is strictly senseless if 'and' has its normal meaning.[1] It may then do no harm, and may even help us to get simpler rules for truth-preserving symbolic transformations, if we arbitrarily use this form 'P and P' to mean exactly what is meant by the plain P.[2] This, however, would not be to identify the sense of P with a logical complication of that sense, but would mean rather that the sense assigned to 'P and P' is *not* a logical complication of that assigned to P. It would only be this if 'and' could and did retain its normal sense in 'P and P', and then the sense of this would *not* be the same as that of P. In any case moves of this sort are scarcely possible with the intertwined 'ands' and 'nots' in our '&', 'et', etc.—one can hardly say that 'and' and 'not' must lose their normal meaning (whatever that is) when they enter into such complexes as our '&', which can therefore be arbitrarily assigned, for purposes of manipulation, the sense of 'and' *simpliciter*.

10. Even unintended interpretations involving non-logical conceptions will meet the inferential and truth-tabular conditions that are supposed to define 'and'. For instance, 'If anyone knew everything he would know that P and Q' follows from the pair of premisses (P, Q) and entails both members of it; and the truth-conditions for 'P and Q' are equally satisfied by 'P ett Q', which is my abbreviation for 'Either P and Q, or Oxford is the capital of Scotland'.

11. But suppose our man said that he intended to use the form 'P and Q' in the *simplest* sense satisfying the usual inferential condi-

[1] Cf. Aristotle, *De Interpretatione*, 21a ff. Also, on the similar form 'P or P', see the discussion in Walter Burleigh's *De Puritate Artis Logicae Tractatus Longior* (Franciscan Institute edition, 1955), p. 119, ll. 20–30. (Burleigh calls the form *improprium, tamen verum vel falsum*.)

[2] Similarly, if quantifications are only intelligible where the variable in the quantifier occurs freely in what follows it, we are free, and have good reason, to assign to a 'vacuous' quantification like '(x) fy' or '(x)(x)fx', the same sense as the formula with the vacuous quantifier deleted—here 'fy' or '(x)fx'.

tions. I imagine that in this case most hearers would soon catch on; but still only because there is something for them to catch on to. That is why the same move will not work with 'tonk'; and in other cases it may not work because the conditions are satisfied by several equally simple notions.

12. In short, it seems that either an 'inferential definition' is a piece of informal pedagogy, in which case it is legitimate enough, but may work or may not; or it is a muddle—essentially a muddle about what you can do with a significant language and what you can do with a symbolic game where the conveying of information isn't in question. It is a muddle when its advocates say 'Being able to do the tricks just *is* knowing the meaning'. In a symbolic game, this is in a way true, but vacuously, because there is no meaning to know. There, we can just *decree* that a couple of wffs with a sign between them is another wff, and lay down what rules we please for this newcomer; and after that there are no more questions to ask. But no one can *make* an expression consisting of two significant sentences joined by 'and' or 'or' or 'tonk' into a significant sentence just by (a) saying it is one, and (b) giving us 'permission' to utter certain other sentences before or after it and insert a few 'therefores'. And if a man who does this says, further, that if we go through these permitted motions we shall never get into trouble (in particular, that we shall never pass from truth to falsehood), we have the right, and would be wise, not to take this on the ticket-seller's say-so, but to try and check up on it. Sometimes checking up on it with the associated sentences whose truth-values we know (because we already understand them) will be enough to make it plain that we are being led up a tree. (This is the case with 'tonk'). But if it is not, and we have also to check up with the newcomers—i.e. if we have to find out whether the ticket-seller has correctly told us when things really are as *these* sentences say they are—it is hard to see how we can even start on this, with nothing but (a) and (b) to guide us. However, if we are prepared to trust the ticket-seller, we might try and turn this *credo* into an *intelligo* by looking for something which we already understand and which fits his story. We may still be stuck, however, by finding not one but several ways of doing this, and we may even be able to prove (as in the case of 'and') that if there is one way (even if we don't know what it is) there *must* be

several. And even if we're lucky and hit on one only, the fact remains that it will be we who have given the new sentences their meaning, not the ticket-seller.

13. But perhaps I have made a fundamental mistake in treating the theory of inferential definition as a theory of meaning rather than of a particular kind of meaninglessness. Perhaps the inferential definers and truth-tabulators really believe (as some certainly seem to have done) that only 'atomic' sentences strictly have meaning at all (i.e. say how things are); the rest are just formulæ expressing our readiness to lurch into inferences, and if they and their rules are suitably chosen these inferences will be safe ones, in the sense of never leading us from true *atomic* sentences to false ones. This being all that is required, we are dispensed from seeking either the meanings or the independently determined truth-values of the non-atomic sentences, and we can also say more happily that 'and', '&' and 'et' in Section 8 have the same meaning, since (a) they all have no meaning at all in the sense of telling us how things are, and (b) they generate and are generated by the same atomic sentences in all the inferences in which we use them. Non-atomic sentences represent pauses in significant discourse rather than parts of it.

14. Logical atomists being considered squares nowadays, I doubt whether many inferential definers will say that this is what they meant all the time; but if they do, I must admit that their position is easier to shrug off than to answer. It is, however, at least established (thank God for Gödel) that it won't work for higher-order quantification theory; e.g. one cannot give any such account of 'There are' in 'There are numbers that divide by two but not by three' (in which we in effect quantify over quantifiers). For there is no finite list of rules from which we can derive all the valid inferential forms in which such quantifications occur, so that if when we use them we are merely poised for making inferences, it is impossible to give any general account of *what* inferences we are poised for making. First-order quantification theory, on the other hand, *can* be thus treated. Are we to say, then, that 'There are prime numbers between two and six' is logically atomic, though 'There are fairies at the bottom of our garden' is not? Kneale in effect says just this, when he argues that the second 'There are' is a logical constant but the first isn't; but this is a hard saying.

17. *The* Cogito *of Descartes and the Concept of Self-confirmation*

The core of Descartes's proof of his own existence, in the *Discourse* and the *Meditations*, has recently been given by A. J. Ayer, in *The Problem of Knowledge* (1956) in the following terms:

'If I believe that I am thinking, then I must believe truly, since my believing that I am thinking is itself a process of thought. Consequently, if I am thinking, it is indubitable that I am thinking, and if it is indubitable that I am thinking, then, Descartes argues, it is indubitable that I exist, at least during such times as I think [. . .]

Neither 'I think' nor 'I exist' is a truth of logic [. . .] What makes them indubitable is their satisfying a condition which Descartes himself does not make explicit, though his argument turns upon it. It is that their truth follows from their being doubted by the person who expresses them. The sense in which I cannot doubt the statement that I think is just that my doubting it entails its truth: and in the same sense I cannot doubt that I exist. There was therefore no need for Descartes to derive *sum* from *cogito*; for its certainty could be independently established by the same criterion.'[1]

I am not going to argue now about whether Ayer correctly represents Descartes's train of thought, though I do not think that on the whole he does. But I want to consider certain aspects of the argument that Ayer presents, whether it be genuinely Cartesian or not.

In the first place, are the propositions 'I think' and 'I exist' really

[1] A. J. Ayer, *The Problem of Knowledge*, ch. 2, sect. iii.

on the same footing, as Ayer suggests at the end, or is there not rather an important difference between them even on Ayer's own account of the matter? It seems to me that there *is* an important difference between them, namely this: That I exist, follows from my doubting it, and also follows from my believing it, only in the sense in which it follows from my doing anything whatsoever—as Hobbes said in effect when invited by Descartes to comment on the *Meditations*, 'I walk, therefore I exist' would have been just as good an argument.[1] But about 'I think' there is the quite special argument which Ayer expresses in his first sentence, which I might restate as follows:

(1) If I think that there is something that I think, then there *is* something that I think.

From this of course it follows that I can never think falsely that there is something that I think. That is,

(2) It cannot be the case that (I think that there is something that I think, but in fact there is nothing that I think).

Whether this means that the proposition that there is something that I think is *indubitable* is another question, to which I shall return later. But at present let us simply note that propositions (1) and (2) are *logically true* in a very straightforward sense, being simply instances of the law of existential generalisation. If we put Tp for 'I think that p',[2] we have

$$CT\Sigma pTp\Sigma pTp$$

(which is just $CTq\Sigma pTp$ with ΣpTp for q) and the clearly equivalent

$$NKT\Sigma pTpN\Sigma pTp.$$

While there is more to this than to the simple 'I do X, therefore I exist', it is clear that the truth of the formulæ is no way depends on

---

[1] Descartes, *Meditations*, 3rd set of objections.

[2] And, for the rest, use the Łukasiewicz forms $Ca\beta$, Na, $Ka\beta$, Σxa, Πxa, for 'If a then β', 'Not a', 'a and β', 'For some x, a', 'For all x, a', respectively.

the *T* standing for 'I think that'. It is equally true, for instance, and for the same reason, that if I *fear* that there is something that I fear, then there *is* something that I fear, i.e. the fear that there is something that I fear cannot possibly be a groundless fear. Again, if I *say* that there is something that I say, then there *is* something that I say—this remark, if made, can never be a false one. In fact, *T* can stand here for any functor which forms sentences out of sentences, and not only for 'psychological' ones: e.g. it can stand for 'It is not the case that'—we have as a law

$$CN\Sigma pNp\Sigma pNp,$$

'If it is not the case that something is not the case, then something is not the case.'

There is, in short, no special 'logic of thinking' or 'logic of psychological attitudes' involved here—nothing but pure quantification theory. One might, indeed, obtain other and not dissimilar examples by means of a slightly more complicated logic. For instance, it is logically true, in a somewhat broader sense of the 'logically', that

(3) If I prophesy that I will have made a prophecy, then I *will* have made a prophecy,

i.e., any such prophecy is bound to be fulfilled. This involves more than simple existential generalisation, as it appeals to the 'tense-logical' law that whatever is the case will have been the case, i.e., using *F* for 'It will be that' and *P* for 'It has been that', the law

$$CpFPp;$$

and to the extensionality of tense-functors, i.e., to the rule that if $Ca\beta$ is a law so are $CPaP\beta$ and $CFaF\beta$. Calling this latter RE, we can prove our implication as follows:

1. $CCpqCCqrCpr$ (syllogism)
2. $C\delta q\Sigma p\delta p$ (existential generalisation)
3. $CpFPp$
4. $CP\delta qP\Sigma p\delta p$ (2, RE)

5. $CFP\delta q FP\Sigma p\delta p$ (4, RE)
6. $C\delta FP\Sigma p\delta Fp FP\delta FP\Sigma p\delta Fp$ (3, subst.)
7. $CFP\delta FP\Sigma p\delta Fp FP\Sigma p\delta Fp$
   ($5 \; \delta/\delta F, \; q/P\Sigma p\delta Fp$)
8. $C\delta FP\Sigma p\delta Fp FP\Sigma p\delta Fp$ (6, 7, 1)

This, with 'I say that' for δ, becomes 'If I say that it will be that it has been that there is something that I say will be, then it will be that it has been that there is something that I say will be', i.e., our implication. Here again, though there is more than quantification theory involved, this more is not a special 'logic of saying'—the δ can be any monadic sentence-forming functor of sentences.

There is, all the same, one way in which the 'attitude' functors have a special interest—an interest, at all events, which is not shared by simple negation. To see this, let us go back to our simpler examples, and look again at the formula

$$CN\Sigma pNp\Sigma pNp.$$

This substitution of N for T or δ has the odd side-effect of making the antecedent the negation of the consequent, so that by the 'law of Clavius' $CCNppp$ we can infer the truth of the consequent (ΣpNp) and the falsehood of the antecedent ($N\Sigma pNp$ or Πpp) *simpliciter*. The interest of the 'psychological' examples lies in the fact that the antecedent *can* occur, and the consequent *can* fail to occur—I *can* think that there is something that I think, say that there is something that I say, fear that there is something that I fear, etc., and I *can* just not think anything, not say anything, not fear anything, so that it is a significant fact that the first thing, in each case, cannot be done at the same time as the second thing (i.e. I cannot say that I am saying something when I am not saying anything, and so on).

But at this point we are liable to hear a chorus of voices—and they once, I must confess, included my own—telling us that one cannot, e.g., say that one is saying something if that is *all* that one is saying. My own earlier, and as I now think erroneous, discussion of this point was provoked by an argument of Mr E. F. Carritt's to the effect that the obligation to keep a promise cannot be denied without self-contradiction, because 'I promise' *means* 'I hereby place myself under an obligation', and this, 'like the statement "I am making a statement", is one of those (statements) that can never be false'.[1] In criticising this, I did not—as I now think I ought to have done—deny the parallel, but accepted it, and then argued that 'I am making a statement', understood as self-referring, is not really a statement at all. For (I wrote)

> 'I am making a statement' means, I take it, that there is some specific statement that I am making when I utter the words; and although I do not say what it is, presumably I know; for if I do not, certainly no one else does; and if no one knows what the statement is, perhaps there isn't any, and then 'I am making a statement' would be false. But Mr Carritt says it cannot be false; and it is plain enough that the answer he intends us to give to the question '*What* statement am I making?' is 'I am making the statement that I am making a statement'. But *what* statement am I making the statement that I am making? The only answer which would make the expression infallibly true would appear to be that I am making the statement that I am making the statement that I am making a statement. There is plainly no end to all this—this 'statement', if it is a statement at all, is a bottomless abyss.'[2]

This, it now seems to me, begins correctly, but after the first semi-colon it is mostly rubbish. 'I am making a statement' does indeed mean that 'there is some specific statement that I am making when I utter the words', and cannot be true unless there is such a statement, but it does not say what that statement is (what that statement is, is *no* part of 'what it means'), nor does it need to; nor do I, nor does anyone, need to know, or be able to say, what that specific statement is, in order for the general statement to be true. The case is exactly as it would be if I said, 'I am being followed by a man'—if I am indeed being followed by a man, there must be some particular individual man who is following me; but I can say that I am being followed by a man, and say so truly, and even know that it is true, without either saying or knowing who the particular man is by whom I am being followed. We might put the point thus: There cannot *be* any merely general fact without there being a

[1] E. F. Carritt, *Ethical and Political Thinking*, pp. 37, 102.
[2] A. N. Prior, *Logic and the Basis of Ethics*, p. 49.

corresponding individual fact, but a merely general fact can quite easily be stated or known without the corresponding individual fact being stated or known. And consequently, an individual object can quite easily *be* what verifies some merely general statement or thought or fear, etc., without anyone stating or thinking or fearing that it is so. In particular, the statement that I am making a statement can quite easily itself *be* the statement that I am making without my stating that it is (or that anything else in particular is), so that there is just no need for the above infinite regress even to get started.

Similarly, if Descartes thought that he thought something, he was right, for he *did* think something, namely that he thought something. But he need not have thought that this was what he thought; just as, if he thought that he was eating something, then if he was in fact eating bacon and bananas, he was right in what he thought (i.e. that he was eating something), even though he did not think that it was bacon and bananas that he was eating (and perhaps had no opinion at all as to what it was). So, having said above 'He was right, for he *did* think something, namely that he thought something', I do not need to add any second 'namely', i.e. I do not need to say 'he *did* think something, namely that he thought something, namely . . .'; for this second 'namely' would not introduce but would be part of what he '*did* think', as if he himself specified what he thought, and this he just need not have done.

I suspect that the reason why people have sometimes been unhappy at this point is that they have confused the present case with what is really a very different one, namely the case in which we have a man saying or thinking that he is saying or thinking something *true*. If I say that I am saying something true (and do not say anything else), I must be either right or wrong in saying this. If I am right, there must be some specific thing which (a) I am saying and (b) is the case—some specific p such that (a) I say that p and (b) p. *Ex hypothesi* there *is* a specific thing that I am saying, namely that I am saying something true [and as far as condition (a) is concerned this could be the end of the matter]; but is this thing that I am saying *true*? [is condition (b) fulfilled?]. It can only be so if there is some specific thing which (a) I am saying and (b) is the case. And now, it is clear, we really are embarked on an infinite regress— condition (b) requires that, behind the fact that there is something true that I say, there be a more specific fact as to what true thing I say, but this turns out to be, if anything, simply the original general fact, that there is something true that I say, for which condition (b) requires that there be, etc.

We might put it this way: if I say that I am saying something true, then this is a specific individual asserting, and so is fit to be the (or a) specific thing said, but its content is purely general, and it is this content which is relevant to the truth of the asserting, and which must be capable of further specification if the assertion is to have any truth at all (and is not capable of it if nothing else is said).

Must I, then, be simply *wrong* if I say that I am saying something true, and say nothing else? This will not do either, for if I am wrong in saying this, the truth of the matter must be that there is nothing true that I am saying. This in turn can only be so if either (i) I am not saying anything at all (and so not saying anything true *or* false), or (ii) there is some specific *false* thing that I am saying. As to alternative (ii), there is *ex hypothesi* one thing and one thing only that I am saying, namely that I am saying something true. But is this false (as alternative (ii) requires)? It can only be so if there is nothing true that I am saying, i.e., if either (i) there is nothing at all that I am saying, or (ii) there is some specific false thing that I am saying. Here again an infinite regress has clearly begun. I cannot, consequently, say either truly or falsely that I am saying something true, if I say nothing else but this. Hence if I say nothing else but this I cannot even say this; though of course I can make the noises which under other circumstances would amount to saying this, and another person can say truly of me that I am saying nothing true (because I am not saying anything at all), or falsely that I am saying something true.[1]

The case is even clearer if I am supposed to say or think that I am saying or thinking something *false*, this being *all* that I am supposed to say or think. This supposition can be easily shown to be simply self-contradictory. It is the same with the vaguer assertion that there are false assertions, and the thought that there are mistaken thoughts. As Socrates notes in his criticism of Protagoras in the *Theaetetus*, there is an inconsistency in supposing the latter thought to occur and to be mistaken; but there is also an inconsistency in supposing

[1] For a similar argument to this one, see P. J. Fitzpatrick, ' "Heterological" and Namely-riders', *Analysis*, October 1961, pp. 18–22.

it to occur at all if no other thought occurs. What Socrates saw was this: If it were false (as it is on the view of Protagoras) that there are mistaken thoughts, then anyone thinking that there are mistaken thoughts would be mistaken, and so there would be *this* mistaken thought; but then it wouldn't *be* mistaken, but true, that there are mistaken thoughts.[1] If I put $T(m)p$ ('It is thought mistakenly that p') for $KTpNp$ ('It is thought that p, but not p'), the reasoning is more or less like this:

1. $CN\Sigma pT(m)pCT\Sigma pT(m)pKT\Sigma pT(m)pN\Sigma pT(m)p$
   ($CpCqKqp$, subst.)
2. $CN\Sigma pT(m)pCT\Sigma pT(m)pT(m)\Sigma pT(m)p$ (1, Df. $T(m)$)
3. $CT(m)\Sigma pT(m)p\Sigma pT(m)p$ ($CT(m)q\Sigma pT(m)p$, subst.)
4. $CN\Sigma pT(m)pCT\Sigma pT(m)p\Sigma pT(m)p$ (2, 3, Syll.)
5. $CT\Sigma pT(m)pCN\Sigma pT(m)p\Sigma pT(m)p$ (4, Comm.)
6. $CT\Sigma pT(m)p\Sigma pT(m)p$ (5, $CCNppp$, Syll.)

But—and this Socrates did not see (or is not depicted by Plato as seeing)—if this necessarily true thought (i.e., necessarily true-if-it-occurs) were the only thought, it would be both false and true. False, because if there is at least one mistaken thought and it is the only thought, it must be mistaken. And so true, because if it is mistaken there is at least one mistaken thought, which is what it says. But it cannot be both false and true, i.e., it cannot both be and not be the case that there is at least one mistaken thought. Therefore this thought cannot occur unless there is at least one other thought.

Even in this case, I am inclined to think, the matter would be completely mended if, let us say, Socrates thought that there was at least one mistaken thought and Protagoras that there were none, and there were no other thoughts beside these two. For then the Socratic thought would be true and the Protagorean one false by the Socratic reasoning—or, alternatively, because at least one of two contradictory beliefs must be mistaken—and the Protagorean thought would supply the specific instance which the truth of the Socratic one requires.

[1] Cf. Geach's modification of the Epimenides paradox in A. N. Prior, 'On a family of paradoxes', *Notre Dame Journal of Formal Logic*, vol. 2, no. 1 (Jan. 1961), pp. 16–32, sect. 8.

However this may be, nothing like our demonstration that the Socratic thought cannot occur in isolation, can be given for the Cartesian thought *that something is being thought*. I take it, therefore, that it would be logically possible for this thought to be the only thought; and it cannot be thought at all (whether it is the only thought or not) without being true. This does not mean, however, that it cannot be doubted, or that there is an infallible recipe for putting all doubt about it to rest, as Descartes seems to have maintained. The recipe that Descartes had in mind, so far as I can see, was simply to go through the argument sketched and defended above—that if a person thinks that there is something he is thinking, then there *is* something he is thinking, namely that there is something he is thinking, so that this thought can never be mistaken. This argument, as I have already admitted, is sound, but that is not enough to make it an infallible recipe for dispelling a man's doubt as to whether he is right in thinking that there is something he is thinking. Is it, all the same, such a recipe?

The Cartesian argument, let me repeat, goes like this:

'I am thinking that there is something that I am thinking.
Therefore there is something that I am thinking'.

But this will only prove its conclusion to someone who is sure of the truth of the premiss, and an essential part of my defence of the Cartesian argument against the infinite-regress criticism was that a man can think that he is thinking something without thinking (let alone knowing) what that something is. Still, it might be maintained that anyone who thinks some specific thing can on reflection discover for certain what it is that he thinks. This principle, if applied universally, entails a possibility of unlimited repetitions—if a man thinks that he is thinking something, he can on reflection discover, and so think, that he thinks this, and then on further reflection discover, and so think, that he thinks that he thinks this, and so on— but this is a repetition that *need* not be started, and can be stopped whenever the man cares to stop reflecting, and so does not constitute a vicious or embarrassing infinite regress. But there seem to me other objections to the principle.

It seems to me, in the first place, quite certain that one may think that one is thinking something when one is in fact not thinking that thing. Suppose—to modify an example I have used before[1]—that I do what I take to be thinking that something false is being thought in Room 7; and suppose that (unknown to myself) I am myself in Room 7 when I do this; that I am alone there, and that I have no thought except the thought that I am thinking this, and possibly this thought itself. Now the thought that I am thinking that something false is being thought in Room 7 is either true or false; can it, under the circumstances envisaged, possibly be true? If it is true, then I really am thinking that something false is being thought in Room 7, and this thought itself is either true or false. But if it were true, then it would be false, for if it were true, something false would be being thought in Room 7, and *ex hypothesi* the only other thought in Room 7, the second-order one, is true, so the false thought must be this one itself. So it cannot be true. But neither can it be false. For if it were, then *nothing* false would be being thought in Room 7, and so not it. But what is not thought truly or falsely is not thought at all. Hence if under these circumstances I were right in taking myself to be thinking that something false is thought in Room 7, I would be wrong. Hence under these (empirically possible) circumstances I would be bound to be wrong in taking myself to be thinking this. Hence a mistake about what one is thinking is possible.

From the fact that I can think that I am thinking that p when in fact I am not and cannot be thinking that p, it does not follow that I can really be thinking that p without being able to discover that I am. But the cases in which I think mistakenly that I am thinking that p seem to be introspectively indistinguishable from at least many of those in which I think so correctly; e.g., the preceding example unaltered except for my not happening to be in Room 7 myself at the time. Since whether I could or could not be thinking the thought in question could depend in part on whether or not I was myself in Room 7, I do not see how I can *know* that I am thinking it if I do not know (as I very well might not) whether I am in Room 7 or not. Hence in this case at least it seems possible that I should think a thing without knowing that I am thinking it; and in general it would seem that if (as seems obviously the case) we can be in this place or that without knowing that we are, we can in at least some cases

[1] A. N. Prior, 'Identifiable individuals', *Review of Metaphysics*, vol. 13, no. 4 (June 1960), pp. 693–4; 'On a family of paradoxes', *Notre Dame Journal of Formal Logic*, vol. 2, no. 1 (Jan. 1961), pp. 16–32, sects. 34 ff.

think this or that without knowing (without being perfectly certain, and entitled to be perfectly certain) that we do.

In sum, then, it seems that although there are thoughts which, if they occur at all, cannot but be true, it is by no means clear that there are any thoughts (even thoughts about our thoughts) which, if they occur, cannot but be *known* to be true.

18. What Do General Statements Refer To?[1]

There is a fashionable philosophical technique of considering the circumstances under which it would be normal to find people uttering sentences of certain sorts, and examining some aspect of what it is that they are then doing. I cannot myself pretend to be a very skilled practitioner of this art; but since I am speaking to this question I mean nevertheless to have a go. Given that someone has made some such remark as 'All John's children are asleep', or 'All trespassers will be prosecuted', or 'All unicorns have a single horn': under what circumstances would it be natural for one of his hearers to ask the question 'To whom' (or 'To what') are you referring?'? I must say I find it very difficult indeed to imagine *any* circumstances in which this would be a very natural question to ask a person who had made one of these statements. In most cases this question, as the saying goes, just doesn't arise.

This is even more obvious if you put the question in the form 'To *which* children' (or 'To *which* trespassers' or 'To *which* unicorns') 'are you referring?' I should have thought that one of the most obvious things about the word 'All' is in statements of the form 'All Xs are Ys' that it *rules out* this question. Certainly this is so if there is any emphasis on the word 'All': '*All* John's children are asleep', '*All* trespassers will be prosecuted', '*All* unicorns have a single horn'. Statements with this emphasis, '*All* Xs are Ys', seem to be tantamount to saying '*No matter what* X you take, you'll find it's a Y'—'No matter what positive integer you take, it will be found to be representable as the sum of four squares'; and so forth. Which items you are referring to, in other words, *doesn't matter*; moreover

[1] [This was a reply to a paper which has never been published, read in Oxford *c*. 1967. We have made various excisions to make the paper self-contained. *Edd.*]

the form is 'Whichever items *you* refer to'—the man who says 'All Xs are Ys' isn't *himself* referring to them; just because *he* says 'all', to ask *which* he is referring to, or even *what* he is referring to, is a silly question.

Still maybe there *is* the odd case in which the question is in order. For example, suppose some adults are gathered in a downstairs room and there's a great clatter of children upstairs, and some member of the party says wistfully, 'All *John's* children are asleep anyhow.' Then if there's more than one John in the room, I suppose someone might ask 'To whom are you referring?', and the particular John intended would then be identified. It's worth noting that in this case it's the reference of the name 'John' that is in question; they're not really, or anyhow not directly, asking which children. In other words, this particular proposition has a singular as well as a general aspect and it is only in its singular aspect that it gives rise to a question about reference.

Or again, I suppose the question 'To which children are you referring when you say "All John's children"?' could be a nasty way of hinting that John's wife had been unfaithful to him, or perhaps that John had more children than he publicly owned. But if this were the case, one might well say that the question was *uncalled for*— that there was really no need to bring that up when John's children were mentioned. Of course there might be a point, I mean a point other than mere nastiness, in bringing it up: if the sentence had been 'All John's children will inherit shares in his estate', you might then say 'To which of John's children are you referring?' But *this* question, whether raised nastily or to settle a legal point, would be only superficially a question of *reference*. I mean, what is really wanted here is not a *list* of children, but an explanation of what you mean by the phrase 'child of John'—do you mean 'legitimate child', 'acknowledged child', 'biological child', or what? It's *sense* rather than reference that is really being asked about here.

In any case it must surely be admitted that these are odd, non-standard circumstances, and that in the normal case part of the point of using 'All' is to forestall any such question, to make it a silly one, to assume that it doesn't arise. And if I'm right about this, this surely lends some support to that quantification-theory interpretation of these statements which has come in for attack. I won't bother with putting this interpretation into symbols; what it amounts to is that 'All Xs are Ys' can be equated, as far as the information it conveys is concerned, with 'If anything is an X it is a Y', or 'Whatever is an X is a Y', where the use of 'X' as well as 'Y' is not referring but predicative, or so to speak hypothetically predicative. I don't mind admitting that reference could in a way come in; but if it does, it comes in hypothetically, and it's not a reference that is made by the *speaker* in saying 'All Xs are Ys', but rather a reference which he invites from the hearer—'*You* name me an X, and I'll tell you it's a Y'. In saying '*All* Xs', I repeat, the speaker is saying in effect 'I'm not referring to any X—I don't need to—I'm prepared to let *you* do the referring; and if you succeed in that, I'm telling you that what you refer to will be a Y.'

Still, perhaps all this is misguided. Perhaps I've got mixed up between philosophy and meta-philosophy, which may well have quite different techniques; perhaps the sort of technique the philosopher applies to everyday utterances, like 'All unicorns have a single horn' and 'All positive integers can be represented as the sum of four squares', is not appropriately applied to the philosopher's own technicalities. If this word 'refers' is being used in the question we started with as part of the technical apparatus of philosophy, then all these illustrations of its use and its non-use in everyday conversation are irrelevant to what the philosopher is doing with it. Well, certainly philosophers do have just as much right to be technical as biologists and grammarians and mathematicians have; I'm all for that. My trouble here is that I don't completely gather just what, in *our* question, the special technical use of the term 'refer' could be. I don't really know of any technical sense of the term 'refer' in which it could be said that *statements* refer at all, let alone general ones.

To be more accurate, I *do* know of one such technical use, but it is fairly obviously not the one intended when people speak of 'referring expressions' and the like. It is a use that has come in from discussion of Frege's view of *Bedeutung*. Frege, as is well known, believed that statements, or at all events sentences, refer to or denote (*bedeuten*) one or the other of a pair of objects called the True and the False. I have never thought that this particular technicality was a very happy one, and I'm glad to drop it. But if we rule out this Fregean referring, what *is* the 'referring' that some people suppose general statements to do? It appears to have something to do with what is called ontological commitment, but not to be quite the same as that; perhaps the difference is that you can refer to what you don't believe exists, but it would be self-contradictory to describe anyone as ontologically committed to what he doesn't believe exists.

One thing that people might mean by saying that a general statement 'All Xs are Ys' *refers to* a certain individual A, is that A is one of the individuals that would have to be a Y for this general statement to be true. And the sorts of individual that qualify as being 'referred to' in this sense will differ a great deal from one sort of general statement to another. In 'All John's children are asleep', only certain individuals now existing are involved; in 'All cats like fish', we also have to consider cats now dead, and perhaps also cats yet unborn. But do reflections of this sort conflict with the analysis which equates 'All Xs are Ys' with 'Whatever is an X is a Y'?

I can see one way in which there *might* be said to be such a conflict. Consider the example about the cats. If 'All cats like fish' is tantamount to saying 'Produce me any cat you like: that cat will like fish', then it could be argued that since you can't now 'produce' dead cats, or anyhow long-dead ones (and the recently-dead ones *don't* like fish any more anyway), and you certainly can't produce unborn ones (apart from foetuses, and once again *these* don't like fish *yet*), the statement, when analysed that way, *must* refer to cats now existing, in fact to cats now alive.

I think this has to be answered in two bits. In the first place, *however* you analyse the proposition 'All cats like fish', it *is* only true of cats now alive that they *like* fish; the thing that is true of the dead ones is that they *liked* fish, and what is true of the unborn ones is that they *will* like fish. Secondly, even allowing this, I think we must agree that the proposition 'All cats like fish' can be, and often is so used as to cover *all* these facts—the facts about the dead and unborn cats as well as the one about the living ones. And I think it must also be admitted that in this use of it the proposition 'All cats like fish' *isn't* equivalent to 'Whatever *is* a cat *likes* fish' but says rather more than that, namely that it is not only *is* the case, but always *has been* the case and always *will be* the case, that whatever is a cat likes fish. I think, in short, that the form 'All Xs are Ys' has different uses in different instances; and we *could* describe these different uses as different ways of referring, though I wouldn't myself think this a particularly happy way of describing them.

One reason why I don't *quite* like this way of putting it, I can try to make clear by adverting again to the 'cats' example. I'd rather avoid the suggestion that existing cats are a sub-class within a wider class that also includes formerly existing cats and cats to be, so that we have to ask, in connexion with a statement like 'All cats like fish', to which of these sub-classes are we referring. And it would be still more objectionable to think of existing animals as a sub-class of a wider class that also includes imaginary ones, and to suppose that when someone says 'All unicorns have a single horn' we have to ask ourselves which province of the animal kingdom we are referring to, the real or the mythical. I'd rather say, in the unicorns example, that what we want to know is whether the man is saying that *it is the case* that whatever is a unicorn has a single horn, or merely that *it is said in the books that* whatever is a unicorn has a single horn. And similarly I'd rather say, in the cats example, that the question is whether the man is merely saying that *it is the case* that all cats like fish, or whether he is also saying that that *always has been the case* and perhaps even that it *always will be the* case. And it does seem to me misleading to put this question in the form 'To which cats—or unicorns—are we referring?' Maybe the moral of the vague use of 'refer' is that we should in most cases drop it.

19. Things and Stuff

Students of Greek philosophy are apt to be bewildered when given as examples of what Aristotle meant by 'substance', in the primary sense, such things as *this horse* and *this man*, and as examples of what he meant by 'substance' in the secondary sense, such things as *horse* or *man* in general. It is fairly clear from the context that he is not here referring to two sorts of *meat*, but to *a horse* or *a man* in general, or perhaps better to *the horse* in the 'institutional' sense, as in 'The horse is an animal that neighs', and to *man* in a similar sense, as in 'Man is an animal that laughs'. We would more happily, today, describe Aristotle's 'first substances' as individual *things* and his 'second substances' as *kinds of things*.

'A substance' nowadays does not mean so much a *kind of thing* as a *kind of stuff*; this is so, e.g. when chemists divide substances into elements and compounds, and list the properties of such substances as sulphur, the various oxides, and so on; equine and human meat are just what *would* be substances in this sense. But, disconcertingly, we find the ancients using 'substance' in the modern sense too; e.g. not only *horse*, but *gold*, may be given as an example of a substance. Thus in *Met.* 1042a6, Aristotle says that the substances 'generally recognised are the natural substances, i.e. fire, earth, water, air, etc. . . . secondly, plants and their parts, and animals and the parts of animals'. Here the first group seem to be kinds of stuff, and the second group kinds of things.

There is the same mistake in Locke's *Essay on Human Understanding* II.xiii.3: 'Thus we come to have the idea of a man, horse, gold, water, etc.; of which substances, whether any one has any other clear ideas . . .' And again: '. . . any particular sort of compound substance, as horse, stone, etc. . . . the thing called horse or stone.' There is here a quite appalling grammatical ineptitude, an indifference to the presence or absence of articles; a course in

Austinian verbalism really would have brought out a philosophical point here.

We clearly cannot follow the ancients, or Locke, in this matter; the distinction between things and stuff has come to stay, and it is worth occupying ourselves with the relation between them.

How little we have yet done so was vividly pointed out in a recent paper by Donald Davidson. Tarski's standard example of the kind of sentence that ought to be derivable from a satisfactory definition of truth is

'Snow is white' is true if and only if snow is white.

But, as Davidson points out, in none of the languages for which Tarski provides a definition of truth is it possible to formulate this particular sentence, let alone prove it. Contemporary workers in logic and semantics have evolved fairly satisfactory ways of formulating the relations between things and their qualities and relations and between things and events and states of affairs, and between things and their parts (mereology), but the logic of the relations between things and stuff, or between things and stuffs (would it be called 'ousiology'?) has still to be worked out.

We might set about filling this gap in various ways. For example, before attempting a rigorous formal treatment we might undertake a more or less Austinian survey of our actual use of thing-words and stuff-words. The first clear distinction between things and stuffs seems in fact to have been made by a grammarian, namely Jespersen, with his introduction of the category of 'mass-words'. It is noteworthy that in Jespersen the discussion is already rather philosophical—it is not for nothing that his book is called *The Philosophy of Grammar*. For him the important point is that with mass-words the distinction between singular and plural makes no sense. (In actual languages some mass-words are singular, like 'silver', 'water', 'butter', and some are plural, like 'victuals', 'dregs', and sometimes a plural in one language corresponds to a singular in another; there may even be this difference with the same word in different dialects, e.g. 'porridge' is singular in English and plural in Scottish.) Jespersen also observes that the same word may be used sometimes as a mass-word and sometimes as a thing-word, e.g. 'a little more cheese' and 'two big cheeses', 'Cork is lighter than water' and 'I want three corks for these bottles'.

This is only a beginning. We might go on, e.g., to contrast contexts in which thing-words and stuff-words *are* interchangeable, e.g. we can say both that snow is white ('This stuff is white'), and that my shirt is white ('This thing is white'), with contexts in which they are *not*, e.g. we can say that my shirt weighs six ounces but not that snow weighs six ounces. We might say, indeed, that such and such a *bit* of snow weighs six ounces, but while snow is a stuff, a bit of snow is a thing. We might, again, examine forms of speech in which things and stuffs are related, e.g. the one just used—*bits* or *pieces* of stuff are things, and possibly all things are bits of stuff; things are said to be *made* of stuff ('This table is made of wood').

Or we might take another line, and say that basically there *isn't* a new problem here, and that stuff-words are dispensable; that if we want to say everything we now say but with a minimum vocabulary, we can do it all with thing-words plus appropriate adjectives, verbs, etc. We might regard this as a 'hypothesis' in the Popperian sense, to be checked against the 'facts' unearthed by investigations of the 'Austinian' sort.

One way of thus eliminating stuff-words as a special category is Quine's—treating stuff-words as referring to a single big broken-up thing consisting of all the bits of that kind of stuff in the universe. Apart from difficulties of detail, I am pretty certain that we are *not* in fact referring to any such object, or indeed to any one object at all, when we use a stuff-word. And when we want to say *which* things are part of the one big thing that is (say) water in Quine's sense, I don't see how we can do it except by saying that it consists of all bits of water (the stuff), so we're back where we were. Quine also, incidentally, follows one of Jespersen's least fortunate suggestions: he assimilates ordinary abstract nouns to mass-words. Jespersen did this on the grounds that we happily use such phrases as 'much experience', 'little talent', 'more admiration'. Maybe; but we don't speak of individuals as made of talent, etc., as we do speak of things as made of glass, and of other genuine stuffs. We might, however, try eliminating stuffs in a slightly subtler way.

Let us compare this case with some more familiar ones. From C. S. Peirce onwards, there have been logicians who have been unhappy about *adjectives* and *common nouns* as irreducible linguistic units, and have contended that they can always in principle be replaced by verbs. It is obvious that they frequently occur as *parts* of verbs or predicates, e.g. in 'This is white' the adjective 'white' occurs as part of the predicate 'is white', and in 'This is a man' the common noun 'man' occurs as part of the predicate 'is a man'. Adjectives and nouns do, indeed, occur in other ways in which they are not patently parts of verbs, e.g. when a common noun occurs as a subject, as in 'Every man is mortal', and when an adjective immediately qualifies a noun, as in 'Every white man is mortal'. But there are well-known ways of exposing the verb-forms which are latent in examples like this, e.g. we can re-write 'Every white man is mortal' as 'Whatever is-a-man and is-white is-mortal'. There are no doubt other cases which present a little more difficulty, but we can reasonably hope to eliminate adjectives and common nouns from a minimum vocabulary (or minimum syntax) by devices of the type illustrated.

Can we do the same with stuff-words? Well, once again, these do enter into verb-forms as parts; in particular, any stuff-word x can occur as part of the verb 'is made of x'. It may be that occurrences of stuff-words in other contexts can be pushed into this context by suitable re-phrasing, e.g. 'Snow is white' is at least roughly equivalent to 'Anything that is-made-of-snow is-white'. This done, we can perhaps define the basic form 'is-made-of-x' in terms of what chemists call the 'properties' of x—to be 'made of snow' is to be white in colour, to melt at such-and-such a temperature, and so on. When this is attempted in detail it rapidly becomes apparent that the definition of 'made-of-x' will in most cases have to be not in terms of occurrent but rather in terms of dispositional properties—powers, tendencies and the like. As Locke says (II.xxiii.37), 'Most of the simple ideas that make up our complex ideas of substances, when truly considered, are only *powers*, however we are apt to take them for positive qualities; viz. the greatest part of the ideas that make up our complex ideas of *gold* are yellowness, great weight, ductility, fusibility, and solubility in *aqua regia*.' Certainly these dispositional terms seem to fall outside any of the languages for which Tarski has provided definitions of truth, but we have at least reduced an apparently new problem to an old one, and powers, dispositions, etc. can perhaps be dealt with satisfactorily by some sort of modal logic.

We may also note one or two other features of the kinds of predicate that generally enter into definitions of stuff-predicates, I mean of predicates of the form 'is made of *x*'. It seems to be the case, for example, that if anything is made of a certain kind of stuff, then at least some of its parts are also made of that kind of stuff, and have the properties of which being made of that kind of stuff consists. If something is made of snow, then in general its parts are made of snow too; though this no doubt has to be qualified when the parts are very small. On the other hand, if something is a horse or even a chair, its parts are not horses or chairs. It seems to follow from this that the things which can be made of such-and-such a kind of stuff must be things having parts which are themselves things. Possibly all things have parts, but it is arguable that some things haven't; for example, if there are such objects as centres of consciousness, it may be doubted whether they have parts, and consequently doubted whether they are made of any kind of stuff; and for all I know, some physicists may think of centres of energy in the same way.

A bit of such-and-such stuff (e.g. a bit of snow) is simply a thing made of that stuff; it may have further properties of interest, but in calling it a bit of such stuff no more is said than that it is made of that stuff; and it may in fact *not* have any further properties of interest—it may be *just* a bit of that stuff. But even if all things are bits of stuff, to call them by their normal names is not always to say merely that they are made of such-and-such stuff, and it may not be to say that at all. Horses and chairs, no doubt, are made of some sort of stuff, but to call a thing a horse or a chair is not to say merely what it is made of, and perhaps is not to say what it is made of at all (this is even clearer with chairs than with horses).

A strong argument *against* the kind of reduction that I have been tentatively advocating has recently been suggested to me. I've suggested in effect that words like 'snow' always occur explicitly or implicitly as part of predicates like 'is made of snow', and that these predicates aren't really further analysable. But sometimes it looks as if they *do* have an internal structure. For example, 'This is made of snow and dirt' doesn't seem to mean the same as 'This is made of snow and is made of dirt', but it's implausible to suggest that 'made of snow and dirt' is simply a third unanalysable predicate into which the separate meanings of 'snow' and 'dirt' don't enter. In other words, it looks as though the words 'snow' and 'dirt' can be *taken out of* the context 'is made of *x*' and separately compounded in logically interesting ways.

If this were the last word to be said on the subject, we would have to admit that an adequate language must contain, beside thing-names and the predicates that go with them, a separate category of stuff-names and the predicates that go with them, and also expressions that link the two kinds of names. But I'm not sure that we *do* have to do this. We might say, for example, that '*x* is wholly made of snow and dirt' means '*x* is partly made of snow and partly made of dirt, and there is nothing else of which *x* is partly made'; and that this in turns boils down to 'Some parts of *x* are made of snow and some parts of *x* are made of dirt and all parts of *x* are either made of snow or made of dirt'. This reduces any suggested discipline of ousiology to what the Leśniewskians call mereology, i.e. the theory of parts of things, supplemented by the theory, whatever it is, of dispositional predicates. And I hope I have at least shown that this reduction can be carried quite a long way—it's a hypothesis that survives *some* criticisms, at all events, though whether it can survive *all* criticisms I don't know.

20. *Intentionality and Intensionality*

1. I share Professor Kneale's view that it is best to regard 'intensionality', or if you like 'non-extensionality', as a rather general phenomenon of which 'intentionality' provides some of the most interesting examples. But I want to make a sharper distinction than Kneale seems to do between the question as to whether there are *intensional functions* and that as to whether there are *intensional objects*. I shall argue, or at all events assert, that there are indeed intensional functions as well as extensional ones, but that there are no such objects as 'intensions', and no such objects as 'extensions' either.

2. To say that a function F of propositions, properties, relations, etc. is an *extensional* one, is to say that it satisfies the appropriate member of the series of formulæ which begins as follows:

(i) $(p) (q) : p \equiv q . \supset . F(p) \equiv F(q)$
(ii) $(\varphi) (\psi) : (x) (\varphi x \equiv \psi x) . \supset . F(\varphi) \equiv F(\psi)$
(iii) $(\varphi) (\psi) : (x) (y) (\varphi xy \equiv \psi xy) . \supset . F(\varphi) \equiv F(\psi)$
(iv) $(\varphi) (\psi) : (x) (y) (z) (\varphi xyz \equiv \psi xyz) . \supset . F(\varphi) \equiv F(\psi).$

It is obvious, I take it, how to continue this series. To take case (i), a function of propositions F is an extensional one, if whenever p and q have the same truth-value ($p \equiv q$), $F(p)$ and $F(q)$ have the same truth-value. Negation is an obvious example. And to take case (ii), a function of properties F is an extensional one if whenever φ and ψ characterise the same objects, $F(\varphi)$ has the same truth-value as $F(\psi)$.

To say that a function F is a *non-extensional* or *intensional* one, is to say that it does not satisfy the appropriate member of this series.

An *extensionalist* may be defined as a person who holds that every function F of propositions, properties, relations, etc. is extensional in this sense, and a *non-extensionalist* or *intensionalist* may be defined as a person who holds that some functions of propositions etc. are not extensional in this sense.

In this sense, both Kneale and I are intensionalists. And we are both, I think, partly led to our intensionalism by the consideration of 'intentional' functions, i.e. ones involving psychological attitudes. For example, the *intentional* function of propositions 'Jones knows that—' is also an *intensional* one; for it is clear that the fact that 'grass is green' and '$\log_{10} 100 = 2$' have the same truth-value does not guarantee that 'Jones knows that grass is green' will have the same truth-value as 'Jones knows that $\log_{10} 100 = 2$'.

It seems to me worth adding, however, that this is by no means the only sort of example that makes extensionalism unplausible, not to say incredible. To take a quite different sort of example, one that is not 'intentional' at all: Everything that is red occupies one or another of certain regions of space, and everything that occupies one or another of those regions of space is red, but who wants to infer from this that since red is a colour, the occupation of those regions is a colour? Is it not, on the contrary, perfectly plain that the occupation of those regions is not a colour but a location? With cases of this sort in mind, I am simply flabbergasted when extensionalists assert that their principles are perfectly compatible with the outlook of Science, though we may be led to question them if we descend to inferior forms of discourse such as Philosophy, Literature and Introspective Psychology.

3. The question as to whether or not there are any such entities as *intensional objects* or *intensions* is an altogether different question, and is part of the wider question as to whether or not there are *abstract* objects, i.e. the question which is sometimes described as that of Platonism *versus* nominalism. If we take the so-called Platonist view that there are indeed abstract objects, we may divide these into *intensions*, which include propositions, properties and relations as ordinarily understood, and *extensions*, which include truth-values, classes and what are called 'relations in extension'. I shall have something to say about extensions later; in the meantime, let us look at the question as to whether there are any such entities as propositions and properties.

In referring to my own views on this subject, Professor Kneale expresses himself in a very generous and accommodating way, though I think it remains clear that he and I are a little further apart on this question than we are on that of intensionalism *versus* extensionalism. But his representation of my version of nominalism is entirely accurate and just. I do still wish to say that in 'Socrates taught that the soul is immortal' we ought not to regard the word 'that' as forming, from the sentence 'The soul is immortal', a name of the object of Socrates' belief, but we ought rather to regard the word 'that' as attaching to the verb 'taught' to form a sort of half-connective linking a name, not to another name, but to a sentence. And I am committed, as Kneale says I ought in consistency to be, to the 'redundancy theory of truth', that is, the theory that 'The proposition that snow is white is true' is merely a blowing up of the plain 'Snow is white'. Talk which is ostensibly about properties and relations I would deal with similarly. I would advocate, for example, what might be called redundancy theories of characterisation and of holding-between; to say that the property of φ-ing characterises the object x is in my view to say no more and no less than that x φs, and to say that the relation of φ-ing holds between x and y, in that order, is to say no more and no less than that x φs y.

Of course we do all talk as if there were such objects as propositions, properties and relations. For example, in the last section I myself said, 'A function of properties F is an extensional one if whenever φ and ψ characterise the same objects, $F(\varphi)$ has the same truth-value as $F(\psi)$'. I would, however, regard such ways of talking as philosophically justified only if they can be given a good sense, i.e. a nominalistic one. For example, the sense of my own bit of Platonistic talk just quoted, or rather the sense of the latter part of it, is given by the symbolic formula (ii) of which it is an English version; in that formula there are no variables that stand for names of properties but only (apart from variables that stand for names of individuals) variables that stand for verbs. (These do, indeed, occur bound by quantifiers, and there are those whose eyebrows lift at this; but that is another topic.) Again, the proposition that 'there are intensional functions of properties' amounts to 'For some F, it is not the case that (ii)'.

4. What is the logical relation between these two issues which I

have been so insistent on distinguishing? There is a rather obvious relation between them which belongs not so much to logic as to the sociology or politics of learning. In the language of William James, extensionalism and nominalism both count as 'tough-minded' philosophies, and tend to be propagated by the same philosophical gang, while intensionalism and Platonism both count as 'tender-minded', and again have a tendency, though in this case not such a strong tendency, to be held by the same people. From this sociological point of view, I am probably a rather deviant type in advocating a combination of intensionalism and nominalism. But I think this particular deviation can be supported by reasons.

It seems to me that the sort of philosophising which aims at being tough-minded at all costs is better called escapist philosophising; the world just isn't simple and tidy enough for *all* the tough-minded theories to be true. Nominalism, in particular, seems to me just hopelessly unplausible *unless* you admit non-extensional functions. It is clear, at all events, that if you get rid of the suggestion that the noun-clause 'that grass is green' names an abstract object, by saying that in 'James believes that grass is green' the expression 'James believes that—' forms a sentence not from a name but from a sentence—if you eliminate Platonistic suggestions this way, you are immediately landed with connectives that are not truth-functional. Since it seems to me that there obviously are non-extensional functions anyway—even *being a colour* and *being a location*, and in general falling under this or that determinable, seem to be obviously non-extensional functions of properties—this consequence of nominalism, or of the way of carrying out nominalistic reductions which I have sketched, seems to me to have nothing awkward about it whatever.

Whether, conversely, being a Platonist would make it easier to escape intensionalism, I do not know; I cannot see how it could; in any case I do not myself have this motive for being a Platonist. Nor, of course, has Kneale, so it is not very clear to me why he is not a nominalist too, though I shall suggest a reason for it at the beginning of Section 6.

5. About some sorts of abstract object, Kneale is quite as nominalistic as I am. I do not entirely understand the principles by which he draws the line between those abstract objects which he regards as

genuinely named by abstract nouns and noun phrases and clauses, and those abstract objects of which he prefers to give a nominalist account. It is clear, however, that what are called extensions fall, for him, into the latter class. I am, of course, entirely in agreement with Kneale about this, but it might nevertheless be useful for me to discuss the subject of extensions in my own way.

Take, to begin with, classes. To say that *x* is *a member of the class of φ-ers* is, in my view, just an inflated way of saying that *x* φs. But I have already indicated that I would give exactly the same brief paraphrase for the assertion that *x* is *characterised by the property of φ-ing*. The difference between classes and properties does not emerge at this point but at another. This difference is sometimes represented as one between the ways in which we *count* these various entities or quasi-entities. There are, for instance, innumerable unexemplified properties but only one null class, although to say that *the property of φ-ing is unexemplified* is just the same as to say that *the class of φ-ers is empty*, both being the same as saying that *nothing φs*. This difference in ways of counting arises from different ways of identification. The class of mermaids is the same class as the class of centaurs, though to be a mermaid is one thing and to be a centaur quite another thing.

There is a difference, then, between the following two identity-statements:

(a) The property of φ-ing is the very same property as the property of φ-ing.
(b) The class of φ-ers is the very same class as the class of φ-ers.

In neither of the statements, I should think, is the word 'same' being used in exactly the same way as it is in

(c) *x* is the very same individual as *y*,

though some of the theses which Professor Kneale lumps together as varieties of extensionalism suggest that he doesn't see much difference between (b) and (c). I would say that (b) differs from both (a) and (c) in that the identity which (b) ostensibly asserts is only a fictitious or figurative identity; for what (b) means can be equally well conveyed without suggesting that anything whatever is identical with anything. For (b) is just a way of saying (b)′ Whatever φs ψs, and whatever ψs φs.

For instance, to say that the class of mermaids is the very same class as the class of centaurs, is just to say that all the mermaids there are are centaurs and all the centaurs there are are mermaids, and this is trivially true because there are no mermaids and no centaurs either.

I do not think that any such account can be given of the identity expressed by (a). We can, however, informally elucidate (a) a little by observing that it is in one way like (c) and in another like (b). It is like (c) in that the identity involved is indefinable—it is what it is and not another thing—but all the same, the identity in (a) is not the same as the identity in (c). That it is the same could, indeed, be asserted by a Platonist, who could say that (a) ascribes the kind of identity that is appropriate to individuals to an individual of a slightly odd sort, namely, a property (that property which is at once the property of φ-ing and the property of ψ-ing). My own view, however, would be that 'the property of ψ-ing' no more forms a genuine name in (a) than it does in 'The property of ψ-ing characterises *x*'; it is, rather, an inseparable part of the whole expression

'The property of ( )-ing is the very same property as the property of [ ]-ing',

which forms a sentence not from a pair of names but from a pair of verbs, just as does the expression

'Whatever ( )s [ ]s and whatever [ ]s ( )s'

in our paraphrase of (b). More or less idiomatic paraphrases of (a) would include

(a)′ To φ is to ψ
(a)′ Whatever φs *ipso facto* ψs, and whatever ψs *ipso facto* φs.

Similar remarks are to be made about the two forms

(d) The proposition that *p* is the very same proposition as the proposition that *q*
(e) The truth-value determined by the proposition that *p* is the

very same truth-value as that determined by the proposition that *q*.

Here (e) is simply an inflation of

(e)′ *p* if and only if *q*,

where the 'if' is, as we say, merely 'material', i.e. where the whole is tantamount to

(e)″ Either *p* and *q*, or it is not the case that *p* and not the case that *q*.

(d) expresses an identity as irreducible as that in (c) or (a), but one which falls into the syntactical category of a connective; that is, (d) is not to be read as predicating ordinary identity of an extraordinary individual, the proposition that is at once the proposition that *p* and the proposition that *q*; rather, this apparent name-former 'the proposition that—' is here an inseparable part of the expression

'The proposition that ( ) is the very same proposition as the proposition that [ ]',

which is not (as '( ) is the very same individual as [ ]' is) a two-place predicate forming a sentence from a pair of names, but is rather a two-place sentential connective forming a sentence from a pair of sentences, just as '( ) if and only if [ ]' does. We could roughly paraphrase (d) as

(d)′ For it to be the case that *p*, is the same as for it to be the case that *q*,

or as

(d)″ If *p* then *ipso facto q*, and if *q* then *ipso facto p*.

In brief, we have invented locutions which represent material and formal equivalences as identity-statements, and extensions are those quasi-objects which are said in these statements to be identical, but in fact the whole force of the apparent identity statements is

7

given by the statements of material or formal equivalence, in which these quasi-objects are not mentioned.

To say what I have just said is to take sides, and to take a slightly unpopular side, in an important issue in the Philosophy of Mathematics; for it is to adopt a form of type theory rather than a form of set theory. It would be chicken-hearted either to attempt to disguise this fact, or to be much abashed by it; I mention it for candour's sake, and pass on.

6. An intensionalist who is a little put off by the foregoing hierarchy of indefinable identity functions might well wish to combine his intensionalism with a comparatively moderate sort of Platonism in which extensions are paraphrased away but intensions regarded as genuine, though abstract, individuals. For the paraphrases in which extensions cease to be even ostensibly mentioned only employ perfectly ordinary functions of sentences and of predicates, namely the truth-functional 'if and only if' and its universal quantification. If we used these to scrap extensions but took intensions seriously as individual objects, the latter could then be regarded as terms of the ordinary relation of individual identity, and my hierarchy of what one might call '*ipso facto* functions' dispensed with.

Professor Kneale's own form of moderate Platonism seems to be quite close to this position. If I have understood correctly his account of 'basic propositions', he would say that of those propositions which appear to be about other propositions, the ones which really *are* about other propositions, and so are in his sense 'non-basic', are precisely all those which are not truth-functions of their constituents. His account of 'basic functions' is, however, more complicated, and so is his account of identity. These complications appear to arise from a desire to escape from Leibniz's principle of the 'indiscernibility of identicals', i.e. the law which may be symbolised as

$$(x)(y)(F): x = y. \supset .F(x) \equiv F(y),$$

with analogues employing variables of different logical types. Kneale seems to regard the acceptance of this principle as a mark of extensionalism, but this seems to me a mistake.

7. Let us consider Leibniz's law firstly as a principle about the identity of individuals. It asserts that if x is the very same individual as y then whatever is true of x is true of y. Possibly this law is not true; I have my own doubts about it, which are connected with the possibility of one individual actually *becoming* two individuals and *vice versa*. (Cf. my 'Time, existence and identity', *Proc. Arist. Soc.* 1965–6.) But the point on which I wish now to insist is that a belief in non-extensional functions of propositions, properties, etc. does not *in itself* provide any reason whatever for having misgivings about Leibniz's law. To take one of the stock examples, if Tully is the very same individual as Cicero, it really does follow that if Tom believes that Cicero denounced Catiline then he believes that Tully did so; at least this follows *if* we so understand 'Tom believes that Cicero denounced Catiline' as to make it a genuine case of $F(x)$. i.e. as really telling us something that is 'true of Cicero', as ascribing *to the man Cicero* the property of being believed by Tom to have denounced Catiline. If we only understand by it that Tom believed that there was someone who was called 'Cicero', who was famous for this and that, and who denounced Catiline, then indeed it does not follow that he also believed that there was someone who was called 'Tully', etc.; but in this case the premiss does not tell us something that is 'true of Cicero'—not because 'Tom believes that —' expresses a non-extensional function of the proposition that someone was called 'Cicero', etc., but because this 'intentional' act of Tom's is not directed towards Cicero or indeed towards any individual in particular. $(\exists y)F(y)$ is not a case of the form $F(x)$, nor is $Ba(\exists y)F(y)$, where $B = $ 'believes that'.

This is not just an *ad hoc* solution to this particular problem. There are independent reasons for not regarding 'Something F's', or of course 'Everything F's', as propositions about particular things that F. For one thing, as Geach has pointed out (*Reference and Generality*, p. 6) their meaning is unaltered if in fact nothing at all F's (though of course this would make them false). And formally we should be led into grave paralogisms if we treated them as cases of $F(x)$. For example, no believer in Leibniz's law would regard it as legitimate to argue as follows:

(1) If x is one and the same individual as y, then for any F, if $F(x)$ then $F(y)$

Therefore

(2) If x is one and the same individual as y then if for all x, $x = x$, then for all x, $x = y$.

But (3) For all x, $x = x$.

Therefore

(4) If x is one and the same individual as y then for all x, $x = y$,

i.e. if x is the same individual as y then *everything* is the same individual as y. The fallacy here would be universally agreed to lie in the step from (1) to (2), i.e. in treating 'For all x, $x = x$' as substitutable for $F(x)$.

We may note, however, that although Tom's believing that someone was called 'Cicero', etc., is not a truth about the man Cicero, the verification of Tom's belief by the man Cicero's being called 'Cicero', denouncing Catiline, etc., *is* a truth about the man Cicero, and incidentally does imply (given the identity of Cicero and Tully) the verification of Tom's belief by *Tully's* being called 'Cicero', denouncing Catiline, etc.

If we turn now to the analogous principle about functions of propositions, i.e.

$$(p)(q)(F): p = q. \supset . F(p) \equiv F(q),$$

this too seems to have nothing specially extensionalist about it. If the proposition that all bachelors are unmarried really is the very same proposition as the proposition that all unmarried men are unmarried, when whoever believes or doubts either *ipso facto* believes or doubts the other, though a man who does not know what 'bachelor' means might doubt whether whatever it is that is expressed by 'All bachelors are unmarried' is true without doubting whether whatever it is that is expressed by 'All unmarried men are unmarried' is true. Though, once again, if we describe a doubt as 'verified' when what is doubted is true, it will follow even in the case of this semantically ignorant man that if his doubt is 'verified' by the fact that all unmarried men are unmarried it is *ipso facto* verified by the fact that all bachelors (i.e. unmarried men) are.

What does entail extensionalism is the identification of the propositional identity expressed by '$p = q$' in the above formula, with material equivalence, and the identification of the property-identity expressed by '$\varphi = \psi$' in the formula

$$(\varphi)\,(\psi)\,(F) : \varphi = \psi . \supset . F(\psi) \equiv F(\psi)$$

with formal equivalence, i.e. characterisation of the same objects. It is also difficult to avoid extensionalism if extensions are treated as genuine individual objects to which Leibniz's law applies. But Kneale no more wishes to make either of these moves than I do.

8. Intentional functions of propositions, properties, etc. are a sub-class of intensional ones. There is also a terminology in which people speak of 'intentional objects'; would these too be a sub-class of intensional ones?

The position here is rather complicated. Intentional objects are, in brief, those objects towards which our thinking, knowing, wanting, hoping, etc. are directed. These certainly include 'intensional' objects in the sense in which these latter include propositions and properties. If James believes that grass is green, we may say that the object of his belief is the proposition that grass is green; though I would repeat that to say this is just to say over again that he believes that grass is green. Propositions as objects of thought, we now know what to do with.

What about properties? I suppose we could say that when Tom ascribes to Cicero the property of denouncing Catiline, this property is at least one of the objects of this rather complicated 'intentional act' of Tom's. But I would wish, naturally, to give this way of talking a harmless sense by providing a paraphrase in which this apparent name of a property is replaced by the corresponding verb. And what can this paraphrase be but: *Tom asserts, or believes* (depending on what sort of 'ascription' we have in mind), *that Cicero denounced Catiline?* Surely for x to ascribe the property of φ-ing to y, is simply for x to assert or believe that y φs.

But we must be careful here. To ascribe the property of φ-ing to *someone* could be rather more than merely to assert or believe *that someone* φs. For to say that Tom ascribes the property of denouncing Catiline to someone could be to say *that there is someone* to whom he ascribes this property, i.e. that there is a *y* of whom he asserts or believes that *y* has it. Whereas to say that Tom asserts or believes *that someone denounced Catiline* could be merely to say that Tom asserts or believes that there has been at least one Catiline-denouncer, without his ascribing such denunciation to anyone in particular. However, in both senses it is easy to get rid of the 'ascription of a property' location—in the one case there is a *y* such that Tom believes that *y* denounced Catiline, and in the other Tom believes that there is a *y* such that *y* denounced Catiline.

To get back now to the question as to whether all intentional objects are intensional ones: in the case in which there is a *y* such that Tom believes *of that y* that it denounced Catiline, it would seem that while this 'intentional act' quasi-relates Tom to the intensional quasi-object denunciation-of-Catiline, it also genuinely relates him to a certain *y* which is not an intensional quasi-object at all but a perfectly ordinary human being (well, one now dead; but let that pass). In general, it would seem that the objects of our beliefs etc., in the sense of the objects that these beliefs etc. are *about*—the *subjects* of these beliefs, etc., as we might more readily say—may be perfectly ordinary individuals. As I insisted in the last section, it is only when the objects of our believing etc. are such individuals that we can expect Leibniz's law for the identity of individuals to apply to them; but it does seem that they sometimes can be such.

9. This seeming, however, may be deceptive. Miss Anscombe opens one of the discussions in her well-known paper on 'The Intentionality of Sensation' by saying, quite in line with what has just been suggested, that 'if I am thinking of Winston Churchill then *he* is the object of my thought'. [*Analytical Philosophy*, Second Series (ed. R. J. Butler, Blackwells, 1965), pp. 160–1.] The italics are mine, but Miss Anscombe herself seems to intend some emphasis here. For when she goes on to consider cases in which the object of thought is non-existent, she dismisses the suggestion that in this case we are really thinking of the 'idea' of the object by saying that

'If the idea is to be brought in when the object doesn't exist, then equally it should be brought in when the object does exist. Yet one is thinking, surely of Winston Churchill, not of the idea of him, and just that fact started us off.'

I am not at all sure what the people Miss Anscombe is attacking mean by 'ideas', but if Miss Anscombe is right in insisting that thoughts of Mr Pickwick and thoughts of Mr Churchill (or, let us say, of Professor Kneale) must be given similar analyses, then surely Churchill and Kneale *cannot* be the objects of my thought in the direct way in which they might be, e.g., the objects of my bumping if I bump into them. At most, certain thoughts of a fundamentally *general* sort which I have—thoughts to the effect that *someone* is φ-ing, maybe that someone is uniquely φ-ing—can be verified by the performances of Kneale and Churchill. For certainly my thoughts of Mr Pickwick can only, in the end, be general ones, and cannot constitute relations between myself and the actual man Pickwick; for there is no actual man Pickwick.

The alternative is to say that the existence of the object does make a difference, and that only what exists can *be thought to* φ, though one can think that something that φs ψs, or that something that uniquely φs ψs, whether or not anything in fact φs (or uniquely ψs) at all. On this view we would also have to say that only what exists can be even *thought by A to be thought by B* to φ, though A might think that there is some φ-er which B thinks to ψ, or that B thinks there is some φ-er that ψs, whether or not there are any φ-ers at all, and in the last case whether or not A thinks there are.

10. Perhaps, then, there are intentional objects which are not also intensional objects, but are individuals of a philosophically ordinary sort, like Churchill; and perhaps there are not. There are, at all events, many cases in which intentional objects—objects of thought, of discussion, of wishing, etc.—*are* also intensional objects, i.e. not ordinary objects but propositions, properties and the like. About these, Professor Kneale has a concluding thesis which I should very much like to think he has succeeded in establishing. As Kneale himself expresses it, this thesis is that 'intentional sentences' always 'express propositions about propositions'. This is Platonistic language, but a nominalistic paraphrase of it is not difficult, and a successful nominalistic programme seems to me almost to depend on its being true.

We speak sometimes of *thinking of* such and such an object, sometimes of *thinking that* such and such is the case; similarly we speak sometimes of *wishing for* or *wanting* such and such an object, sometimes of *wishing that* such and such was the case; and similarly with other intentional verbs. I take it that what Kneale's final thesis amounts to is that every genuine case of 'thinking *of*', 'wishing *for*', etc., is also a case of 'thinking *that*', 'wishing *that*', etc. He gives the example 'I was dying for a cup of tea', for which his paraphrase is 'I very much wished (that) there were a cup of tea I was drinking'; and his contention appears to be that this sort of thing can be done in all cases. To this, I can only say that I hope it is true. For the objects that we may ostensibly think of, wish for, etc. include some very strange ones—abstract objects, fictitious propositions, the philosopher's stone—and the strangest of all are perhaps those which might be described as *concrete but indefinite*, like 'a cup of tea', or 'a saucer of mud', when there isn't any particular cup of tea or saucer of mud that I think of or want, but I just think of or want *a* cup of tea or *a* saucer of mud. There is, clearly, no such object in the real world as a cup of tea which is just a cup of tea without being any cup of tea in particular; and yet it does seem perfectly possible to think of or want a cup of tea without thinking of or wanting any cup of tea in particular. These *individua vaga* do disappear when we replace 'wishing for (thinking of) a φ-er' by forms like 'wishing that (imagining that) something φs', or by more complicated forms of this general type; and moreover this is the *only* way to make them disappear that I can think of (apart from violently *ad hoc* solutions like treating '( ) is thinking of a [ ]-er' as an expression, forming a sentence from a name and a verb, which is just not analysable.) That is why I hope that Kneale's final thesis is true.

The thesis does, all the same, have certain difficulties about it which I'm not *quite* confident can be resolved, though I hope they can. One (put to me by P. T. Geach) is this: Suppose there is an F.B.I. agent who would like to catch a Communist, though there is no particular Communist he is after (he possibly doesn't even know who the Communists are). It would clearly be wrong to say that in this case there is an *x* such that *x* is a Communist and the F.B.I. agent would like it to be the case that he has caught *x*; for *ex hypothesi* there is no such *x*. But is it then the case that the F.B.I. agent would like it to be the case that for some *x*, *x* is a Communist and has been caught by him? This would seem to imply that the agent would like it to be the case that there are Communists, but surely our original proposition needn't imply this. The best solution

I can think of is that the suggested analysis doesn't imply it either, i.e. that 'a wishes that for some x, both φx and ψx' doesn't imply 'a wishes that for some x, φx'; but I cannot pretend to be wholly happy about this, and if Kneale has a better solution I should welcome it.

21. The Possibly-true and the Possible

In the first two items in the eighth chapter of his *Sophismata*, John Buridan argues that the sentence 'No proposition is negative' cannot be true, since to be true it must be there, and if it is there, there is at least one negative proposition, namely itself. On the other hand, though not 'possibly true', it is 'possible', in the sense of describing a possible state of affairs, since God might have annihilated all negative propositions, including that one. This leads Buridan to raise a few questions about the inferences 'Every proposition is affirmative, therefore no proposition is negative' and 'No proposition is negative, therefore some proposition is negative': he ends up by defending the former and rejecting the latter.

It may appear that in this reasoning about 'No proposition is negative' Buridan is guilty of some sort of confusion between use and mention, or between object-language and metalanguage. No such confusion, however, is involved in his argument at this point, though it may be elsewhere in this chapter of the *Sophismata*. We could say, if we like, that the characterisation of a proposition as 'negative', unlike its characterisation as 'true', is a syntactical rather than a semantic matter, and that there is nothing against a language containing its own syntax, though there may be plenty against its containing its own semantics. This defence could possibly be carried out in detail by using Gödelian arithmetisation and the like, but the detailed defence I shall offer here will be simpler. I shall distinguish sharply between an object-language L and a metalanguage M, the former consisting of a certain limited class of Latin sentences which ars used to describe the physical appearance of certain marks on sheets of paper, these including those of the Latin sentences themselves which are written on the sheets. The metalanguage M is the English in which the sections of this article which follow are written. I am prepared to be told, and indeed myself believe, that it is not quite standard English. For example, I shall make free use of such non-standard phrases as 'true on a sheet', and saying that a sentence is true on a sheet will be a description of the physical appearance of the sheet. It will be too complicated a description to go into the language L, and the latter language does not contain the word *verum*. Even with this comparatively meagre apparatus, it will be possible to make quite precisely the rather subtle distinctions in which Buridan was interested.

1. *Truth-conditions of some inscriptions about inscriptions*

Suppose we have several sheets of white paper on which there are black marks arranged in lines. We may classify the marks according to their shapes. Those of certain shapes we call terms; and in particular any marks of these shapes:

> *propositio*
> *affirmativa*
> *negativa*

are terms. Marks of any of these shapes:

> *Omnis*
> *Quaedam*
> *Nulla*

are called signs of quantity, and marks of these shapes:

> *est*
> *non est*

are called copulæ. A line of marks is called a sentence if and only if it consists of a sign of quantity followed by a term followed by the copula *est* (or by *non est*, if the sign of quantity is *Quaedam*) followed by a term. Thus sentences are any lines of marks of these four shapes

> *Omnis A est B*
> *Quaedam A est B*
> *Nulla A est B*
> *Quaedam A non est B*,

where A and B are marks of the shapes called 'terms'.

Sentences are divided into those which are true on their sheets and those which are not. Whether sentences are or are not true on their sheets is determined by the shapes of the marks on their sheets. In this sense, the sentences are 'about' the shapes of the marks. Each term is associated with a particular group of shapes, which it may be said to *connote*, though this means no more than that the presence on a sheet of marks of certain shapes will determine, in ways which we shall shortly detail, whether or not sentences containing certain terms are to be counted as 'true on their sheets'. The shapes connoted by the term *propositio* are all those which count, by the rules given above, as shapes of sentences. The shapes connoted by the term *negativa* are those of sentences which either begin with *Nulla* or have *non est* for their copula, and the shapes connoted by the term *affirmativa* are those of all sentences which do not either begin with *Nulla* or have *non est* for their copula.

The rules by which we classify sentences as true or false on their sheets are as follows:

(1) A sentence of the type *Omnis A est B* is true on a sheet if and only if (i) it is written on the sheet, (ii) there is at least one mark on the sheet of a shape A (i.e. of a shape connoted by the term A) and (iii) there is no mark on the sheet of a shape A which is not also of a shape B. For example, the sentence

Omnis propositio est affirmativa

is true on a sheet if and only if (i) it is on the sheet, (ii) there is at least one sentence on the sheet and (iii) there is no sentence on the sheet which begins with *nulla* or has *non est* for its copula. If the only sentence on a sheet is this sentence itself it will clearly be true on that sheet, since it is on the sheet, is a sentence, and does not begin with *Nulla* or have *non est* for its copula. It would also be true on a sheet containing no sentences except itself and the sentence

Quaedam propositio est negativa,

since this also does not start with *nulla*, etc.

(2) A sentence of the type *Quaedam A est B* is true on a sheet if

and only if (i) it is on the sheet, and (ii) there is at least one mark on the sheet which is at once of a shape A and of a shape B. For example, the sentence last mentioned, i.e.

Quaedam propositio est negativa

is true on a sheet if and only if (i) it is on the sheet, and (ii) there is at least one mark on the sheet which is a sentence and either begins with *Nulla* or has *non est* for its copula. If it were the only sentence on a sheet it would not be true on that sheet, since it does not begin with *Nulla*, etc.; though it would be true on a sheet which contained both itself and the sentence

Nulla propositio est affirmativa

since that does begin with *Nulla*.

(3) A sentence of the type *Nulla A est B* is true on a sheet if and only if (i) it is on the sheet, and (ii) no mark on the sheet is both of a shape A and of a shape B. For example, the sentence last mentioned, i.e.

Nulla propositio est affirmativa,

is true on a sheet if and only if (i) it is on the sheet and (ii) no mark on the sheet is a sentence which neither begins with *Nulla* nor has *non est* for its copula. If it were the only sentence on a sheet it would be true on that sheet, but it wouldn't on a sheet which also contained, e.g. the sentence *Quaedam propositio est negativa*.

(4) A sentence of the type *Quaedam A non est B* is true on a sheet if and only if (i) it is on the sheet and either (ii) no mark on the sheet is of a shape A, or (iii) some mark on the sheet is of shape A but not of shape B. (The alternative (ii) is only brought in to preserve the standard rules of opposition; we can here ignore it, as it will not affect any of the points we shall be bringing forward.) For example, the sentence

Quaedam propositio non est negativa

is true on a sheet if and only if (i) it is on the sheet and either (ii) no mark on the sheet is a sentence (this alternative is, of course, in this instance ruled out by (i)) or (iii) some mark on the sheet is a sentence which neither begins with *Nulla* nor has *non est* for its copula. If it is the only sentence on a sheet it will obviously be false on that sheet, since it has *non est* for its copula, but it would be true on a sheet which also contained the sentence *Omnis propositio est affirmativa*.

A sentence which is written on a sheet but is not true on that sheet may be said to be false on it.

Sentences of the forms *Omnis A est B* and *Quaedam A non est B* (with the same terms in the same order) may be called 'contradictories' of one another, and similarly with the forms *Quaedam A est B* and *Nulla A est B*. It is easy to verify that if both of two contradictories are written on a sheet, one of them will be true on that sheet and the other false on it.

2. *Conditions of possible-truth and of possibility*

It may be observed that certain sentences will be true, by the above rules, on any sheets on which they are written; e.g.

1. *Nulla affirmativa est negativa.*

Certain others will be false on any sheets on which they are written, e.g. the contradictory of 1, namely

2. *Quaedam affirmativa est negativa.*

And it may be thought to be a general rule that if a sentence is true on all sheets on which it is written, its contradictory is false on all sheets on which it is written, and *vice versa*. This, however, is not the case. Consider, for example, the sentences

3. *Quaedam propositio non est affirmativa*
4. *Quaedam propositio est affirmativa.*

These will both be true on any sheets on which they occur, simply because their own presence on the sheet will suffice to satisfy their truth-conditions. But their contradictories, namely

5. *Omnis propositio est affirmativa*
6. *Nulla propositio est affirmativa*

need not be false on all sheets on which they occur. Each of them would, for example, be true on a sheet on which there was no other sentence but itself; 5 would also be true on a sheet containing no sentence but itself and 4, and 6 on a sheet containing no sentence but itself and 3. Consider, again, the sentences

7. *Omnis propositio est negativa*
8. *Nulla propositio est negativa.*

These would both be false on any sheets on which they occurred, their mere presence on a sheet sufficing to contravene their truth-conditions. But their contradictories, namely

9. *Quaedam propositio non est negativa*
10. *Quaedam propositio est negativa*

need not be true on every sheet on which they occur; for example, 9 would be false on a sheet on which it was the only sentence, or on which there were no sentences but itself and 8, and 10 would be false on a sheet on which it was the only sentence, or on which there were no sentences but itself and 7.

A sentence on a sheet may be said to be *possibly-true* on that sheet if and only if there is some sheet (that one or another) on which it is true, and *possibly-false* on that sheet if and only if there is some sheet (that one or another) on which it is false. It is clear that 1, 3 and 4 can none of them be possibly-false, nor any of 2, 7 and 8 possibly-true. But whereas the contradictory of the not-possibly-false 1 is not-possibly-true, the contradictories of the not-possibly-false 3 and 4 will come out as possibly-true if our sheets are suitably inscribed; and whereas the contradictory of the not-possibly-true 2 is not-possibly-false, the contradictories of the not-possibly-true 7 and 8 will come out as possibly-false if our sheets are suitably inscribed.

A sentence on a sheet may be said to be *possible* on that sheet under the following conditions:

(1) If it is of the shape *Omnis A est B* it is possible on a sheet X if and only if (i) it is on the sheet X, and (ii) there is some sheet Y such that (a) some mark on Y is of a shape connoted by A, and (b) no mark on Y is of shape A but not of shape B.

(2) If it is of the shape *Nulla A est B* it is possible on a sheet X if and only if (i) it is on the sheet X, and (ii) there is some sheet Y such that no mark on Y is at once of shapes A and B.

The possibility-conditions for the other forms may be worked out similarly; the important point to notice is that for a sentence S on a sheet X to be 'possible' in virtue of what is on Y, the sentence S does not itself have to be on Y. This differentiates the 'possibility' of a sentence from its 'possible-truth', and the difference it makes in practice becomes clear when we consider the sentences 7 and 8, *Omnis propositio est negativa* and *Nulla propositio est negativa*. Let us suppose sheet X contains only sentence 7 (*Omnis*, etc.) and sheet Y only sentence 8 (*Nulla*, etc.). Then 7 is possible on sheet X, since (i) it is written on sheet X, and (ii) there is a sheet, namely Y, on which (a) there is a sentence but (b) there is no sentence which neither begins with *Nulla* nor has *non est* for its copula (the only sentence on Y, namely 8, does begin with *Nulla*). And 8 is possible on sheet Y, since (i) it is written on sheet Y, and (ii) there is a sheet, namely X, which contains no sentences which either begin with *Nulla* or have *non est* for the copula. Both 7 and 8 are of course false on their own sheets, and would be false on any sheets on which they occurred, i.e. neither of them is possibly-true on any sheet— though, as just shown, each of them is possible on its sheet.

We might also arrive at the conditions for the 'possibility' of a sentence on its sheet by considering the sentence, not just as describing the marks on its own sheet but also as describing the marks on other sheets. We might say, for example, that a sentence of the form *Omnis A est B*, occurring *on* a sheet X, is true *of* a sheet Y if and only if (a) there is a mark of a shape connoted by A on sheet Y, and (b) there is no mark of shape A on Y which is not also of shape B. The conditions under which sentences of other forms than *Omnis A est B* on sheet X may be said to be true of sheet Y, can be worked out on similar lines. We may then say that a sentence S on sheet X is possible *on* that sheet if there is a sheet Y *of* which S is true. Thus if the only sentence on sheet X is 7. *Omnis propositio est negativa*, and the only sentence on sheet Y is 8. *Nulla propositio est negativa*, we can say that 7 is true of sheet Y on the sheet on which it occurs, namely X, and that it is therefore possible on X; and that 8 is true of sheet X on the sheet on which it occurs, namely Y, and that it is therefore possible on Y. These sentences have the peculiarity of never being true of sheets on which they themselves occur, and this precludes their being 'possibly-true', but they may be true of other sheets than their own, and thus come to be counted as 'possible' even on their own.

We may say, similarly that a sentence is *necessary* on the sheet on which it occurs if it is true of every sheet, and that it is *necessarily-true* on any sheet on which it occurs if it is true on every sheet on which it occurs. Whatever is in this sense necessary on a sheet is necessarily-true on that sheet, but not always *vice versa*. For example, 4. *Quaedam propositio est affirmativa* is true on any sheet on which it occurs (its presence there being its own verification), and so is 'necessarily-true' on any sheet on which it occurs, but it would fail to be 'necessary' in any set of sheets which included one on which nothing was written but, say, *Nulla affirmativa est negativa*; for *Quaedam propositio est affirmativa* would not be true of that sheet, and so not true of all sheets, and so not necessary. The contradictory of a necessary sentence is never possible, for no sentence and its contradictory are ever true of the same sheets, so if a sentence S is true of all sheets its contradictory will be true of none. But the contradictory of a necessarily-true sentence may be possibly-true, since the condition of a sentence's being necessarily-true is only its being true of (and so on) every sheet on which it is written, and the contradictory might be true of (and so on) some other sheet on which the original is not written (and so not true). We have seen this exemplified in the case of 4. *Quaedam propositio est affirmativa* (which is necessarily-true) and its contradictory 6. *Nulla propositio est affirmativa* (which is possibly-true if there is a sheet with only itself on).

3. *Some limitations and their irrelevance*

All the metalinguistic terms we have used so far about these sentences—'true', 'false', 'possibly-true', 'possibly-false', 'possible', 'necessary'—have been relative to (a) the sheet on which a sentence occurs, and to (b) the set of sheets of which this one is a member. A sentence might turn out, e.g., not to be possible on its sheet simply because no other sheet in our set is of the sort which would make the sentence possible, according to our rules. I ought strictly speaking to have used terms like 'possibly-true on a sheet in a set of sheets', 'possible on a sheet in a set', 'true of a sheet in a set', and so on. For instance, *Nulla propositio est negativa* is not strictly speaking possible on its sheet in a set unless there actually is some sheet in the set which contains no sentences beginning with *Nulla* or having *non est* for their copula. However, many of our characterisations are ones which are bound to obtain in any set of sheets where the inscriptions are sorted according to our rules; e.g. in any such set sentences 1, 3 and 4 will come out true on any sheets on which they occur, and 2, 7 and 8 false on any sheets on which they occur. And at other points, to make some of the distinctions in which we are interested it suffices that there can be sets of sheets on which the marks are of such and such a kind; e.g. sets which will make 7 and 8 possible but not possibly-true on sheets on which they occur. Moreover, we might play this game with bigger pieces. We might let one of our 'sheets' be the entire physical universe, and our sentences be any patterns of dark lines on light surfaces (anywhere in the universe) of the prescribed shapes. To call a sentence 'true' on this 'sheet' is simply to state a physical fact (or falsehood) about the physical universe; e.g. it is to say that either the sentence itself is not of the shape *Quaedam propositio est negativa* or there are in the universe light surfaces on which dark lines form patterns of sentence-shape which either start with the shape *Nulla* or have the shape *non est* in the copula position. And to say that something is true of or on 'another sheet' is (in this 'big' game) to say that it is logically compatible with existing physical laws that the dark lines on light surfaces which occur in the universe should have been, or should not have been, of such and such patterns. For example, to say that there is a sheet of which *Nulla propositio est negativa* is true is to say that existing physical laws do not rule out the possibility of certain dark lines on light patterns (namely ones of sentence shape and either beginning with *Nulla* or having *non est* in the copula position) just not occurring.

Having made this clear, we may return to sheet-and-sentence games of a more modest sort.

4. *The definition of validity*

We may wish to say of the sentences on our sheets not only that they are true, false, etc. but also that certain of them may or may not be validly inferred from others. What might we mean by this, and how is the conception of validity related to the others we have been considering?

The most satisfactory definition of validity (on a sheet in a set of sheets) is to say that a sentence on a sheet may be validly inferred from other sentences on this sheet if and only if there is no sheet (in the set) of which all the premiss-sentences are true but of which the conclusion-sentence is false. In what follows we shall only be concerned with the relation of valid inferability between a conclusion-sentence and a single premiss-sentence, but the definition just given will validate, on any sheets on which the sentences involved occur, all the traditional immediate inferences and syllogisms.

Given this definition, moreover, it can be proved that in no set of sheets will a sentence which is not possible on its sheet be validly inferable from one which is. On the other hand, there could be a set of sheets in which a sentence which is not possibly-true on its sheet is inferable from one that is. We might consider, for example, a set which contains just two sheets, X and Y, the sentences on sheet X being the pair

7. *Omnis propositio est affirmativa*
8. *Nulla propositio est negativa,*

while sheet Y contains just sentence 7. 8 will be validly inferable from 7 on sheet X, since the only sheet of which 7 is true, namely Y, is one of which 8 is (the inference of 8 from 7 will in fact be a valid one, on any sheet on which these sentences occur, in any set of sheets). But the conclusion 8 is not possibly-true on sheet X (or, for that matter, anywhere), whereas its premiss 7 is possibly-true on that sheet X, since it is plainly true on sheet Y.

Again, given our definition, any sentence whatever will be validly inferable on a sheet from one which is not-possible (on that sheet and in that set), but not always from one which is not-possibly-true. For example, *Omnis propositio est affirmativa* is validly inferable from *Quaedam affirmativa est negativa* (on any sheet in which they both occur, in any set of sheets), since one cannot so inscribe a set of sheets as to make *Quaedam affirmativa est negativa* true of any of them, and hence cannot so inscribe them as to make *Quaedam affirmativa est negativa* true of a sheet of which *Omnis propositio est affirmativa* is false. On the other hand, one can so inscribe a set of sheets as to prevent, say, *Quaedam propositio est negativa* from being inferable from the not-possibly-true sentence *Nulla propositio est negativa*. Just write these two on sheet X, and the first one only on sheet Y; *Nulla propositio est negativa* will be true of sheet Y (though not of course true *on* sheet Y) but *Quaedam propositio est negativa* will be false of it; hence our condition for validity will not be met. This inference would have been let through if it had been said that an inference is valid if its premiss or premisses cannot be true without its conclusion being true; for *Nulla propositio est negativa, ergo quaedam propositio est negativa* meets *this* condition twice over— first because *Nulla propositio est negativa* cannot be true anyway, and secondly because the very existence of the sentence *Nulla propositio est affirmativa* on any sheet satisfies the condition for truth on that sheet of *Quaedam propositio est negativa* (once this latter is there).

We may, again, validly infer a necessary sentence from any sentence whatever on its sheet, but there can be sets of sheets in which we cannot validly infer a necessarily-true sentence from every sentence on its sheet. For example, if we have just two sheets X and Y, and X has on it only the pair

6. *Nulla propositio est affirmativa*
4. *Quaedam propositio est affirmativa,*

while Y has on it just 6, the necessarily-true sentence 4 is not inferable in our sense from 6, since 6 is true on sheet X of sheet Y while 4 is not true on sheet X of sheet Y.

5. Buridanian semantics

I conclude by enunciating a series of metatheorems which will be true of any set of marked sheets whatever, given the above definitions of 'sentence', 'true on a sheet', and so on. S and T represent any sentences. In the proof of metatheorems 5, 7, 11, 13, 15 and 17, it is important to remember that 'S is true on a sheet X' means 'S is true of X on sheet X', so that if S is not true *of* sheet X it is not true *on* sheet X. For example, we may use this in the proof of 5 as follows:

If S is possible on sheet X there is a sheet *of* which it is true, but if S is not possibly-true on sheet X there is no sheet *on* which it is true; but if it were on the sheet of which it is true, it would be true on that sheet; therefore (under these conditions) it is not on that sheet. Hence if S is possible but not possibly-true on sheet X, there is a sheet which it is not on. It may be noted that none of the metatheorems assert that any sentence is possible on a sheet without being possibly-true on it, or that any sentence is necessarily-true on a sheet without being necessary on it; whether anything of this sort is so will depend on how the sheets we have are decorated. Some of the metatheorems do, however, say what else will be true of a set of sheets if these things are true of it. Here, now, are the metatheorems:

1. If S is true on sheet X, S is on sheet X.
2. S is false on sheet X if and only if S is on sheet X and is not true on sheet X.
3. S is neither true nor false on sheet X if and only if S is not on sheet X.
4. If S is possibly-true on sheet X, S is possible on sheet X.
5. If S is possible but not possibly-true on sheet X, there is a sheet which S is not on.
6. If S is necessary on sheet X, S is necessarily-true on sheet X.
7. If S is necessarily-true but not necessary on sheet X, there is a sheet which S is not on.
8. If T is validly inferable from S on sheet X, and S is true on sheet X, so is T.
9. If T is validly inferable from S on sheet X, and T is false on sheet X, so is S.
10. If T is validly inferable from S on sheet X, then if S is possible on sheet X, so is T.
11. If T is validly inferable from S on sheet X, and S is possibly-true on sheet X but T is not, then S is false on sheet X and there is a sheet which T is not on.
12. If T is validly inferable from S on sheet X, then if S is necessary on sheet S, so is T.
13. If T is validly inferable from S on sheet X, and S is necessarily-true on sheet X but T is not, then T is true on sheet X and there is a sheet which S is not on.

14. If S is not possible on sheet X, then if T is on sheet X, T is validly inferable from S on sheet X.

15. If S is not possibly-true on sheet X, and T is on sheet X but is not validly inferable from S on sheet X, there is a sheet which S is not on.

16. If T is necessary on sheet X, then if S is on sheet X, T is validly inferable from S on sheet X.

17. If T is necessarily-true on sheet X, and S is on sheet X but T is not validly-inferable from S on sheet X, there is a sheet which T is not on.

22. *Self-perception and Contingency*

On p. 94 of his book 'Self-Knowledge and Self-Identity' (1963), Mr Sydney Shoemaker has the following argument, designed to show that no one can possibly perceive himself perceiving anything:

'The relation "perceives" (or "is perceived by"), if I can observe it holding between two things, must be an empirical relationship, and hence a contingent one. This being so, it seems apparent that if I can perceive a self and an image, and observe that the self perceives that image, then it ought to be possible for me to perceive a self and an image and observe that the self does *not* perceive that image. But clearly this is not possible.'

For

'it is self-contradictory to suppose that I could perceive an image, and perceive, as a fact about it, that I do not perceive it.'

Very similar arguments appear on pp. 101 and 110, and it is clear that Shoemaker attaches considerable importance to them. But whether or not the conclusions which he arrives at are correct, these arguments seem to me quite worthless for the purposes to which he puts them.

If I am right about this, it will suffice to examine Shoemaker's first argument, the one that I have quoted. The nerve of it seems to lie in the first sentence, or rather in an unstated premiss behind it, to the effect that 'relationships', such as 'perceiving', are *as such* classifiable as contingent, necessary and impossible. (He also hints at a connected classification into 'empirical' and something else, but as I have never been able to discover what empiricality is, I shall largely ignore this.) What this seems to mean is that if *anything* of

215

the form '*x* φs that *p*', where 'φ-ing' is some 'relationship' of the appropriate sort (*e.g.* perceiving), is contingent, then *everything* of that form must be so; and in particular, if '*x* φs that *p*' is contingent, then '*x* φs that not *p*' must be equally so, and cannot be, for example, impossible. And there is perhaps a suggestion that this is particularly obvious where *p* and not-*p* are themselves both contingent, and certainly when '*x* φs that *p*' entails that they are (as may well be the case with perceiving). Applied to perceiving, the argument then goes as follows: Since it is in general a contingent matter whether *x* perceives that *p*, there can be no true *p*, and certainly no contingent *p*, for which it would be (logically) impossible that *x* perceives that *p*; and in particular if it is a contingent matter whether *x* perceives that *p*, it cannot be impossible for *x* to perceive that not *p*. But it is impossible for *x* to perceive that he is not perceiving anything, or for him to perceive that he is not perceiving anything about *y* (for if he perceives this to be so, it *is* so, i.e. if he *isn't* perceiving anything about *y*, then he can't be perceiving *this* about *y*). Therefore, by the principle, it cannot be a contingent fact, either, that he is perceiving that he *is* perceiving something, or that he is perceiving that he is perceiving something about *y*, i.e. perceiving *y*; and since this would be a contingent fact if it were a fact at all, it cannot be a fact.

I should have thought that Shoemaker's argument was a perfect proof that the principle he uses is false. Whether or not this is so, there certainly *are* refutations of the principle that whenever '*x* φs that *p*' is contingent, '*x* φs that not *p*' must be equally so. Nor ought this to be at all surprising. For even when the propositions for which *p* can stand, in the form '*x* φs that *p*', are restricted to contingent ones, they may very well stand for propositions involving φ-ing, and perhaps also involving *x*, which could get into logical tangles with the prefix '*x* φs that'. But the point will be clearer if we look at some other examples.

For one such example, let our φ-ing be *thinking correctly that*, and *p* '*y* is being thought about'. It surely *can* happen, and yet does not *have* to happen, that *x* is thinking correctly that *y* is being thought about, i.e. it is a contingent matter (and perhaps even an empirical matter) whether or not *x* is thinking this, and therefore whether he is thinking it correctly. Yet it is impossible that *x* should be thinking correctly that *y* is *not* being thought about. For if this thought of *x*'s were correct, *y* would not be being thought about, and so *x* would not be thinking, correctly or otherwise, that *y* is not being thought about. This point was seen by Berkeley, who argued, notoriously, from the fact that, whatever *y* might be, nobody can correctly think that *y* is not being thought about, to the false conclusion that whatever *y* might be, it cannot *be the case* that *y* is not being thought about.

Again, it can happen, but does not have to happen, that *x* thinks *in*correctly that *y* is not being thought about. But it cannot be the case that *x* thinks incorrectly that *y* *is* being thought about. For if *x* thought this incorrectly, *y* would *not* be being thought about, and *x* would therefore not be thinking, correctly or incorrectly, that *y* *was* being thought about. And again, it is possible, but not necessary, that *x* should think incorrectly that there is nothing that he is thinking, but it is not possible that *x* should think incorrectly that there is *something* he is thinking. For if *x* thought this incorrectly, there would be nothing that he was thinking, and therefore not this. This, I think, is something that Descartes saw, though it does not follow from it (as I think Descartes thought it did) that if there is something that *x* is thinking, *x* must *know* that there is.

Nor do we have to confine our form '*x* φs that *p*' to statements of a broadly 'psychological' or 'intentional' sort in order to refute the principle that if '*x* φs that *p*' is contingent, '*x* φs that not *p*' must also be so. For example, we could let 'φ-ing that' be 'ψ-ing while it is the case that', and let *p* be '*x* ψs'. It is a contingent matter (and I should have thought an 'empirical' matter) whether *x* is red while *x* is red, i.e. whether *x* is red, but it is impossible that *x* should be red while *x* is not red. And in general '*x* ψs while *p*' can be a contingent matter (and will be if '*x* ψs' is itself one, or if *p* is itself one), though 'x ψs while not *p*' will be impossible, in all those cases in which x's ψ-ing entails that *p*. This example makes it clear that even in quite trivial cases a logical relation between a proposition and a compound proposition of which it is a part may be such that replacing a *contingent* part by its equally *contingent* negation will turn the proposition as a whole from a *contingent* to a *non-contingent* one. For example, although 'Grass is green' and 'Grass is not green' are equally contingent, '*Grass is green and* grass is green' is contingent but '*Grass is green and* grass is not green' is impossible. Similarly if our replacements were the pair of equally contingent propositions 'Something is green' and 'Nothing is green'. Why should the same thing not occur with the rather different sort of composition which Shoemaker examines? He does not give us a single cogent reason why it should not.

The nearest thing he gives to such a supporting argument is this: he observes that we do not have these logical oddities when more than one percipient is involved. If x perceives that some *other* person y perceives that p, or perceives that y perceives z, and it is a contingent fact that x perceives this, there is no reason why it should not be an equally contingent fact, when it is a fact, that x perceives that y does *not* perceive that p, or that y does not perceive z, i.e. does not perceive anything about z. And Shoemaker argues, or seems to argue, that because we do not have this 'equal contingency' when we replace y by x, it cannot be true, as it appears to be, that x's perceiving x to perceive something is a special case of the general sort: x's perceiving y to perceive something. This is like arguing that 'x is taller than x' is not a special case of the form 'x is taller than y' because when x and y are different it is a contingent matter whether one is taller than the other, but nothing can be taller than itself. But if xRx were *not* a special case of xRy it would be nonsense to talk of reflexive, irreflexive and non-reflexive relations. Again, what Shoemaker says is like arguing that 'Some Xs are not Xs' cannot be a special case of the form 'Some Xs are not Ys' because there is no reason why there should not be true propositions of the form 'Some Xs are not Ys', but there cannot be true propositions of the form 'Some Xs are not Xs'. The fact is that 'Some men are not men' *is* of the form 'Some Xs are not Ys', but it has a further formal feature (the identity of the two terms) which gives it logical peculiarities that are not possessed by, say, 'Some men are not albinos', which is also of the form 'Some Xs are not Ys'. Self-perception, similarly, if there is such a thing, has (and may be expected to have) logical peculiarities which are not shared by other cases of perception; this does not prove that self-perception is not one kind of perception, or that there is no such thing (does not *prove* it—there may of course *be* no such thing). And the particular logical peculiarities that Shoemaker has shown self-perception, if there is such a thing, to have, are certainly not, as he suggests, quite outrageous ones which nothing at all can have; on the contrary, plenty of other things *do* have them.

Bibliography of the philosophical writings of A. N. Prior by Olav Flo

1937
a 'The nation and the individual', *Australasian Journal of Psychology and Philosophy*, vol. 15 (1937), pp. 294–8.

1941
a 'Sense and sentences', *National Education*, March 8, 1941.

1942
a 'Can religion be discussed?', *Australasian Journal of Psychology and Philosophy*, vol. 20 (1942), pp. 141–51. Reprinted in *New Essays in Philosophical Theology*, ed. A. G. N. Flew, London, 1955, pp. 1–11. Norwegian translation by Anfinn Stigen in *Gud i moderne filosofi*, ed. Anfinn Stigen, Oslo, 1968, pp. 7–16.

1944
a 'The meaning of good', *Australasian Journal of Psychology and Philosophy*, vol. 22 (1944), pp. 170–4.

1945
a 'The subject of ethics', ibid., vol. 23 (1945), pp. 78–84.

1946
a 'Eighteenth-century writers on twentieth-century subjects', ibid., vol. 24 (1946), pp. 168–82.

1947
a Review of Clive S. Lewis, *Abolition of Man*, *Landfall*, vol. 1 (1947), pp. 63–7.

b   Review of Karl R. Popper, *The Open Society and its Enemies*, vols. I and II, ibid., pp. 136–42.
c   Review of D. Daiches Raphael, *The Moral Sense*, ibid., pp. 314–18.

1948
a   'Adam Gib and the philosophers', *Australasian Journal of Philosophy*, vol. 26 (1948), pp. 73–93.
b   'Facts, propositions and entailment', *Mind*, n.s. vol. 57 (1948), pp. 62–8.

1949
a   *Logic and the Basis of Ethics*, Oxford, 1949, xi + 111 pp. Second ed., 1956.
b   'Argument a fortiori', *Analysis*, vol. 9 (1949), pp. 49–50.
c   'Categoricals and hypotheticals in George Boole and his successors', *Australasian Journal of Philosophy*, vol. 27 (1949), pp. 171–6.
d   'Determinables, determinates and determinants', *Mind*, n.s. vol. 58 (1949), pp. 1–20, 178–94.

1951
a   'The ethical copula', *Australasian Journal of Philosophy*, vol. 29 (1951), pp. 137–54.
b   'The virtue of the act and the virtue of the agent', *Philosophy*, vol. 26 (1951), pp. 121–30.

1952
a   'In what sense is modal logic many-valued?', *Analysis*, vol. 12 (1952), pp. 138–43.
b   'Łukasiewicz's symbolic logic', *Australasian Journal of Philosophy*, vol. 30 (1952), pp. 33–46.
c   'The *parva logicalia* in modern dress', *Dominican Studies*, vol. 5 (1952), pp. 78–87.
d   'Modality *de dicto* and modality *de re*', *Theoria*, vol. 18 (1952), pp. 174–80.
e   'This quarter', *Landfall*, vol. 6 (1952), pp. 49–53.
f   Review of J. A. Passmore, *Ralph Cudworth: An Interpretation*, *Australasian Journal of Philosophy*, vol. 30 (1952), pp. 133–7.

1953
a   'Negative quantifiers', ibid., vol. 31 (1953), pp. 107–23.
b   'The logic of negative terms in Boethius', *Franciscan Studies*, vol. 13 (1953), pp. 1–6.

c 'On some consequentiae in Walter Burleigh', *The New Scholasticism*, vol. 27 (1953), pp. 433–46.

d 'Three-valued logic and future contingents', *The Philosophical Quarterly*, vol. 3 (1953), pp. 317–26.

e 'On propositions neither necessary nor impossible', *The Journal of Symbolic Logic*, vol. 18 (1953), pp. 105–8.

f Review of Boleslaw Sobociński, *L'Analyse de l'antinomie russellienne par Leśniewski*, ibid., pp. 331–3.

g Review of I. M. Bocheński, *Non-analytical Laws and Rules in Aristotle*, ibid., pp. 333–4.

1954

a 'Entities', *Australasian Journal of Philosophy*, vol. 32 (1954), pp. 159–68.

b 'The interpretation of two systems of modal logic', *The Journal of Computing Systems*, vol. 2 (1954), pp. 201–8.

c 'The paradoxes of derived obligation', *Mind*, n.s. vol. 63 (1954), pp. 64–5.

1955

a *Formal Logic*, Oxford, 1955, ix + 329 pp. Second rev. ed., 1962, xi + 341 pp.

b 'Curry's paradox and 3-valued logic', *Australasian Journal of Philosophy*, vol. 33 (1955), pp. 177–82.

c 'English and ontology', *The British Journal for the Philosophy of Science*, vol. 6 (1955–6), pp. 64–5.

d 'Diodoran modalities', *The Philosophical Quarterly*, vol. 5 (1955). Cf. 1958h.

e With Mary Prior, 'Erotetic logic', *The Philosophical Review*, vol. 64 (1955), pp. 43–59.

f 'Many-valued and modal systems: An intuitive approach', ibid., pp. 626–30.

g 'Is necessary existence possible?', *Philosophy and Phenomenological Research*, vol. 15 (1955), pp. 545–7.

h 'Berkeley in logical form', *Theoria*, vol. 21 (1955), pp. 117–22.

i Review of B. B. von Freytag Löringhoff, 'Zur Logik als Lehre von Identität und Verschiedenheit', *The Journal of Symbolic Logic*, vol. 20 (1955), p. 55.

j Review of Sadeo Shiraishi, 'The structure of the continuity of psychological experiences and the physical world', ibid., pp. 169–170.

k Review of Arata Ishimoto, 'A set of axioms of the modal propositional calculus equivalent to S3', ibid., p. 169.

l Review of Shumpei Ueyama, 'Development of Peirce's theory of logic', ibid., p. 170.

m 'Definitions, rules and axioms', *Proceedings of the Aristotelian Society*, n.s. vol. 56 (1955–6), pp. 199–216, with addendum.

1956

a 'Logicians at play: or Syll, Simp and Hilbert', *Australasian Journal of Philosophy*, vol. 34 (1956), pp. 182–92.

b 'Modality and quantification in S5', *The Journal of Symbolic Logic*, vol. 21 (1956), pp. 60–2.

c 'The consequences of actions', *Proceedings of the Aristotelian Society*, *Supplementary volume* 30 (1956), pp. 91–9. Cf. 1968a.

d Review of Jerzy Kalinowski, 'Teoria zdań normatywnych' and 'Théorie des propositions normatives', *The Journal of Symbolic Logic*, vol. 21 (1956), pp. 191–2.

e Review of B. Sobociński, 'Studies in Leśniewski's mereology', and of Czesław Lejewski, 'A contribution to Leśniewski's mereology', ibid., pp. 325–6.

f 'A note on the logic of obligation', *Revue philosophique de Louvain*, vol. 54 (1956), pp. 86–7.

1957

a *Time and Modality, Being the John Locke Lectures for 1955–56 delivered in the University of Oxford*, London, 1957, lx + 148 pp.

b 'Is it possible that one and the same individual object should cease to exist and, later on, start to exist again?' (Analysis Problem No. 11, Report), *Analysis*, vol. 17 (1957), pp. 121–3.

c 'The necessary and the possible', the first of three talks on 'The logic game', *The Listener*, vol. 57 (1957), pp. 627–8. 'Symbolism and analogy', the second of three talks on 'The logic game', ibid., pp. 675–8. 'Many-valued logics', the last of three talks on 'The logic game', ibid., pp. 717–19.

d 'Opposite number', *The Review of Metaphysics*, vol. 11 (1957), pp. 196–201.

e Critical notice of Alfred Tarski, *Logic, Semantics and Mathematics*, *Mind*, n.s., vol. 66 (1957), pp. 401–10.

f Review of the fourth edition of Lewis Carroll, *Symbolic Logic, Part I, The Journal of Symbolic Logic*, vol. 22 (1957), pp. 309–10.

g Review of Arata Ishimoto, 'A note on the paper "A set of axioms of the modal propositional calculus equivalent to S3",' and 'A formulation of the modal propositional calculus equivalent to S4', ibid., pp. 326–7.

h   Review of Ronald J. Butler, *Language Strata and Alternative Logics*, ibid., p. 383.

1958
a   'Escapism: The logical basis of ethics', *Essays in Moral Philosophy*, ed. by A. I. Melden, Seattle, 1958, pp. 135–46. Reissued as paperback, 1966.
b   'Łukasiewicz's contribution to logic', *Philosophy in the Mid-century*, *Volume I*, ed. by R. Klibansky, Florence, 1958, pp. 53–5.
c   ' "The good life" (The East-West meeting in Canberra)', *Australasian Journal of Philosophy*, vol. 36 (1958), pp. 135–6.
d   'The syntax of time-distinctions', *Franciscan Studies*, vol. 18 (1958), pp. 105–20.
e   'Peirce's axioms for propositional calculus', *The Journal of Symbolic Logic*, vol. 23 (1958), pp. 135–6.
f   'Epimenides the Cretan', ibid., pp. 261–6.
g   'Time after time', *Mind*, n.s. vol. 67 (1958), pp. 244–6.
h   'Diodorus and modal logic: A correction', *The Philosophical Quarterly*, vol. 8 (1958), pp. 226–30. Cf. 1955d.
i   Review of Patrick Suppes, *Introduction to Logic*, and J. W. Blyth, *A Modern Introduction to Logic*, *Australasian Journal of Philosophy*, vol. 36 (1958), pp. 146–50.
j   Review of Robert G. Turnbull, 'A note on Mr Hare's "logic of imperatives" ', *The Journal of Symbolic Logic*, vol. 23 (1958), p. 442.
k   Review of Walter Burleigh, *De Puritate Artis Logicae*, ed. by Ph. Boehner, *The New Scholasticism*, vol. 32, (1958), pp. 127–30.
l   Review of H. D. Lewis, ed., *Contemporary British Philosophy*, 3 (Series), *Philosophy*, vol. 33 (1958), pp. 361–4.

1959
a   'Notes on a group of new modal systems', *Logique et analyse*, vol. 2 (1959), pp. 122–7.
b   'Thank goodness that's over', *Philosophy*, vol. 34 (1959), pp. 12–17.
c   'Mr Cohen on thanking goodness that p and q', ibid., pp. 362–3.
d   'Creation in science and theology', *Southern Stars*, vol. 18 (1958), pp. 82–9.
e   'Formalized syllogistic', *Synthese*, vol. 11 (1959), pp. 265–73.
f   Review of Alan Ross Anderson and Omar K. Moore, 'The formal analysis of normative concepts', *The Journal of Symbolic Logic*, vol. 24 (1959), pp. 177–8.
g   Review of Alan Ross Anderson, 'A reduction of deontic logic to alethic modal logic', ibid., p. 178.

224   *Bibliography*

h   Review of Alan Ross Anderson, 'The logic of norms', ibid., p. 178.

i   Review of Frederic B. Fitch, 'Self-referential relations', ibid., p. 240.

j   Review of J. Porte, 'Deux systèmes simples pour le calcul des propositions', ibid., p. 247.

k   Review of Jens Erik Fenstad, *Notes on Normative Logic*, ibid., pp. 247-8.

1960

a   'The runabout inference-ticket', *Analysis*, vol. 21 (1960), pp. 38-9. Reprinted in *Philosophical Logic*, ed. by P. F. Strawson, Oxford, 1967, pp. 129-31.

b   'The autonomy of ethics', *Australasian Journal of Philosophy*, vol. 38 (1960), pp. 199-206.

c   'Identifiable individuals', *The Review of Metaphysics*, vol. 13 (1960), pp. 684-96. Cf. 1968a.

d   Review of Sören Halldén, *On the Logic of 'Better'*, *Philosophy*, vol. 35 (1960), pp. 359-61.

1961

a   'Symmetry, transitivity and reflexivity', *Journal of the Philosophical Association*, vol. 7 (1961), pp. 67-9.

b   'On a difference between "betweens" ', *Mind*, n.s. vol. 70 (1961), pp. 83-4.

c   'On a family of paradoxes', *Notre Dame Journal of Formal Logic*, vol. 2 (1961), pp. 16-32.

d   'Some axiom-pairs for material and strict implication', *Zeitschrift für mathematische Logik und Grundlagen der Mathematik*, vol. 7 (1961), pp. 61-5.

1962

a   *Changes in Events and Changes in Things*, University of Kansas, Lawrence, 1962, 13 pp. Cf. 1968a.

b   'Nonentities', *Analytical Philosophy*, ed. by R. J. Butler, Oxford, 1962, pp. 120-32.

c   'Quantification and Ł-modality', *Notre Dame Journal of Formal Logic*, vol. 3 (1962), pp. 142-7.

d   'Possible worlds', *The Philosophical Quarterly*, vol. 12 (1962), pp. 36-43.

e   'The formalities of omniscience', *Philosophy*, vol. 37 (1962), pp. 114-29. Cf. 1968a.

f   'Limited indeterminism', *The Review of Metaphysics*, vol. 16 (1962), pp. 55-61. Cf. 1968a.

g 'Współczesna logika w Anglii' (Contemporary logic in England), *Ruch filozoficzny*, vol. 21 (1962), pp. 251–6.

h 'Tense-logic and the continuity of time', *Studia logica*, vol. 13 (1962), pp. 133–51.

i 'Some problems of self-reference in John Buridan', *Proceedings of the British Academy*, vol. 48 (1962), pp. 281–96. Reprinted in *Studies in Philosophy*, selected by J. N. Findlay, London, 1966, pp. 241–59.

j Review of Andrzej Grzegorczyk, 'The systems of Leśniewski in relation to contemporary logical research', *The Journal of Symbolic Logic*, vol. 27 (1962), pp. 117–18.

1963

a 'Is the concept of referential opacity really necessary?', *Acta philosophica fennica*, vol. 16 (1963), pp. 189–99.

b With C. A. Meredith. 'Notes on the axiomatics of the propositional calculus', *Notre Dame Journal of Formal Logic*, vol. 4 (1963), pp. 171–87.

c 'Indirect speech again', *Philosophical Studies*, vol. 14 (1963), pp. 12–15.

d 'Rejoinder to Professor Lachs on omniscience', *Philosophy*, vol. 38 (1963), pp. 365–6.

e 'Oratio obliqua I', *Proceedings of the Aristotelian Society, Supplementary Volume* 37 (1963), pp. 115–26.

f 'The theory of implication', *Zeitschrift für mathematische Logik und Grundlagen der Mathematik*, vol. 9 (1963), pp. 1–6. Cf. 1965d.

1964

a 'Some exercises in epistemic logic', *Knowledge and Experience*, ed. by C. D. Rollins, Pittsburgh, 1964, pp. 21–7.

b 'The algebra of the copula', *Studies in the Philosophy of Charles Sanders Peirce, Second Series*, ed. by E. C. Moore and R. S. Robin, Amherst, Mass., 1964, pp. 79–94.

c 'Conjunction and contonktion revisited', *Analysis*, vol. 24 (1964), pp. 191–5.

d 'Two additions to positive implication', *The Journal of Symbolic Logic*, vol. 29 (1964), pp. 31–2.

e 'On the unity of Professor Carnap', *Mind*, n.s. vol. 73 (1964), pp. 268–9.

f 'The done thing', ibid., pp. 441–2.

g 'Axiomatisations of the modal calculus Q', *Notre Dame Journal of Formal Logic*, vol. 5 (1964), pp. 215–17.

h 'K1, K2 and related modal systems', ibid., pp. 299–304.

8

i 'Indirect speech and extensionality', *Philosophical Studies*, vol. 15 (1964), pp. 35–8.

j With C. A. Meredith, 'Investigations into implicational S5', *Zeitschrift für mathematische Logik und Grundlagen der Mathematik*, vol. 10 (1964), pp. 203–20.

k Review of Joseph Dopp, *Logiques construites par une méthode de déduction naturelle*, *The Philosophical Quarterly*, vol. 14 (1964), pp. 280–1.

1965

a 'Existence in Leśniewski and in Russell', *Formal Systems and Recursive Functions*, ed. by J. N. Crossley and M. A. E. Dummett, Amsterdam, 1965, pp. 149–55.

b 'The cogito of Descartes and the concept of self-confirmation', *The Foundation of Statements and Decisions*, ed. by K. Ajdukiewicz, Warsaw, 1965, pp. 47–53.

c With C. A. Meredith. 'Modal logic with functorial variables and a contingent constant', *Notre Dame Journal of Formal Logic*, vol. 6 (1965), pp. 99–109.

d 'The theory of implication: two corrections', *Zeitschrift für mathematische Logik und Grundlagen der Mathematik*, vol. 11 (1965), pp. 381–2. Cf. 1963f.

e Review of B. Sobociński, 'On the single axioms of protothetic', *The Journal of Symbolic Logic*, vol. 30 (1965), pp. 245–6.

f 'Time, existence and identity', *Proceedings of the Aristotelian Society*, n.s. vol. 66 (1965–6), pp. 183–92. Cf. 1968a.

1966

a 'Postulates for tense-logic', *American Philosophical Quarterly*, vol. 3 (1966), pp. 153–61.

b Critical notice of G. E. Hughes and D. G. Londey, *The Elements of Formal Logic*, *Australasian Journal of Philosophy*, vol. 44 (1966), pp. 224–31.

1967

a *Past, Present and Future*, Oxford, 1967, x + 217 pp.

b 'Correspondence theory of truth', *The Encyclopaedia of Philosophy*, ed. by Paul Edwards. London, 1967, vol. 2, pp. 223–32.

c 'Existence', ibid., vol. 3, pp. 141–7.

d 'Logic, deontic', ibid., vol. 4, pp. 509–13.

e 'Logic, history of' (editor), ibid., pp. 513–71. Within this (author): 'Peirce, C. S.', pp. 546–9.
'The heritage of Kant and Mill', p. 549.

'Keynes, John M.', pp. 550–1.
'Johnson, W. E.', p. 551.
'Polish logicians', pp. 566–8.
'Bibliography', pp. 568–71.
f 'Logic, many-valued', ibid., vol. 5, pp. 1–5.
g 'Logic, modal', ibid., pp. 5–12.
h 'Logic, traditional', ibid., pp. 34–45.
i 'Negation', ibid., pp. 458–63.
j 'Russell, Bertrand A. W.: Logic and mathematics', ibid., vol. 7, pp. 244–51.
k With Paul Edwards and William P. Alston, 'Bibliography' (to Russell), ibid., pp. 256–8.
l 'On spurious egocentricity', *Philosophy*, vol. 42 (1967), pp. 326–35. Cf. 1968a.
m 'Stratified metric tense-logic', *Theoria*, vol. 33 (1967), pp. 28–38. Cf. 1968a.
n Review of M. A. E. Dummett and E. J. Lemmon, 'Modal logics between S4 and S5', Iwao Nishimura, 'On formulas of one variable in intuitionistic propositional calculus', and D. C. Makinson, 'There are infinitely many Diodorean modal functions', *The Journal of Symbolic Logic*, vol. 32 (1967), pp. 396–7.
o Review of Keith Lehrer and Richard Taylor, 'Time, truth and modalities', ibid., pp. 401–2.
p Review of Storrs McCall, *Polish Logic*, *The Oxford Magazine*, n.s. vol. 8 (1967), pp. 111–12.

1968
a *Papers on Time and Tense*, Oxford, 1968, 176pp. Reprints of 1956c, 1960c, 1962a, 1962e, 1962f, 1965f, 1967l, and 1967m, and the following new papers: 'Contemplation and action', pp. 45–50; 'The logic of ending time', pp. 98–115; 'Tense logic and the logic of earlier and later', pp. 116–34; 'Quasi-propositions and quasi-individuals', pp. 135–44; 'Tense logic for non-permanent existents', pp. 145–60.
b 'Imperatives and truth', *Akten des 14. Internationalen Kongresses für Philosophie*, Vienna, 1968, vol. 2, pp. 291–6.
c 'The logic of tenses', ibid., pp. 638–40.
d 'Intentionality and intensionality', *Proceedings of the Aristotelian Society, Supplementary Volume* 42 (1968), pp. 91–106.
e 'Fugitive truth', *Analysis*, vol. 29 (1968), pp. 5–8.
f With C. A. Meredith, 'Equational logic', *Notre Dame Journal of Formal Logic*, vol. 9 (1968), pp. 212–26. Cf. 1969j.

228 *Bibliography*

g   'Now', *Nous*, vol. 2 (1968), pp. 101–19. Cf. 1968i.

h   'Egocentric logic', ibid., pp. 191–207.

i   ' "Now" corrected and condensed', ibid., pp. 411–12. Cf. 1968g.

j   'Time and change', *Ratio*, vol. 10 (1968), pp. 173–7. Appears as 'Zeit und Änderung' on pp. 145–9 of German *Ratio*, vol. 10 (1968).

k   'Modal logic and the logic of applicability', *Theoria*, vol. 34 (1968), pp. 183–202.

l   'Comment on "A knock at prelims logic" ', *The Oxford Magazine*, n.s. vol. 9 (1968), pp. 68–9.

m   Review of Łukasiewicz, *Elements of Mathematical Logic*, *The Journal of Philosophy*, vol. 65 (1968), pp. 152–3.

1969

a   With E. J. Lemmon, C. A. Meredith, D. Meredith and I. Thomas, 'Calculi of pure strict implication', *Philosophical Logic*, ed. by J. W. Davis, D. J. Hockney and W. K. Wilson, Dordrecht, 1969, pp. 215–50.

b   Critical notice of Richard Gale, *The Language of Time*, *Mind*, n.s. vol. 78 (1969), pp. 453–60.

c   Review of Gerold Stahl, 'Le problème de l'existence dans la logique symbolique', 'Temps et existence', and 'Une formalisation du "dominateur" ', *The Journal of Symbolic Logic*, vol. 34 (1969), pp. 140–1.

d   'Worlds, time and selves', *L'Age de science*, no. 3 (1969), pp. 179–91.

e   'Tensed propositions as predicates', *The American Philosophical Quarterly*, vol. 6 (1969), pp. 290–97.

f   'The possibly true and the possible', *Mind*, n.s. vol. 78 (1969), 481–92.

g   'Propositional calculus in implication and non-equivalence', *Notre Dame Journal of Formal Logic*, vol. 10 (1969), pp. 271–2.

h   'On the calculus MCC', ibid., pp. 273–4.

i   Review of G. H. von Wright, *Time, Change and Contradiction*, *The British Journal for the Philosophy of Science*, vol. 20 (1969), pp. 372–4. Norwegian translation by Knut Bjørngård in *Norsk filosofisk tidskrift*, vol. 5 (1970), pp. 1–21.

j   'Corrigendum to C. A. Meredith's and my paper, "Equational logic" ', *Notre Dame Journal of Formal Logic*, vol. 10 (1969), p. 452. Cf. 1968f.

k   'Self-perception and contingency', *Analysis*, vol. 30 (1969), pp. 46–9.

l   'Recent advances in tense logic', *The Monist*, vol. 53 (1969), pp. 325–39.

m   Review of G. E. Hughes and M. J. Cresswell, *An Introduction to Modal Logic*, *The Oxford Magazine*, n.s. vol. 10 (1969), pp. 50–1.

1970

a 'I', *Jowett Papers 1968–1969*, ed. by B. Y. Khanbai, R. S. Katz and R. A. Pineau, Oxford, 1970, pp. 1–10. French translation by Pierre Dubois in *Revue philosophique de la France et de l'étranger*, vol. 158 (1968), pp. 427–37.

b 'The notion of the present', *Studium generale*, vol. 23 (1970), pp. 245–8.

Index

231

DATE DUE

OCT. 11 1984			